too many to Mourn

One Family's Tragedy
in the Halifax Explosion

James Mahar and Rowena Mahar

NIMBUS
PUBLISHING LTD
nimbus.ca

Nimbus Publishing Limited
PO Box 9166, Halifax, NS   B3K 5M8
(902) 455-4286

Cover design: Heather Bryan
Cover photo: Ada (Jackson) (Moore) with her husband Howard Sperry, taken in 1920, shortly after their marriage. Photo courtesy of the author.
Book design: Terri Strickland

Printed in Canada
Previously printed under ISBN 1-55109-240-9
NB0807

Library and Archives Canada Cataloguing in Publication

Mahar, James G.
Too many to mourn : one family's tragedy in the
Halifax Explosion / James Mahar and Rowena Mahar.

ISBN 978-1-55109-668-1

1. Halifax (N.S.)—History—Explosion, 1917. 2. Jackson family. I. Mahar, Rowena II. Title.
FC2346.4.M35 2008   971.6'22503   C2008-902476-1

Canada Council Conseil des arts
for the Arts   du Canada

Nimbus Publishing acknowledges the financial support for its publishing activities from the Government of Canada, the Canada Council for the Arts, and from the Province of Nova Scotia. We are pleased to work in partnership with the Province of Nova Scotia to develop and promote our creative industries for the benefit of all Nova Scotians.

With great respect, compassion and love,
this book is dedicated to the memory
of the Jackson family of Richmond.

They endured unimaginable horror with faith;
they suffered the greatest loss
with courage and dignity.

Within these pages their story is told for the first time.
May they rest in eternal peace.

Acknowledgements

The authors extend special thanks to the Arts Awards Division of The Canada Council for the generous financial assistance granted.

In addition, gratitude is expressed to the Department of Veteran Affairs for special permission to examine the restricted files of the Halifax Relief Commission. These files supplied extraordinary insight into the lives of both the victims and survivors of the Halifax Explosion.

We also gratefully acknowledge the assistance of the following organizations and individuals in the writing of this book:

Anglican Diocesan Centre—Rev. William Bishop and Staff
Archdiocese of Halifax, Catholic Pastoral Centre
    Rev. Martin Currie, Vicar General and Chancellor;
    Karen White, Archivist
Rita (Jackson) Aubie
Dorothy Blythe
Sybil (Hollet) Carter
Aloysius Chaffey
Church of Saint Peter and Saint Paul, Wilmington, California
    Father G. Peter Irving, Pastor; Helen Workman Mora, Archivist
Edith (Orr) Clattenburg
Jane (Hadley) Cocaine
William Cowan and Marie (Daine) Cowan
Lenora (Marsh) Cross
Gwendolyn E. Daine
Harry E. and Shirley Daine
James W. G. and Louise Daine
Dalhousie University Archives—Dr. Charles Armour, Archivist
James R. Edmonds
Halifax Regional Fire Department—Capt. Donald R. Snider
Halifax Regional Library, Halifax and Dartmouth branches
Halifax Regional School Board—Dr. Donald Trider, Superintendent
Anne (Whalen) Isenor
Jennifer Lambert
T. J. William and Noreen Latham

Robert Lloy
Jane (Mills) MacLellan
Heather MacLellan
Mrs. Dorothy McDonald
Maritime Museum of the Atlantic—Graham McBride & staff
Mount Saint Vincent Motherhouse Archives,
    Sisters of Charity; Sister Mary Martin, Archivist
Hector Newport
William Orr
Marian (Whittaker) Peevy
Reg Rasley
Violet (Newport) Rothwell
Lorraine (Daine) Rozee
Gordon Shanks
Suzanne Seager
St. Agnes Roman Catholic Church—Rev. Lloyd J. Robertson
St. Joseph's Roman Catholic Church—Father Gordon MacLean;
    Thelma LeBlanc, Secretary
St. Mark's Anglican Church—Rev. J. Smith
St. Mary's University—Professor Paul A. Erickson
St. Patrick's Roman Catholic Church—Father John Hayes;
    Catherine Hutt, Secretary
St. Theresa's Roman Catholic Church—Rev. Lloyd E. O'Neill
The Los Angeles Times, Dave Laventhol, Publisher;
    Jonathan Miller, Ad Sales
The New York Times, NYT Pictures, Photo Syndicate, New York, N.Y.
Tourism Nova Scotia—Allan Doyle
John Versteege—IMPACT Videographic Services Limited
Diane M. Walker
Muriel Wesley

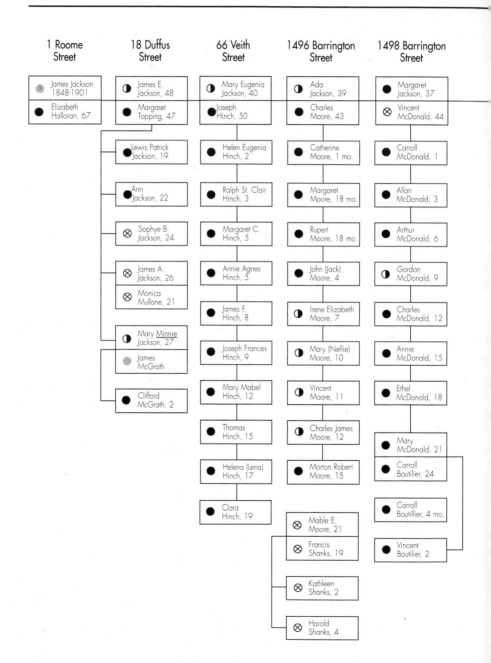

1 Roome Street	18 Duffus Street	66 Veith Street	1496 Barrington Street	1498 Barrington Street
James Jackson 1848-1901	James E. Jackson, 48	Mary Eugenia Jackson, 40	Ada Jackson, 39	Margaret Jackson, 37
Elizabeth Halloran, 67	Margaret Topping, 47	Joseph Hinch, 50	Charles Moore, 43	Vincent McDonald, 44
	Lewis Patrick Jackson, 19	Helen Eugenia Hinch, 2	Catherine Moore, 1 mo.	Carroll McDonald, 1
	Ann Jackson, 22	Ralph St. Clair Hinch, 3	Margaret Moore, 18 mo.	Allan McDonald, 3
	Sophye B. Jackson, 24	Margaret C. Hinch, 5	Rupert Moore, 18 mo.	Arthur McDonald, 6
	James A. Jackson, 26	Annie Agnes Hinch, 5	John (Jack) Moore, 4	Gordon McDonald, 9
	Monica Mullane, 21	James F. Hinch, 8	Irene Elizabeth Moore, 7	Charles McDonald, 12
	Mary Minnie Jackson, 27	Joseph Frances Hinch, 9	Mary (Nellie) Moore, 10	Annie McDonald, 15
	James McGrath	Mary Mabel Hinch, 12	Vincent Moore, 11	Ethel McDonald, 18
	Clifford McGrath, 2	Thomas Hinch, 15	Charles James Moore, 12	Mary McDonald, 21
		Helena (Lena) Hinch, 17	Morton Robert Moore, 15	Carroll Boutilier, 24
		Clara Hinch, 19	Mable E. Moore, 21	Carroll Boutillier, 4 mo.
			Francis Shanks, 19	Vincent Boutilier, 2
			Kathleen Shanks, 2	
			Harold Shanks, 4	

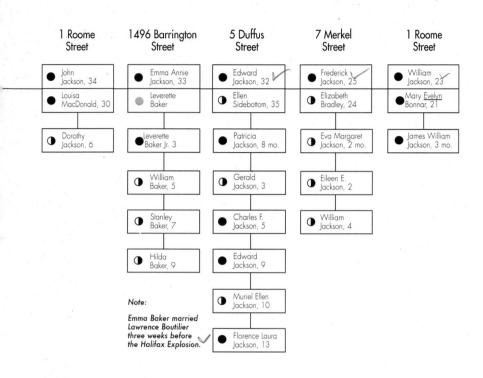

1 Roome Street	1496 Barrington Street	5 Duffus Street	7 Merkel Street	1 Roome Street
● John Jackson, 34	● Emma Annie Jackson, 33	● Edward Jackson, 32	● Frederick Jackson, 25	● William Jackson, 23
● Louisa MacDonald, 30	● Leverette Baker	◐ Ellen Sidebottom, 35	◐ Elizabeth Bradley, 24	● Mary Evelyn Bonnar, 21
◐ Dorothy Jackson, 6	● Leverette Baker Jr. 3	● Patricia Jackson, 8 mo.	◐ Eva Margaret Jackson, 2 mo.	● James William Jackson, 3 mo.
	◐ William Baker, 5	◐ Gerald Jackson, 3	◐ Eileen E. Jackson, 2	
	◐ Stanley Baker, 7	● Charles F. Jackson, 5	◐ William Jackson, 4	
	◐ Hilda Baker, 9	● Edward Jackson, 9		
		◐ Muriel Ellen Jackson, 10		
		● Florence Laura Jackson, 13		

Note:

Emma Baker married Lawrence Boutilier three weeks before the Halifax Explosion.

Of the sixty-six members of the Jackson family who were in the Richmond area on the morning of December 6th, 1917, forty-six were killed. Of the surviving twenty, the majority were seriously injured. This was the largest loss of life suffered by one family group in the Halifax Explosion.

～

The family of Joseph and Mary Hinch sustained the largest loss of life for a single family unit. Mary (Jackson) Hinch was severely injured and buried under debris for twenty-four hours. Her husband and all ten of their children were killed.

● Died before 1917
● Killed
◐ Injured
⊗ Away from Richmond

Prologue

There is a very special kind of courage. Most of us are unaware we possess it; fortunately, only a few will ever need it. It is the deep, spiritual courage that bestows upon humanity the fortitude to suffer the insufferable, bear the unbearable and accept the unacceptable. Triggered by tragedy, nourished by anguish and strengthened by suffering, quiet courage bestows upon humanity the resilience to rebound from the ashes of broken lives and shattered dreams. It is the most precious of all human attributes.

This story is about the quiet courage that sustained the people of Halifax and Dartmouth during and after the most violent and destructive disaster in Canadian history—the Halifax Explosion. This catastrophic event killed more than two thousand, injured nine thousand others and destroyed thousands of properties. Almost two hundred people lost their sight to the daggers of flying glass and nearly twenty thousand were left homeless.

In particular it is the story of the Jackson family in the community of Richmond. Richmond occupied a square in north-east Halifax, stretching one-half mile from the waterfront to Gottingen Street and a half mile from Duffus Street to North Street—an area of barely one-quarter square mile. It is fitting to focus attention here for this was the epicentre of the disaster.

Richmond bore the undiminished brunt of the Halifax Explosion. Facing broadside to the blast, this was the locale for the most horrendous forms of death; the most grievous injuries. Every street, home, business and person in Richmond was within two thousand feet of the explosion centre. Although it comprised less than one-fiftieth of the city proper, Richmond residents accounted for more than 75 per cent of the recorded deaths and suffered the majority of the serious injuries. Property damage was absolute; not one building, fit for habitation, survived.

The people were predominantly working class, a mixture of ethnic groups, who lived in relative harmony close to their places of employment. Most worked as stevedores on the waterfront, or as brakesmen, engineers or freight handlers on the railway. There was a strong representation of English and Scots, but the predominant ethnic group was Irish, primarily first and second generation descendants of those who had been forced from their country during the potato famines of the previous century. Now, seventy years later, many of their children and their children's children lived in Richmond.

It was a close-knit community. In the days before the automobile it remained fairly insular. People stayed mainly in their own area; even a shopping trip to downtown Halifax was a noteworthy occasion. A special closeness between families, generated by the earlier years of mutual suffering through the degradation of poverty and discrimination, had melded the residents of Richmond into a unique entity within the city of Halifax.

By the time of World War One the memories of the famine and suffering, never to be completely forgotten, had at least mercifully dimmed. In the third year of the war, times were good for the working class. With full employment there was hope for the future, a person's fate was limited only by the capacity to dream and the willingness to work and sacrifice in pursuit of that dream. Plans were made for their children's future that a few years before would have been fantasy.

By today's standards many Richmond families were large; eight to twelve children were not uncommon. Prior to the discovery of antibiotics and vaccinations, many families had been decimated by the ravages of scarlet fever, diphtheria, pneumonia, tuberculosis and other diseases. A large family was a hedge against total loss, a hope that most would survive. Sons and daughters of one family married into other large families they had known since childhood within their own area. They, in turn, produced a large family. Catholics married Baptists, Irish married English; over the years barriers of religious and ethnic differences had been largely eliminated by understanding. Prejudice and discrimination only exist in an environment of ignorance and fear. In Richmond this environment was transcended by matrimony.

The people affected by the explosion were neither saints nor sinners, but an intricate blend of each. They patronized their churches and social clubs, made sure their children had the advantage of an education they themselves had largely been denied. They were no different from working class people everywhere, except there was a closer bond through family ties. Before the day was over they would be bloodied in battle by forces beyond their comprehension.

One of the largest, if not the largest, of these families was the Jacksons. At the time of the Halifax Explosion the extended family of James Jackson and his wife, Elizabeth Halloran, consisted of nine children, their spouses, forty-eight grandchildren and five great-grandchildren. Sixty-six members of the Jackson family were within the

Richmond area on that day. Forty-six were killed and nineteen of the remaining twenty were hospitalized with injuries. Only one escaped unharmed.

This was the greatest loss of life, suffered by one family group, during the catastrophe. The greatest single-family loss also occurred within the Jackson group. The eldest of Elizabeth's daughters, Mary Jean Jackson, mother of one of this book's authors, lost her first husband, Joseph Hinch, and all ten of their children. Until now, neither story has ever been told. This book will tell the story of the Jackson family before, during and after the most tragic event in Canadian history—the Halifax Explosion.

CHAPTER
1

In the pre-dawn darkness of Thursday, December 6th, 1917, the Mont Blanc *lay at anchor near the mouth of Halifax Harbour. Not a glimmer of light was showing. The black hulk creaked and groaned as it rose and fell slowly to a gentle Atlantic swell. The few crew members on duty at that hour, treaded the deck lightly and spoke in hushed tones, as if by silence they might thwart the awakening of the sleeping monster beneath their feet.*

Nothing outwardly distinguished this ship from the many others that daily arrived and departed the East Coast Canadian port. Only a handful of people in the area knew it was there; even less were privy to the nature of its frightful cargo. Not even one person was remotely aware this ship was about to become the key player in a tragic drama that would shock the entire world.

THE FLYING SHUNT swayed rhythmically as it rolled toward the string of boxcars. The clickety-clack of the wheels, passing over the space between rails, added a tempo to the rhythm, interrupted now and then by a discord, as the boxcar lurched through a switch. It was an hour and a half before daylight.

James Jackson was attuned to the music of the tracks, the perfect partner to the dancing boxcar beneath his feet. At forty-nine he was a lean, gangly man, half an inch short of six feet; his rugged, angular features were highlighted by a dark, bristling moustache, now showing a few streaks of grey. Even with summer long gone, his face was bronzed from exposure to sun and wind. The otherwise stern visage was occasionally softened by hazel eyes twinkling with an inherent good humour. On flat, level ground he had the ungraceful gait of a shore-bound sailor, but on the boxcar he was in his element. With his legs widespread and bent slightly at the knees, he gracefully absorbed the sway and lurches of the car.

Bundled against the morning chill in a heavy wool overcoat, his gloved hands gripped the brake wheel for additional safety against any unforeseen movement by the freight car. The peak of his ear-lug cap had been pulled down to protect his eyes from the ever-present soot and cinders that flew from the huffing, puffing engines in the Richmond Railyard.

With practised skill James braked the shunting cars until they coupled with a resounding thump into the line of cars ahead. All motion ceased and for a moment he relaxed. From his vantage point he looked over the Narrows toward Dartmouth. There was not a cloud in the sky; it appeared the city was in for a beautiful clear, cold, autumn day. There was enough moonlight for him to see some of the ships waiting for a convoy in Bedford Basin. A voice, from the tracks below, cut through his reverie. "Hey! You dumb Irishman. Are you plannin' on spendin' the rest of the day up there pretending you're a statue of St. Patrick, or are you going to join the rest of us poor working slobs in our never-ending battle against the Kaiser?"

James Jackson looked down at his brother-in-law, Lawrence Boutilier, waiting for him at the side of the tracks. He quickly climbed down the ladder and the two men fell in step as they made their way back to the idling engine. There was still time, before their shift ended, to return to Rockingham for more cars.

Without the trace of a smile James replied, "You know, Larry, you are one very lucky fella. Why even as little as three weeks ago that dumb Irish crack would have earned you at least a month in hospital. But now that you're family I'm going to overlook that snide remark made by, in your own words, a poor working slob."

Lawrence Boutilier was far from being a slob. He was an inch shorter than his new brother-in-law, but shared the same lithe grace that defined most brakesmen. At twenty-five, Larry was half James's age but this made little difference to their relationship. The men had been friends for several years and enjoyed an easy-going comradeship that had both men chuckling as they climbed into the engine cab to return to the Rockingham Yard for the next lot of freight cars. Jim peeled off his gloves and warmed his hands in front of the open boiler door, deftly pulling them back each time the fireman threw another shovel of coal into the boiler. It was the one aspect of being a brakesman he did not enjoy; his hands were forever cold.

The engineer gave a blast of the train whistle and with a screeching spin of drive wheels the engine began to move. "At the tail-end of a long, hard night I'm not really overjoyed to run into a comedy team— what's so funny?" Larry smiled innocently. "I'm just trying to educate this dumb Irishman, and it's an uphill battle. I have it on good authority, that most Irishmen are in their twenties before they learn how to tie their left shoe lace, and probably won't live long enough to learn how to tie the right one."

"You seem to forget, 'Boots,' replied the engineer with mock severity, that my name is Clancy and my fireman is Flynn—you're surrounded by Irish. This also seems to be as good a time as any to remind you, and it must be for about the ten-thousandth time—there are only three types of people in this whole world. There's the Irish, those who wish they were Irish and then there's the poor unfortunate heathens like you. For a recently married man with four step-children depending on you staying alive you sure do love to live dangerously."

Lawrence clapped a hand to each side of his head, "Oh! Lord forgive me, I've offended a bunch of bleedin' shamrocks. Tell you what, as soon as we reach the yard, I'll jump out and paint your locomotive green. Will that pacify the Sons of Erin?"

James Jackson threw a proprietary arm over Larry's shoulder. "It's all right, Clancy; now that this poor soul has married my youngest sister, he's family. The Jackson clan will soon drum some sense into his head. In another month you'll hardly recognize him."

The fireman shovelled more coal into the boiler, then turned to Larry. "Someone said you and Emma moved in with Ada. That true?"

"Yeah, we've got three rooms with Ada and Charlie until we can get a place of our own in the spring—we pay twelve dollars a month." Flynn looked shocked, "Twelve dollars a month! Good God, the wife and I rent a whole house for eight. Besides, you would have to pay me to live in the same house with Ada."

James jumped to the defence of his sister. "Oh, Ada's okay, she's got a heart of gold, really. She just should've been a man—she knows exactly what she wants, just don't stand in her way while she gets it. She has a temper I'll admit, but there's always a reason for anything she does. Besides, Charlie let me in on the secret of how to get along with Ada. There are two things you have to do. First, you must always let her do all the talking." He turned away and looked out the window of the cab. After a minute of silence Clancy prompted him, "So, what's the second thing?" With a great bellowing laugh, James said, "While she does all the talking—you don't listen to a word she says."

When the laughter died down, Clancy turned to Larry. "Why did Emma marry you when she's already had one brakesman chopped up under the wheels a couple years ago; now she's taken on another clumsy clot. It doesn't make sense. A brakeman's job is a class-A widow-maker."

"It could be any number of things," Lawrence joked. "My terrific good looks, or my delightful personality; or maybe she's fascinated with

3

my young muscular body." Clancy nudged James, "Do you want to get him off my engine, otherwise the Clancys and Flynns will be helping the Jacksons whip this kid into shape—he may not survive the lessons."

The four men were still laughing as the engine, with a squeal of protesting wheels, rounded the curve of Fairview Cove. As they approached the Rockingham Yard, the engineer and fireman turned their attention to the train. James turned to Lawrence, "Are you looking to buy a house, or build one come spring?" Lawrence became serious for a moment. "Emma thinks we should build, it would be cheaper and we can get the kind of house we want. She has a bit of money from Leverette's insurance and I put a little away each week, so we should have enough by now to pour the foundation and buy the stuff for the framing in."

James was silent for a moment then said, "Ed, Willie and Fred want to start a contracting business when the weather gets better. You should consider giving them the job. They're your brothers now too and we may as well keep the money in the family. I also want to get a house built, as soon as I can, for my daughter Minnie and her son Clifford. I finally made up my mind last night and thought I'd go over this morning to tell them to go ahead with it. They're at Pier Eight or Nine. They'll still stevedore for the winter but they plan on being in business for themselves by early spring."

Lawrence nodded, "Why not? I'm sure they'll do a good job and treat me fairly. But isn't it the darndest thing, all I did was stand alongside of Emma a few weeks ago and say, 'I do' and, from being a nobody, I now have a wife, four kids, five brothers-in-law, three sisters-in-law, at least sixty nieces and nephews, and a horde of other relatives I don't even know about yet."

James punched him playfully on the arm, "See, I told you, you're a very luck fella."

Had any of them looked to their right they might have seen a ship at anchor in Fairview Cove with huge letters on each side, spelling the words BELGIUM RELIEF. But they had seen thousands of ships; there was no particular reason to notice this one.

Few ocean ports are as fortunate as Halifax. It is blessed with one of the finest harbours in the world connected to another huge body of water called Bedford Basin. They are joined by a narrow channel of water, appropriately called the Narrows and are arranged in an hour-glass configuration, the harbour to the south, the basin to the north.

Bedford Basin, at two miles long and one mile wide, is four times the area of Halifax Harbour. In peacetime it is a mecca for small yachts, sailboats, racing shells and other pleasure craft owned by the members of nearby aquatic clubs. In wartime its usage changes to the serious business of war. The Basin then becomes the congregation point for ships awaiting convoy. Here, heavily laden with supplies and equipment, they are safe from the enemy.

The 5,043 ton Imo was not laden with supplies and equipment; it was empty. Neither was it concerned with the safety offered by Bedford Basin. Captain Haakon From believed the words BELGIUM RELIEF would protect the Imo and its thirty-nine crew members from the enemy. His ship's job was the delivery of blankets and clothing to the war-weary victims of the European conflict. Almost twelve hundred British ships had been torpedoed and sunk in that year alone, but it was very unlikely the Imo would present a target enticing enough to warrant the enemy's wrath. Far better to conserve their deadly torpedoes for destruction of a target more damaging to the British war effort.

The Imo had left Rotterdam, crossed the Atlantic and entered Halifax on December 5th to replenish its supply of coal before continuing the journey to New York. There it would load relief supplies for the return trip. The coal barge had been late. By the time refuelling was complete, the submarine net across Halifax Harbour had closed for the night and would not reopen until daylight the next day, December 6th.

The same submarine net that stopped the Imo from leaving the Harbour had prevented the Mont Blanc from entering. At this moment, an hour and a half before daybreak, Imo was anchored seven miles away in Fairview Cove, Bedford Basin; Mont Blanc was anchored in McNab's Cove at the mouth of Halifax Harbour. Both ships were impatiently awaiting the first streaks of dawn. Neither ship knew of the other's existence, and no one suspected the role Imo would play in the forthcoming tragedy.

MARY JEAN (JACKSON) Hinch was taking advantage of the lull before her family awoke. With a husband who worked all night in the grease and dirt of the Graving Dock on the waterfront and with ten very active children, one washday a week was hardly enough. Earlier she had opened the front door and looked at the sky above the roof of Hillis Iron Foundry, across Veith Street from her home, and determined this would be an ideal wash day. Joe would not be home from work for at least two hours, more if he got into one of his long-winded conversations with his buddies, and the children would stay in bed for another hour. That should allow her time to do the wash and maybe even hang some of it on the line.

She had cut slivers of lye soap into the pots of water that were now heating on the kitchen and hall stoves, stirred the fire in both stoves, added more coal and as she waited for the wash water to heat, was seated quietly at the kitchen table with a freshly made cup of tea.

She was a remarkably pretty woman. Her long, auburn hair framed a heart-shaped face with delicate, even features and a clear, almost translucent complexion. Despite having borne fourteen children, at age forty she had not lost her youthful looks; people invariably guessed her to be five to ten years younger, and Mary Jean was still considered by many to be "the prettiest girl in the North End." As a young girl her sister Ada had nicknamed her "Dude" because of her fastidious appearance.

She had just finished her tea when nine-year-old Joseph touched her elbow and startled her. "Good Lord, child! You startled me. What are you doing out of bed?" He put one arm around his mother, leaned against her, and said, "I have a sore throat and it hurts to swallow. Can I have a piece of brown bread and molasses?" Mary Jean felt his forehead. It was not feverish and if he wanted to eat bread and molasses he couldn't be feeling too badly.

"All right, you can have your bread and molasses." She stood up and, with a quick swoop, clasped the child in her arms. "But first, it's time for a dance lesson." So saying, she held him off the floor with one arm tight around his waist and took his hand in hers. Then, despite his giggles and wriggles, waltzed him around the kitchen table, singing softly in his ear:

"Ohhh, Casey would waltz with the strawberry blonde
While the band played on,
He'd glide 'cross the floor with the girl he adored
While the band played on,
His brain was so loaded it nearly exploded
The poor girl fair shook with alarm
He'd ne'er leave the girl,
With the strawberry curl,
While the band played on."

By now they were both laughing so hard there was a danger of waking everyone in the house. She set him down, "There, my young man, someday you may be almost as great a dancer as your Dad." She gave him a tight hug, spread molasses generously on a thick slice of home-made brown bread and gave it to her son.

Despite her gaiety, the mere mention of illness had caused Mary Jean to feel anxious. In the early years of her marriage four of her children had died from scarlet fever, two within hours of each other on the very same day. This had been the worst day of her life.

This morning her two oldest girls, Clara and Lena, were staying in bed; Lena was just getting over a bad cold and Clara had caught it from her. Before Christmas arrived, everyone in the house would probably have it, but, thankfully it was just a cold. Perhaps, after Joe was home, she could run down to Creighton's store and get some lemons and a bottle of Minard's Liniment. Maybe there might even be time to go over to Frances Hale's candy store and buy a bag of penny candies for the children. Even the older ones liked a little treat when they were not feeling well.

Still thinking of the children she had lost she silently asked God to spare her from the grief of ever losing another child.

In addition to the Imo *and the* Mont Blanc *there were many other ships in the harbour that morning. Some were at the drydock awaiting repairs, others were loading or unloading the necessities of war. The British ship* Colonne *was at Pier Nine, the American ship* Curaca *was at Pier Eight. Both had been loaded with grain and were now taking on a cargo of horses. These poor creatures were used to haul the cannons and the supply wagons on the battlefields of Europe. They were expendable to the ravenous appetite of war. These particular animals would be spared death on the battlefront.*

Three vessels, the J. A. McKee, Middleham Castle, *and the* Douglas H. Thomas, *were moored side by side at the drydock. The steel tugboat* Douglas H. Thomas, *212 tons gross weight, owned by the Dominion Coal Company, was moored alongside the* Middleham Castle.

Two smaller, wooden tugs, the Hilford *and the* Regus, *were moored at the Sugar Refinery wharf. Also at the Sugar Refinery wharf was the SS* Picton. *This ship carried a cargo of explosives, sufficient to cause enormous damage, given the wrong set of circumstances.*

Permanently moored at the Halifax Dockyard was the Canadian cruiser HMCS Niobe. *No longer used as a warship, it served as a training and depot ship. It housed the offices of the Chief Commanding Officer, Commander Frederick Wyatt, and was headquarters for Naval Control and Intelligence. Extra accommodations had been added to the deck of the* Niobe *to house trainees. It no longer had the sleek lines of a cruiser.*

The Stella Maris *was waiting, near the Dockyard, to tow two barges to Bedford Basin. Originally a British gunboat and later a mine-sweeper it now served in any capacity needed. At the moment it was a tugboat and it soon would enjoy a brief tenure as a frustrated rescue vessel. The Norwegian vessel* Hovland *was in drydock.*

All of these ships had two things in common. They would all be bit players in the drama about to start and all of them were within eight hundred feet of Pier Six.

Three American ships were also in the immediate vicinity, the USS Old Colony, *the U.S. Cruiser* Tacoma *and the U.S. Coastguard ship,* Morrill. *The* Old Colony *was a hospital ship with 150 beds; all three vessels had highly trained medical personnel.*

THE FAMILY OF James and Elizabeth (Halloran) Jackson was a close-knit group. Originally numbering twelve children, the father, James Sr., and three of the children had died prior to 1917. Elizabeth, a widow for the past sixteen years, had imbued her remaining five sons and four daughters with her own Irish traits. Each had a delightful sense of fun, even when times had been tough; they all were fiercely loyal to, and protective of, each other. There was the occasional argument and the inevitable flaring of Irish temper but never severe and never long last-ing. They were all adults now, ranging in age from forty-nine to twenty-three, and all were married. With the exception of one son, Frederick, his wife and three children, they all lived close to each other. In total they had produced fifty-three children and five grandchildren. They lived in an area of Richmond bounded by Veith and Barrington Streets, to the east and west, and Richmond to Duffus Streets, north and south.

The matriarch of the Jackson family, sixty-seven-year-old Elizabeth (Halloran) Jackson, lived at 1 Roome Street, on the corner of Barring-ton within a few doors of Ada and Margaret. With her at that address were two of her sons, John and William, their wives and two children. One other person was living there as a border, Howard Sperry, but he was away at the time.

Ada, her husband, Charlie Moore, and nine of their ten children lived at 1496 Barrington Street. The youngest sister, Emma, her new husband of three weeks, Lawrence Boutilier, and the four children by her first marriage, had rented rooms from Ada.

Next door, at 1498 Barrington, lived Ada's sister Margaret, her hus-band, Vince McDonald, and their eight children. The oldest daughter, Mary Elizabeth, was married and her husband and two children also were occupants of the home. Vincent's mother, Mary Squires, and his half-brother, Richard, completed the roster. This house contained fifteen people.

Around the corner from Ada and Margaret, at number five Duffus Street, was another brother, Edward, his wife and six children. In addition to immediate family, at this address, there was an extended family of cousins and their families who had moved in during wartime lack of other housing. There were sixteen people living in this one home.

Further up Duffus Street, at number eighteen, lived the oldest son, James, his wife and three of their five children. His eldest daughter, Minnie McGrath was a widow. She and her son Clifford, had moved back with them after the death of her husband.

Frederick Jackson, his wife Elizabeth and their son and two daughters, lived at seven Merkel Street. This was the home furthest from the others. It was just on the border of the Richmond area.

Mary Jean, her husband Joe Hinch, and their ten children lived at sixty-six Veith Street, directly in line with Pier Six and distanced from it by less than eight hundred feet. In total, these seven homes housed sixty-eight members of the extended Jackson family: twenty-one adults; forty-four grandchildren and three great-grandchildren. Ada Moore's joking contention that this area of Richmond should be renamed 'Jacksonville' did have some basis in fact.

There was no part of Richmond more than a half mile from the end of Pier Six. In Richmond, there was no part of 'Jacksonville' more than twelve hundred feet from the end of the same wharf.

The Mont Blanc *had arrived off the mouth of the harbour in late afternoon on December 5th. Harbour Pilot Francis Mackey transferred from an outgoing vessel and guided* Mont Blanc *to the Incoming Ship Examination point. There, after the ship's papers were cleared by the authorities, it started toward the submarine net. It was too late to enter by a matter of minutes. The ship then retraced its course, a mile and a half, to the shelter of McNab's Island and there spent the nighttime hours.*

On board, in addition to Francis Mackey, was Captain Aime LeMedec, and his crew of forty-one seamen. At the examination point Mackey had become privy to the knowledge, shared by few other than those on board, of the devil's brew stored below deck. The New York City manifest and export papers listed the cargo on the Mont Blanc *as:*

2,366 tons of wet and dry picric acid; 250 tons of TNT; 62 tons of guncotton; 246 tons of benzol. In addition there were three hundred live shells as ammunition for the two deck guns. The benzol had been added at the last moment and was stored in drums on the forward deck. In total there was more than 2,924 tons of the most unstable and destructive explosive forces ever devised by mankind stored on the Mont Blanc.

HENRY TURNER AND his wife, Annie, were the caretakers of the Lorne Amateur Athletic and Rowing Club, established in 1873. The club was located on Renforth Street, a short street running below and parallel to Barrington. In peacetime it had been one of the most popular places in the north end of Halifax, with a full and very active membership.

Each July the club sponsored an annual regatta that created a carnival-like atmosphere, with crowds of spectators lining the harbourfront. Now, due to wartime restrictions and the end of the boating season, Henry and Annie's current responsibilities were reduced to preparing the club's facilities for social functions.

The annual meeting was scheduled to take place the following day, December 7th, to coincide with the anniversary of the opening of the clubhouse. Today, there was no hurry to get up. Their son, Allan, who lived with them, would help. Their other son, William, and his wife Mary, were coming over early tomorrow morning. Five sets of hands would make short work of the cleaning. Henry pulled the bedclothes up to his chin and snuggled down for a few more hours sleep. There was no reason to look out his bedroom window, the view of the harbour and the Basin was still obscured by darkness and there was no activity at Pier Six, less than two hundred feet from the Lorne Club. It was just an ordinary morning, with the exception that he could sleep in.

A few hundred feet from the Lorne Club the bulk of the fifteen- storey Sugar Refinery was in darkness. The tallest building in Richmond had been responsible for the name "Richmond" being given to this community. Bales of raw sugar from Richmond, Virginia, were unloaded here to be processed into the finished product. The name Richmond, emblazoned on the bales, soon became synonymous with the area in which it was prepared. At this hour the factory was silent. The lone figure of the nightwatchman stood just outside the main door, smoking his pipe and awaiting the spectacle of dawn.

Not far, to the north of the Lorne Club at Pier Eight and Nine, the British ship *Colonne* and the American ship *Curaca* were taking on cargoes of horses. The animals were removed from cattle cars, fitted with body slings and lifted aboard the ships. At the Sugar Refinery wharf a small gang of men were beginning the job of securing the cargo of explosives on board the SS *Picton*.

Two of the major industries in Richmond, the Hillis Iron Foundry and the Richmond Printing Company, were also experiencing the calm before the arrival of employees and the starting of the day's production. None of the activities, or lack thereof, were beyond the norm. It had the appearance of a typical day.

Just above the Richmond Printing Company and on the same street as the Hillis Foundry was the Protestant Orphanage. This was a large, sprawling, two-storey building that contained the orphanage, hospital and one-room school. There were thirty-six children and three adults in attendance. The majority of the children were under age six.

William Hayes reluctantly rolled out of bed. He had been robbed of a proper sleep by the captain's dog howling most of the night. Somewhere he had read that a dog howling was an omen the dog's master was about to die; he wanted to dismiss this as superstitious nonsense, but the howling was not like any he had ever heard, there was an eerie attribute that had set his nerves on edge. He should have been off the Imo *yesterday afternoon and home in his own bed last night, but the delay in refuelling had prevented that. Now he was tired, impatient to finish this job and above all, to get away from that dog. He dressed quickly; it was still a half-hour to daybreak, maybe he could get a quick breakfast or at least a cup of tea before they wanted him on the bridge. As he opened the door of the cabin the dog started howling again.*

ARTHUR EDMONDS, HIS wife Letitia and their seven children lived on Duffus Street, not far from the home of James and Margaret Jackson. Over the years the two families had become friends. Arthur was one of the most widely known and liked persons in the area. Every day of the week except Sunday he plied the streets with his horse and wagon bringing his wares to the people. The children of Richmond, including the Jacksons, would line up for the privilege of feeding an apple to Molly. Now, with winter approaching, Arthur was busy changing the horse's harness over from a wagon to a sleigh.

This morning Letitia was annoyed. The fire in the kitchen stove had burnt down to a few measly embers and there was no kindling by the coal scuttle. The kindling supply was young Arthur's job, which he had shirked once already in the past week.

Both Letitia and her husband believed that sharing domestic chores helped to instil a sense of responsibility in their children. By and large they were good children and she was proud of them.

However, at sixteen, young Arthur was thoroughly obsessed by the war, in particular with the navy. He could name every naval vessel in the harbour and list off her vital statistics as well. His naval passion had begun to wreak havoc with his school work, as well as interfere with his chores, and in the past year his grades had slipped to an all-time low. His father had stepped into him with some vigour and Arthur's last report card had shown considerable improvement. He seemed to listen only to his father. Well, thought Letitia, he would hear from his dad about the kindling.

Scowling, Letitia went down to the cellar and fetched the kindling herself. She added it to the coals, removed the stove cover, and put the kettle on to boil. Opening the back door, she took a deep breath of the crisp, cold air to clear the cobwebs from her head. Even though it was still a half-hour to daybreak, and despite the heavy frost on the back steps, it looked to be the beginning of a fine, clear day. She shivered, closed the door, and moved back to the friendly warmth of the stove. For a few more minutes she would have the kitchen to herself. The elder girls, Annie and Alice, would be down for breakfast at the last possible moment before they left for work; Elizabeth, Arthur, Henry and William would be even later, school didn't start until 9:30. Emily, the youngest, would stay home today and nurse her cold. Letitia's mood lifted as she drank her second cup of tea. Perhaps she would take Arthur aside after supper and remind him about the kindling herself. He really was a good boy, she reflected, thinking of the times when, as a young child, he would shyly offer her bouquets of dandelions and buttercups that he'd picked on his way home from school. All too soon he would be grown up, married and have children of his own. He would be a fine catch for any woman, thought Letitia. Yes, she decided, it was hardly worthwhile upsetting her husband over a little thing like kindling.

Captain LeMedec had also been deprived of a good night's sleep. There was no howling dog on the Mont Blanc *but there was the ever-threatening presence of the demonic beast below the deck. Aimee LeMedec had been a captain for only two years. This was his first experience carrying explosives and the only thing he knew for sure was that no one, not even the experts, knew anything for sure about explosives; their key features were their instability and uncertainty.*

He was aware that shells and bombs had a detonator that triggered the main charge and the thing was safe as long as this detonator was not subject to impact. Years ago someone, who seemed to be an authority on the subject, told him that a stick of dynamite, if put in a fire, would burn but not explode. LeMedec was inclined to doubt this and he certainly had no intention of ever being the person to verify this by experimentation.

The men who loaded the cargo in New York seemed to know little more than he did. In building the bulkheads they had used copper nails to eliminate the danger of sparks, and they had cautioned him against fire. Before they left port all matches and cigarettes had been confiscated from the crew and it was strictly forbidden to smoke anywhere on the ship. And, now, fifteen minutes before daybreak, he nervously paced the bridge and contemplated the real danger, being hit by a torpedo after they left Halifax. That would be the detonator. He certainly didn't need to worry about fire.

CHAPTER
2

The first faint blush of dawn lightened the sky above the hills of Dartmouth. The golden glow kissed the skyline, whispering the promise of a clear, bright, sunny day. With the dawn, the concealment of darkness was lost to the Mont Blanc. *Captain Aimee LeMedec ordered the anchor raised and called to the engine room for slow ahead. He then turned command of his ship over to the Harbour Pilot, Francis Mackey.*

At the other end of the hour-glass configuration, the captain of the Imo *was making basically the same decisions at almost the same moment. The anchor had been weighed and the ship, under the command of Harbour Pilot William Hayes, was slowly moving toward the guard ship near the centre of Bedford Basin.*

With the lifting of the curtain of darkness, the two key players, Imo *and* Mont Blanc, *began the journey to tragedy. They were now six miles apart.*

FREDERICK AND EDWARD Jackson were waiting on the corner of Barrington and Roome for John and William. They were behind schedule. Fred pulled his watch from his vest pocket, glanced at the time, and impatiently said, "We seem to spend most of our time these days waiting for Willie. He gets later every day. It's almost twenty to eight, we're going to be late again." Fred shook his watch and held it to his ear to make sure it was still ticking. At that moment, William and John Jackson both came out the back door of number one Roome Street and all four brothers started south on Barrington. William greeted his older brothers with a cheerful, "Good morning Ed." He turned to Fred, "And the top o'the morning to you too, partner."

Edward grumbled, "Willie, you are going to have to get started earlier, we're always rushing to get some place on time." William snapped back, "What's put a bee in your bonnet? I was ready, it was you guys who were late getting here. If you'd been here sooner I would've been ready. Anyways, we're early, not late. They want us at the Refinery

Wharf for about an hour, we can be there in ten minutes. Then we go to Furness Withy."

Edward moved up alongside William. "Willie, did you talk to Jim last night about building the house for Minnie?" William sighed, "This starting up a contracting business is enough to give you the screaming pips. You might say we discussed the subject, but it was in between playing cowboy with Clifford, I was the horse, and listening to about an hour-long piano recital by Annie. She plays real good, but I only like waltzes and she does all that fancy high-brow stuff. When we finally had a few minutes to ourselves Jim said he wants a small house, maybe four or five rooms; he figures Minnie'll get married again within a few years and he'll let her and Clifford have it till then. You know the three houses he owns already all have nine rooms and he wants one that is easier to sell later on."

Edward looked thoughtful. "Maybe it'd be better for us anyways. We should start out small." William put a hand on Edward's shoulder, "Don't get you're hopes too high, big brother; he didn't say yes and he didn't say no. He said he wanted to sleep on it. I think he might let us know today. Meantime we better keep on stevedoring." He looked at Edward's hands, stuffed in his pockets. "How come you don't have your lunch pail?"

Ed stopped dead, "Oh, damn, damn, damn, Ellen made me a roast beef sandwich and left my lunch pail on the hall tree and I forgot to pick it up. Damn. If she had left it on the kitchen table, like she usually does, I would've remembered. Damn. Oh well, it's too late to go back now."

They started walking again. William gave him a sugary sweet smile "It's okay, big brother, seeing as we are partners now, if you're really good, work hard and don't sass anyone, I might give you one of my cookies." Fred chipped in with, "Not to be outdone by any brother o'mine, I'll let you have a sip of my tea so you don't choke on Willie's crumbs."

As they reached Richmond Street, John turned and started to walk away from them, across Barrington, toward the pedestrian bridge over the railyard tracks. "Well, I must away to some highly technical work while you poor working class buffoons get on with your no-brain labour. See you tonight." Fred yelled after him, "How much brain does it take to fall off a boxcar?" John's reply was lost in the rumble of a horse and wagon over the cobblestones of Barrington Street.

MARGARET (JACKSON) MCDONALD, Mary Jean's younger sister, watched her husband from the doorway of her home on Barrington

Street. Despite the chill in the air, she watched Vince until he reached the pedway over the tracks. He turned, sure that she was watching, and gave a final wave. Having concluded their morning ritual, she closed the door and walked to the hall stove and enjoyed its friendly warmth for a few minutes while she mentally planned her day. That Ada had thrown a wrench into the works by talking her into looking after baby Catherine this morning. Ada was just too bossy sometimes. She made you feel like a real dummy if you didn't do what she wanted; she could cut through your arguments like a hot knife through butter. "Oh well, she is my sister, and I guess sisters should stick together," she mumbled to herself as she walked to the kitchen.

Her seven-year-old son, Gordon, was seated at the kitchen table with Vincent's mother, Mary Squires. These two shared a special bond. At the moment they were having a late breakfast together and were solemnly discussing Christmas as it used to be when Mary was the age of Gordon. Lost in a world of their own, they were hardly aware that Margaret had entered the room. Margaret's eldest daughter, Mary Elizabeth, stood at the kitchen sink, washing the dishes she and her husband, Carroll, had used for breakfast. She turned to her mother with a mischievous smile, "So I hear you and Aunt Mary Jean, started a war with the army last night." Margaret sighed, "My, how these rumours do get around. You know, the army should start sending messages by rumour, they travel a lot faster than wireless. Whoever told you a thing like that?"

Mary put the last of the plates in the cupboard, "Daddy told us; he said it was a sight to behold, the two mildest ladies in the entire North End engaged in battle with a genuine general." Margaret frowned at her daughter, "Well, I didn't think it was the least bit funny. We listened to that man for over an hour, him with his fancy uniform and his gold braid, telling us about the glory of war and how we should be honoured to have our children serve our country. He kept telling us how brave Canadian soldiers were and how they took this hill and that hill and only a couple of thousand of them were killed. I never heard such nonsense in my life. I felt positively sick. There is no hill in the whole world that is worth having a single young man die for, never mind a couple of thousand. And I bet the German mothers feel the same way. Sometimes I agree with Ada, men are such fools. I don't see anything glorious about those boys who come home missing arms or legs, or gassed or shell-shocked. I wanted to cry. I pictured how I would feel if I got one of those telegrams saying young Charlie was killed or lost his legs and I just felt like bawling." Mary Elizabeth walked over and put her arm around her mother. "Mom, Charlie is only twelve, and Al's barely nine, the war will be over long before they are old enough, don't upset yourself."

Margaret refused to be mollified. "Someday, when your two babies are in their teens, after you have nursed them and sat up many a night when they're sick, you'll know how a mother would feel. Besides, despite what your father says, we were not nasty to the man, Mary Jean simply asked him how many of his own children were in the trenches, and he said he didn't have any children. All I said was, so, why do you want to send ours?"

Margaret absently poured a cup of tea and said, "For the first time in a long time things are going pretty good for us—and all the other families around here—our men are working, there's money to pay the bills, you kids have it better than we ever did. Surely there must be a way to end this without sending our young people thousands of miles to fight and die in a foreign country."

As the Mont Blanc *entered the harbour through the now open submarine net, Captain LeMedec breathed a huge sigh of relief. He felt the tension that had gripped him for the past five days melt away as the early frost had melted with the arrival of the morning sun. Last night had been particularly nerve-racking. The five-day voyage from New York had been bad enough, but at least his ship was on the move and had some degree of manoeuvrability in the event of attack. Last night, at anchor, he felt like a sitting duck.*

He turned to the harbour pilot, who was now in charge of his ship, and they exchanged relaxed smiles. Francis Mackey, now aware of the cargo beneath his feet, was also relieved they had gained the protection of the harbour. In less than an hour they would be at anchor in Bedford Basin. The Mont Blanc *and its crew gratefully embraced the protection offered by the Port of Halifax. But no power on earth could protect the Port of Halifax from the* Mont Blanc, *and the satanic cargo below its deck.*

ADA MOORE WAS not a happy woman and her black mood permeated the atmosphere at the breakfast table. Her husband, Charlie, was the primary object of her displeasure but the strain was felt by the children too, and particularly the boys. Even four-year-old John, despite his tender age, had the sagacity to realize this was not the opportune moment to mention the spinning top with the red and blue swirls that he would dearly love for Christmas.

It had started early last evening and raged until bedtime. The initial dispute was a variation of the familiar "men have it easy" grievance. Ada had been feeling the restraints of being mother to nine young children.

"Men are free to come and go as they damn well please. If a man wants to go shopping he just up and goes; he's not tied to a bunch of kids." Charlie tried to reason, "Your sister has more kids than we have and you don't hear her complaining." Ada took a deep breath in readiness for a long-winded explanation. "Dude wouldn't complain if she had twice as many kids as the orphanage. She never complains about anything, she's a bloody saint, we can't all be bloody saints. Dude lets everyone walk all over her; besides, Clara and Lena can look after most of them, except for Helen and Ralph, and Dude can take them with her in the carriage if she wants to." Her voice took on a slightly whining inflection, "I don't have anyone to help me. Cathy is only a month old, I have to be with her every moment. The twins are only a year-and-a-half old, who do you think I can leave them with?"

Ada's frustrations had not worked themselves out by the morning. Breakfast had presented a dilemma. She couldn't let her man work all day on the waterfront without a good breakfast. She had served him eggs and sausages with a large portion of hash-browned potatoes and a strong cup of tea—everything just the way he liked it. But she was damned if she would let him enjoy it, and as she worked she slammed the plates around just short of smashing them.

The battle continued over breakfast, beginning with "Women Are Second Class Citizens," Ada's favourite campaign. "We don't even have the right to vote for gawdsake! The last time they tried to pass a law to let us vote it was defeated by one vote, one stupid vote, mind you, by a bunch of stupid old codgers. We're second class citizens; we'll never get to have a say in how the country is run."

Charlie gave a long, resigned sigh as he buttered his toast, and patiently explained, "The reason is, as I have told you a million times before, is that men are the wage-earners. We are the ones who have to decide how things are done. Besides, if you give women the vote, the first thing you know they'd elect somebody just because they liked his moustache. Women don't know anything about politics." Ada's hackles rose even further, "What gives you the stupid idea we'd vote for a man? The brilliant bunch you voted for is doing really great. Some stupid old fogy at the top has us in a war he wasn't smart enough to avoid and is killing thousands of kids just so he can put more medals on his chest. No woman in the world is that dumb."

As she cleared the table, Charlie appeared again, dressed for work, his lunch pail in his hand and the kitchen door half open. "Someone said the Prime Minister's in town today, if I meet him—or any of those other stupid old fogies—I'm going to invite them home for supper.

Might I tell them what delicious little goodies you plan on serving?" Ada gave him a withering glance, "The children and I will be having roast chicken with all the trimmings—you and your guests will be dining on rat-poison soufflé." Going out the door, ready to run if any of the dishes or cutlery became airborne, her husband retorted, "Sounds a treat after some of the meals I've had lately. I must away to the peace and quiet of the waterfront, see you tonight." A few minutes after he left Ada smiled, the tempest was over. Charlie was okay; he never got mad when she got mad. She would make sure he had a good supper waiting for him tonight. The waterfront was a hard place to work, it certainly was neither peaceful nor quiet.

At a few minutes after eight most work places were humming with activity. The waterfront was bustling as stevedores and freight handlers unloaded the freight from the boxcars that had arrived early that morning and transferred the cargo to the many ships waiting to transport it across the Atlantic. There, in the fields of conflict, it would be greedily consumed by the ravenous gods of war.

EDWARD JACKSON, STILL grumbling over the missing lunch pail, worked alongside his younger brothers, Frederick and William. The three generally managed to work in the same gang. In the Richmond and Rockingham rail yards, the daytime crews of engineers, firemen and brakesmen had taken over from the night shift, with scarcely a pause in motion. Jim Jackson's younger brother, John, had taken over as brakeman and was even now easing another car into the string at the Richmond yard. Jim's youngest child, nineteen-year-old Lewis Patrick, had a sheaf of papers on his clipboard and was busily checking the cars by serial number. He was looking for one particular car that seemed to be lost. Lew decided it must have been left in Rockingham, he wouldn't worry about it at the moment. His uncle John would be heading for Rockingham in a few minutes, he's ask him to have a look for the wayward car.

As the Imo *made its way toward the guard ship in Bedford Basin, the* Mont Blanc *passed the inner submarine net at George's Island. Five miles of water separated the two ships.*

VINCE MCDONALD LEANED his shovel against the coal bin and opened his lunch pail. He was still hungry despite a full breakfast at home; one sandwich and a cup of tea would hit the spot and there was plenty left for noon, Margaret always packed enough lunch for a large horse. Vince was in an exceptionally good mood. He loved his job as fireman on the I.C.R. locomotives, constantly reminding his brother-in-law, Joe Hinch, it was the only sensible railway job to have. It carried neither the onus of responsibility of the engineer, nor the dangers and discomfort of waltzing along tops of heaving boxcars that was the lot of brakesmen. Now, with winter approaching, he was kept toasty warm, shovelling in all the coal he wanted and being paid for it, to boot.

There was another aspect of his job that Vince enjoyed tremendously. The railway firemen had a unique barometer for measuring the flux of the local economy. When times were tight, as they had been prior to the war, the children of poor families in the Richmond area would line the railway tracks and throw rocks at the engines going by. The firemen, in turn, heaved lumps of coal at the kids. This mock battle was fought to a stringent set of rules. No child would dream of hitting the cab windows and none of the firemen came even close to hitting any of the children. In the years of conflict there had been no casualties, and many of the homes were heated through the winter by the benevolence of the I.C.R. firemen. There were fewer children lying in ambush these days, an indication that better days were at hand.

With the blade of the shovel, Vince flipped open the boiler door and added another dozen scoops of coal to the fire. At forty-four he was a powerfully built man; many years of labour had developed tremendous upper body strength. He handled the shovel as many would a teaspoon, and he was proud of his strength. Slamming the fire door shut, Vince leaned on his shovel and looked out toward the Basin as the engine rounded the Fairview Cove curve. His engine was on the way to the Rockingham Yard to continue the work started by the night crew.

There were a number of ships, at anchor, awaiting formation of a convoy. Vince pointed to them and said, "Now, ain't that a pretty sight? All those ships are loaded with stuff that had to come here by train, making lots of work for us which, in turn, makes lots of money to hand over to the wife to feed and clothe the kids, pay the rent and buy all kinds of goodies." The engineer took his eye off the rails long enough to glance at his fireman. "Is that what has you in such a good mood this morning—getting rid of all your money?" Vince grinned. "That's part of it" he said. "Last night Margaret told me she thinks she may be having another, she's going to see the doc on Monday to make sure."

"Oh the saints preserve us! Just what you need for Christmas—another kid. What are you—in some kind of contest with Joe Hinch?

What does that make, nine…ten?"

"If it's true it'll make nine, Joe's got ten. But we have him beat anyhow, our oldest daughter, Mary, has her two kids living with us, so, counting grandchildren we'll have eleven kids in the house." He paused long enough to throw a huge lump of coal at a ragged young boy by the side of the track. "There, that'll save me from having to break it up, and by the time he does, his old lady will have enough coal to cook dinner." He laid the shovel down, "You know, counting me and Margaret, there's fifteen of us in that house. My mother and my half-brother have been living with us since Dad died, and we have Mary and her husband, Carrol Boutilier, and their two youngsters. But it works out. My mother loves being a granny and a great-granny—she says it gives her all the fun of having kids without any of the wear and tear."

The engineer looked shocked, "Good Lord! Fifteen! Aren't you tripping over each other? Cripes, if I had that many people around me they would drive me crazy." Vincent shook his head. "Well no, not really, it seems to work out pretty good. Mary, Carrol, and their two kids, will be moving out in the spring. Mary's a big help to her mother now and my Mum helps with the younger kids. Ethel's seventeen already and whenever she is not busy flirting with the young guys, she washes a dish or two. Emma's fifteen and I swear she's training to be a maid, she keeps the place so spotless. No, it's working out pretty good. There are lots of willing hands. Everybody pitches in when something needs doing and makes short work of it. I don't think I'd ever want to be without a large family around me."

"Well, to each his own," replied the engineer, with some disbelief. "But I tell you, I'd go off my rocker. Doesn't it bother Margaret?" Vince picked up his shovel, flung the firedoor open and shovelled in more coal. He gave a delighted chuckle. "Nothing bothers Margaret. She believes everything is God's will. No matter what happens she just accepts; that's her way. It must be nice to have that kind of faith. She loves everybody and thoroughly enjoys her life. Yup, my Margaret is one contented lady."

The engineer was thoughtful for a few minutes and then shook his head, "This God's will business is a nice cosy belief, but buddy, it's a lot of baloney. There's a hell of a lot of things happening in this world that the God I believe in would have nothing to do with."

The recently acquired chemical pumper was the object of much admiration at the West Street Fire Station. The Fire Chief, Edward Condon, and his deputy, William Brunt, were as delighted as two children with a brand new toy. The Patricia *was the most up-to-date piece of equipment for fighting oil, gas, and chemical fires, and the men lovingly ran their hands along her gleaming fenders and breathed in the fresh, clean smell of new leather and oil. The chief turned to his deputy and said, somewhat wistfully, "Far be it from me to wish any poor soul hard luck, but I sure would love to see this little lady in action."*

WHEN EMMA BOUTILIER looked out the kitchen window of Ada's home on Barrington Street the last of the frost was disappearing from the back steps. The sun had been up for almost three-quarters of an hour. But even the touch of frost remaining in the shade of the banister caused her to shudder. It had been on a frosty fall morning just a little more than two years ago her first husband, Leverette Baker, had fallen beneath the boxcar and had been killed. The accident had taken place in the Richmond Yard, not two hundred feet from their home. He was knocked unconscious by the fall and caught up in the brake mechanism and dragged a good distance before the train could be stopped. He was badly injured and died in hospital that night.

As she stood, transfixed by the shimmer of the frost, she muttered to herself, "Why any woman in her right mind would marry a brakeman is beyond me. And here I've gone and done it again. Larry is a good man and he loves the kids, but every time someone comes to the door I jump out of my skin. Mrs. Lawrence Boutilier, Mrs. Lawrence Boutilier. It does have a nice ring. If he dies on that track I swear I'll kill him."

CHAPTER

3

FOR THE FOURTH time, in as many minutes, Ada went to the door and impatiently looked for Mabel. Barrington Street was busy as usual, but there was no sign of her daughter. The New York Cloak Company had been closed all day yesterday in preparation for their sale which would begin when the doors opened at nine o'clock. Charlie had given her the money to buy the coat she wanted for Christmas, but now it looked as if the plans she had made were falling apart. That coat wasn't going to last long; someone else would grab it.

As she had made very clear to Charlie at breakfast, a simple shopping trip could be an insurmountable mission for a woman with young children. But, for Ada, there were few problems that were insurmountable. Her ability for organization was an accepted fact by the family. First, she'd managed to convince her sister, Margaret, that taking care of one-month-old Catherine would be a breeze. Ada would feed the baby just before she left and would be back within two hours at the most. Morton, fifteen, was the oldest of the children and had left for work with his lunch pail tucked under his arm. The rest would be watched over by Mabel. The toddlers, Margaret and Rupert, were good as gold, and would probably not even notice she was gone—as with many twins, they seemed to live in a world of their own. This left only four-year-old John, who adored Mabel and would eat worms if she asked him to. Besides, Emma was here now, with her four children; there were lots of helping hands.

The only flaw in her preparations was that they depended on Mabel to turn up on time. Although Mabel's husband, Francis Shanks, was overseas, she insisted on staying in the house they rented in the West End, on Willow Street, owned by her mother-in-law. Why she didn't move back with her parents was beyond Ada's understanding. It would be so much cheaper for Mabel—and so much more convenient for Ada. She paced back and forth in the hallway and flung open the door as she heard the tram stop. Seven people got off but Mabel was not one of them. Ada closed the door a little harder than necessary and muttered, "Damn. If a bloody man wanted to go to a bloody sale all he would have to do is put on his bloody hat and walk out the bloody door."

The atmosphere on the Imo *was thick with tension. Both the captain and the pilot were anxious to reach the guard ship. Captain From's annoyance had been building since the previous evening; his ship was more than eighteen hours behind its scheduled departure time for New York. They were reluctant to waste more time with the red tape occasioned by leaving port.*

William Hayes's nerves were also on edge, having slept poorly thanks to a dog that had howled all night. As well, the ship was handling sluggishly due to the lack of ballast. The harbour pilot struggled to maintain course, cursing the rudder that was half out of the water. He would increase his running speed down the harbour. That might help with the steering.

As the ship turned south she immediately began to pick up speed. Hayes relaxed; in less than an hour he'd be at the net and turning command back to the captain. Someone else would have to listen to the howling on the way to New York.

The two lead players, Imo *and the* Mont Blanc, *were now steaming toward each other on reciprocal courses. Both were heading for a spot near Tuft's Cove, in the Halifax Narrows. They were three-and-a-quarter miles apart.*

JIM JACKSON WAS half an hour late knocking off from his night shift. The last carload of coffins had been coupled to the string; and, even as he and Larry Boutilier walked away, an engine was already hauling the boxcars toward the Deepwater piers. After parting from Larry, he went to the Sugar Refinery wharf to find his three brothers. The place was bustling and Jim followed William around as his brother worked. "Willie, I'll go ahead with Minnie's house and you guys can have the job. It's too late for this year, but you can start whenever you're ready." The two brothers shook hands on the deal.

William turned to Edward and Fred. "You hear that, boys? The Jackson Brothers Contracting Company is officially in business." The foreman, Frank Carew, was within earshot. Grinning, he said, "If the Jackson brothers don't put their backs into it they'll be looking for employment elsewhere, real soon." Fred grinned back at him, "We wouldn't do a thing like that to you Frank, you're too nice a fella. You'd have to hire three dozen guys to replace us."

As he turned to leave Jim said, " Willie, one other thing; there's a pile of two-by-fours on my lot that needs covering—the weatherman's predicting snow for tomorrow." Fred gave a snort of derision, "They're never right, Jim. There won't be any snow tomorrow—look at that sky, it couldn't be clearer." Willie gave him a warning glance and cut him off. "We'll throw a tarp over it as soon as we knock off here. Don't worry, brother, you can count on us."

The first in a series of questionable decisions began as the Imo *was about to enter the Narrows from the north. An American freighter was exiting midway between Halifax and the Dartmouth shores. From the* Imo *it was difficult to judge its speed, and Captain From and Pilot Hayes made the decision to pass the steamer starboard to starboard. This was contrary to the laws of navigation, but they thought it was a better decision than crossing the bow of the oncoming steamer without knowing its speed. The manoeuvre placed the* Imo *slightly on the wrong side of the Narrows.*

The name Narrows is a bit of a misnomer. Certainly it is narrower than either Bedford Basin or the harbour, but even at its narrowest point it is over two thousand feet across. There was room for forty-five vessels the width of Mont Blanc *or* Imo *to fit side by side without touching either shoreline. Hardly a tight squeeze.*

AFTER HE LEFT his brothers, Jim Jackson was almost to the railroad pedestrian bridge when Joe Hinch came up behind him. "Hey there, how's it going?" They walked toward the stairway together, Joe stretching to match the longer stride of his brother-in-law. "Hey yourself, Joe, just knocking off?" Joe spat in disgust, "I've been all night in the Graving Dock on that ship with the jammed gun. We can't get the damn thing to work." Jim laughed, "The German Navy will love you for that, maybe they'll give you guys an Iron Cross." They walked in silence until they came to the pedway over the tracks. Then, abruptly Joe said, "Mary Jean was wondering how Sophye's getting along in New York, you heard from her lately?"

"We had a long letter from her last week," Jim replied. "She seems happy enough, and she's coming home for Christmas on the twentieth. She's finished her training now, so we've got a full-fledged nurse in the family. She's taken a shine to some doctor at the hospital." Joe smiled, "You never know when it will come in handy to have a nurse in the family. Sophye will do okay. She's smart enough and a real go-getter, to boot. She's a bit on the bossy side maybe—I think she got that from watching Ada. Then again, a lot of women these days seem to be getting bossier than they used to be."

Jim Jackson nodded, "She was never happy around here; too small-town for her. Sophye will probably want to live in Boston or New York. Young Jim's the same. Sooner or later he'll up and leave for greener pastures. It's funny, these young people today don't seem to know how lucky they are—they can have and do almost anything they want. Mum and Dad used to tell us stories about the old days that would curl your hair. The English ousted the poor Irish from their own damn country, but when they got here they were still treated like scruff. They couldn't get jobs and it was years before they got rid of the drunken bum image. Times are good for us now, but the young people don't want to know about it."

It was on the tip of Joe's tongue to make an Irish joke, but he decided it wasn't the time and instead asked, "Have you done anything yet about the house for Minnie?" Jim Jackson sighed and rolled his eyes upward, "Oh, God, if that's not the same question Maggie asks me a dozen times a week. Clifford is a great little guy and we love him to pieces, but we're not used to toddlers around anymore and the kid gets into everything. The place is a madhouse since Minnie moved home with him. The sooner we get her place finished the better. I just turned the job over to Willie and the boys, but I don't think there's much they can do until spring. Meanwhile, I've a pile of lumber that's going to warp all to hell unless I can get a tarp over it."

They stopped on the rail bridge. "You know, Joe, my family never ceases to amaze me. Those two daughters of mine, Minnie and Sophye, couldn't be more different if they tried. There's Minnie, gentle as a lamb, while her sister's made of steel. The whole family's split like that. Mary Jean and Margaret are both soft as silk—if the devil himself knocked on the door they'd invite him in for tea and crumpets and treat him like a gentleman. But, Sophye takes after Ada and Emma. If God knocked on the door they'd haul Him into the kitchen, sit Him down and set Him straight on a thing or two. I tell you, Joe, it keeps a man on his toes trying to figure out what's what when he's surrounded by Jackson women."

They paused half-way across the pedway. Joe smiled, "And it gets even more complicated, old buddy. Some of 'em are like you, hail-fellow-well-met until someone crosses you and sets off that Irish temper, causing all hell to break loose." Looking thoughtful, he added, "You know, Jim, your sister's not as soft as you think. When our first two kids died that day within an hour of each other, I was the one who went to pieces. Mary Jean was the pillar of strength. It tore her heart out, but she still had the strength to comfort me; without her I would've been lost. And when the other two kids died it was the same thing. I ranted and raved while your sister held things together. Don't kid yourself. That lady has a steel core when she needs it, and I suspect Margaret and Minnie are the same. If something is important enough, any of the women in your family would fight like bloody demons."

If the two men had looked behind them they might have seen the *Mont Blanc* steaming through the Narrows toward Bedford Basin at a leisurely four knots per hour. But neither Jim Jackson nor Joe Hinch had any particular reason to notice one nondescript tramp steamer.

As Mont Blanc *entered the Narrows from the south, she passed HMS* Highflyer, *a British Cruiser on Atlantic escort duty. The munition ship dipped her colours and the naval vessel lowered her ensign in acknowledgement of the salute. On board the* Highflyer, *Lt. Richard Woolams gazed in disapproval at the deck cargo of fuel drums. He did not know what the drums contained but assuming it was oil or gas, and considering, to his critical eye, the clumsy way it was secured, he was glad he was not a member of the* Mont Blanc's *crew.*

A few minutes later the Mont Blanc *came opposite the Halifax Dockyards, almost the midpoint in the Narrows. Here it was overtaken and passed by the SS* Stella Maris.

Originally a British gunboat, the Stella Maris *had recently served as a mine-sweeper but on this day was delegated to the role of tugboat. At that moment she was towing two barges north to Bedford Basin. As they passed the* Mont Blanc *two of the crew members, Sidney Malone and Robert Pearce, were standing on the aft deck keeping a watchful eye on the tow line. Pearce, seeing the barrels of benzol, turned to his companion and said, "I hope there are no heavy smokers on board that tub." Malone laughed, lit a cigarette, and replied, "If there are they're in for a long trip—straight up." Both men were laughing as they turned back to their job. There was no way they could know that before Malone could finish smoking his cigarette, the SS* Stella Maris *would be called upon for a brief but futile career as a rescue vessel.*

STOPPING TO PRIMP in the hall tree mirror, Ellen Jackson saw Edward's lunch pail. "Mercy Maude, that man would forget his head if it wasn't fastened to his neck." She turned to her daughters, Florence and Muriel. "Girls, your dad's forgotten his lunch again. You'll have to take it to him at the wharf on your way to school. If you can't find him leave it with one of your uncles, or the foreman. Now, mind you, go straight there and then directly to school. I won't have you dilly dallying around the waterfront and I'm not fooling, do you hear me?"

There immediately began a small battle as to which girl would carry the lunch pail. Being the elder by three years, and in her own eyes at least, rapidly approaching the status of "responsible young lady," Florence won out. Muriel was designated as her chief assistant, which seemed to mollify her somewhat.

The pilot on the Mont Blanc, *noticing the* Stella Maris *and the two barges had a combined length of over four hundred feet, decided to give it a bit more sea room. Already well on the correct side of the channel, Mackey gave orders for a slight change in course which brought the ship even closer to the Dartmouth shore. In a few minutes, the* Stella Maris *would also influence the path of William Hayes on the* Imo, *which was now two-and-a-quarter miles away, and increasing speed.*

IN THE KITCHEN of the Edmond's home, on Duffus Street, twelve-year-old William was sitting delicately balanced on the rear legs of a kitchen chair with his feet propped up on the open oven door. He rocked gently to and fro, absorbed in his book and absent-mindedly scratching the cat stretched out on his lap. Annie and Alice had left for work almost an hour before and Elizabeth was beginning to gather her school books together. Young Arthur, somewhat subdued after a scolding from his mother for again neglecting the kindling, had just left with Henry to buy a new scribbler at Creighton's store on their way to school. And nine-year-old Emily sat huddled at the kitchen table, sniffling and coughing, another victim of the flu season.

Letitia looked at her and remarked, "Young lady, the best place for you today is in your own little bed. I think you had better go there right now." Giving a tremendous sigh, Emily hauled herself up and started for the hall steps. She turned as she was leaving the kitchen to ask, "Can I take Fluffy with me?" "No." Her mother answered, "Not just now, you can see he's helping Willie read his book—he has to pronounce all the big words for him." Then, seeing the disappointment in her daughter's face, she softly added, "After William goes to school I'll bring Fluffy up and put him on your bed." Content with the compromise Emily made her weary way upstairs.

Letitia lifted the cover of the stove and stirred the bed of hot coals. It was just right for making toast. She pulled the toasting fork out of the kitchen drawer and cut a few thick slices of bread.

"Willie, how about some toast and jam with a glass of milk?" The words took a moment to penetrate. "Yes, please." Letitia opened the cellar door and called down to her husband, "Arthur, would you like some toast and jam with another cup of tea? I've opened a new bottle of strawberry preserves." His voice drifted up the steps. "Not right now, love. I'm working on Molly's harness and I don't want to stop. I may have some before I go out."

Letitia returned to the stove, skewered a slice of bread on the toasting fork and held it over the coals. She tried to make out the title of William's book. "So what are you reading, Willie? It must be good by the looks of you." The boy surfaced long enough to say, "It's called *The Swiss Family Robinson* and it's about this family that gets shipwrecked and they are living on a deserted island." His mother very logically pointed out, "If they are living there then it can't be deserted." Willie gave an exasperated sigh, "No, what I mean is it was deserted before they got there and they lost everything in the shipwreck and now they have to build everything all over again; and you know what they did?" Without waiting for a reply he went charging on, "They built a tree house, that's what they did, they built a tree house in a tree." Letitia, matching the seriousness of her son, said, "Well now, that was clever, if I were going to build a tree house that is exactly where I would build it too, because the very best place to build a tree house is in a tree, everybody knows that."

Distracted by the smell of burning, she turned her attention back to the toast. Scraping off the worst of the charcoal, she turned it over to toast the other side. Unfazed by his mother's humour, Willie added, "Do you know what? We could build a tree house in that old oak at the end of the yard. Do you think Dad would help?" Letitia ruffled his hair and laughed, "I don't think so, sweetheart, every time you get your dad to help you with something he winds up doing the whole thing himself. He's busy enough now taking care of the horses and wagons; he has enough on his plate without getting into the construction business. Anyway, this is hardly the time of year to be building tree houses, maybe we should wait until June and talk about it then." William rescued his book from Fluffy's claws. "I wonder what it would be like to lose everything like that in a shipwreck? What would we do if we had to start out again from nothing?" Letitia looked at the clock. "I wouldn't worry about it if I were you. I've no intention of getting shipwrecked. I plan on staying on dry land, safe and snug right here in Richmond. Now you better put that away and get ready for school. And take Fluffy up to your sister before you go."

William Hayes made the same evaluation of the Stella Maris *and its barges as Mackey made a few minutes before. It represented a potential hazard. If the barges should break loose or be caught by a rogue current swirling near the mouth of the Narrows they could obstruct the path of the* Imo, *perhaps cause a collision. Even with the increased speed, the* Imo *was sluggish to the helm; Hayes instructed the helmsman, Johansen, to come a few more degrees to port. Again the decision was made to pass on the starboard side of the oncoming ship and barges rather than attempt crossing its bow. This placed the* Imo *even closer to the Dartmouth shore.* Imo *and* Mont Blanc *were now one-and-a-half miles apart, converging on a collision course at a combined speed of 15 nautical miles per hour. They would meet in five minutes.*

MABEL MISSED THE tram by only a minute. It may as well have been an hour. From her stop on Windsor Street she watched it until it turned out of sight. Her mother would be furious and no excuse would save Mabel from her sharp tongue. Ada was a stickler for everything being on schedule, being what it was supposed to be, being where it was supposed to be and when it was supposed to be there. Excuses, other than the end of the world, didn't cut the mustard. Mabel moaned audibly. "Lord knows how long I'll have to wait for another tram. It was just in the paper last night that they're cutting back on service 'cause there's not enough motormen and conductors. If they cut back much more there won't be a tram service either. If I hadn't lost my hat pin Saturday night and spent so much time looking for another one, I would have been here in plenty of time. I can't walk it in these shoes, it has to be three miles, I'd kill my feet. If I don't get there in the next half-hour I won't have to worry about my feet—Mum will kill me anyways."

She stamped her foot in frustration and began pacing restlessly, continuing to mutter out loud. "How do I always feel like a little kid caught with my hand in the cookie jar when my mother is around? I'm a married woman with two children for heaven's sake. She's going to be after me again to move back home now that Francis is gone. Well she can forget that idea. I am not moving back in under her thumb. When Francis comes home we'll get a house of our own, far enough away so that we can only visit now and then."

Mabel closed her eyes and sighed, thinking of her husband overseas. "When Francis comes home, she repeated to herself. If he comes home." Last week she'd seen a boy she'd gone to school with who had lost both his legs. A shiver ran down her spine and she whispered,

"Please God, bring him back to me safe and sound."

She scanned the length of Windsor Street; there was not a tram car in sight. Again she stamped her foot, "Damn, damn, and double damn."

None of the navigational decisions, taken separately could definitely be called wrong. The harbour pilots on both vessels were highly skilled men with no blemishes on their records. The fact that the Imo, *under command of William Hayes, was on the wrong side of the Narrows is justifiable when the alternative, a possible head-on collision with either the American freighter or the* Stella Maris, *is considered. That two such decisions had to be made in a short time was unfortunate. At first glance the rules of navigation would presumably place the blame on the* Imo; *but rules can be broken under extenuating circumstances, and these certainly existed.*

Francis Mackey, in command of the Mont Blanc, *cannot be faulted for being in the right position. With an unblemished record dating back twenty-four years he had guided thousands of ships into and out of the harbour. He had moved closer to the Dartmouth shore than originally intended and had no desire to risk grounding the* Mont Blanc *by moving even closer. He was playing strictly by the book and was firm in his belief that the* Imo *would turn to his port and regain its proper channel.*

A contributing factor had to be the conflicting attitudes on the two ships: impatience on the Imo, *with the unforeseen delay causing them to be behind schedule; a state of relief on the* Mont Blanc *with the presumed safety of being off the high seas and protected from harm. Each attitude, although different, produced a common factor—carelessness.*

Years later a Supreme Court would pass judgement that both ships were equally to blame.

THE MATRIARCH OF the Jackson family, Elizabeth, was sitting at the kitchen table in her home at number one Roome Street. Her daughter-in-law, Louisa, was talking about Emma's recent marriage to Lawrence Boutilier and the danger of his job. "If I had lost a husband to the trains, I don't think I would be eager to marry another who is in the same line of work—I just wouldn't be able to handle the worry." Elizabeth set her tea cup back on the table. "Sure, and Emma will be just fine. Men do what they have to do to provide for their family. There is no reason for Emma to fret herself. There is no job that is 100 per cent safe. Even doctors and lawyers get killed sometimes. Of my five sons, two work on the railroad and three work on the waterfront, and there is not a night goes by I don't say a prayer asking the good Lord to keep them from harm. Just last week one of the stevedores working alongside of Fred was hit in the head by a tea chest that fell from the top of a pile. It killed him outright. Fred was very upset, he knew the man well and only moments before had been standing where his friend was. When it is the Lord's will, it will be."

Despite being born and raised in Halifax, Elizabeth's voice carried the musical lilt of Ireland. At age sixty-seven, her manner of speech still reflected her Irish parentage. Normally, Louisa loved to listen to the charming cadence of her mother-in-law's voice, but this morning the morbid subject matter distracted her.

Louisa poured a glass of milk for her daughter, Dorothy, who had joined them, then turned her attention back to Elizabeth. She gave a shudder and wrapped her arms across herself. "For heaven's sake let's talk about something pleasant, it's a beautiful day and all's well with the world—at least here. Did you hear how Mary Jean lashed out at the recruiting man at the hall last night?"

Elizabeth looked up with a start. "Mary never lashed out at anyone in her life—I'd sooner believe in a mouse roaring at a cat. She is the gentlest of all my children. What in heaven's name was it all about?" Louisa helped herself to tea and refilled Elizabeth's cup. "Well, some English Army general or whatever was trying to convince Richmond mothers how wonderful it was to send their boys to fight for their country." Elizabeth snorted in derision, "You mean send them to die for dear old Blighty."

She gave a deep sigh, as she thought of the island she would never see. "My father, may he rest in peace, left County Kilkenny a few years before the Famine. But the tales Dad would tell of how the Irish were treated by the English landowners are enough to chill your soul. The poor devils were chased off the land, herded into boats like so many cattle and shipped away from their home. They were treated worse than cattle—hundreds died on those boats and hundreds more died of disease after they got here. Families my parents knew well were torn apart; some were shipped one place and some another. It was cheaper to ship them to this side of the ocean to get rid of them than to feed them."

She paused for a moment, idly rubbing the tea cup given to her by her mother many years ago, as if by touching it she could reach the past. "How like the English to expect us to sacrifice our children, for their own benefit, in a war that never should have been."

Louisa had finished drying the breakfast dishes and placed the towel on the rack as Elizabeth ended her denunciation of the English. "Oh, come now, Mother Jackson, surely you don't mean that. Why, many of our very best friends and neighbours are English and you couldn't meet nicer people."

Elizabeth turned to her. "My dear, I don't blame or dislike the common English people; I'm talking about the higher-ups. The ones who try to say how everyone else may live. Even the English who are here don't like them, that's why they left England in the first place, to get away from class distinction. Of course the ones we know are nice people, they're like us. I'm angry at the high muckety-mucks, like that general Mary Jean stepped into last night."

William's wife, Evelyn, who had just entered the kitchen and was starting to cube last Sunday's roast to make hash for supper, wheeled around laughing. "Mary Jean stepped into a general?" Louisa explained the incident and by now the three women were laughing. Louisa said, "The general was just lucky Ada wasn't there. If that lady got on her high horse the general would have been busted down to private, tarred and feathered and ridden out of town on a rail—and his whole army couldn't save him!"

As the laughter died down six-year-old Dorothy crept up to her grandmother, tugged at her sleeve and whispered, "Granny, if you would like some toast I could make it for you. I know how and I have plenty of time before I go to school." Elizabeth smiled. "Why yes, child, and sure that would be very nice, but mind you don't go burning yourself, and won't I have another cup of tea to go with it." Louisa poured the tea and placed it in front of her mother-in-law. "Mama, all of us have been hinting around for the last month trying to find out what you would like for Christmas. There must be something you want." Elizabeth was silent for a moment, thinking again of the tragedy of the Irish famine. Then she spoke softly but fervently, as if in prayer.

"Yes, there is something I wish for with all my heart. But I don't think you or the other children can grant it. I wish that the Jackson family, their wives and children and their children's children, never have to face the hardships of those who have gone before them. I wish they may find happiness and fulfilment during long and fruitful lives—and, above all, that they stay together always, united by love. There, that is my Christmas wish."

The last five minutes were squandered in indecision and panic. Each ship waited for the other to give way and change course. The Imo *blew a signal that indicated its intention to pass starboard to starboard as it had with the American vessel and the* Stella Maris. *The* Mont Blanc *had no intention of risking grounding on the Dartmouth shoreline and whistled for the* Imo *to* pass on its port side in accordance with marine regulations. Neither ship altered course. In the final minute there was a frantic cacophony of horns and whistles, and even shouts, that had no affect on the outcome. In the last few moments the Mont Blanc desperately started a turn to port, far too late, and each ship reversed engine, an equally useless gesture. The prow of the Imo ploughed into the deck of the Mont Blanc.

The wound was far from fatal. Neither ship was rendered unseaworthy and the damage, in comparison to most marine accidents, could be considered negligible. But the prow of the Imo had penetrated the deck of the Mont Blanc a sufficient distance to strike the outer barrels of benzol. These split under the impact and the volatile liquid cascaded to the deck.

For a minute the two vessels were locked in an embrace. Then the force of the propellers, churning in reverse, tore them slowly apart. The ragged metal of the gouge in the Mont Blanc, scraping against the steel side of the Imo, acted as a flint sending a shower of sparks into the flammable fluid. Only one spark was needed to begin the chain of events. The volatile liquid ignited in an explosive burst of light and heat. The heat would in turn became the catalyst that pushed the immense cargo of explosives toward an intolerable degree of instability. With the first flash of flame the point of no return was passed. Disaster was now inevitable.

There was more than a touch of irony. The two ships, now so closely coupled, were on opposite ends of humanity's scale. The Mont Blanc loaded with the means to inflict death and destruction; the Imo dedicated to the humane task of bringing relief and hope to the victims of such terror. This grotesque paradox would pass unnoticed by the participants in the mind-numbing horror fast approaching.

CHAPTER

4

The exploding barrels of benzol shot ribbons of flame high into the whorls of steam and smoke; there, they flashed and twisted, contracted and expanded, in a kaleidoscope of brilliant colour. Each bursting barrel added its own intensity to this overwhelming pyrotechnical extravaganza. Halifax had never seen fireworks to rival this. Children were irresistibly halted on their way to school; tradesmen cheerfully laid aside their tools; factory workers closed down machinery and work ground to a halt along the waterfront and railyard. All moved closer for a better look. Hundreds watched from behind their windows, while some even ventured to factory rooftops for an unobstructed view. After the monotonous months of dull drudgery, the dreary years of supplying the demands of war, who could resist this break from the ordinary? Within moments there was a carnival-like atmosphere. Few, if any, saw it as an ominous precursor of doom. Meanwhile, below the burning deck, where nearly 3,000 tons of TNT, picric acid, and guncotton were stored, the temperature steadily and irreversibly began to rise. The devil's brew was about to awaken.

JIM JACKSON AND Joe Hinch heard the shrieking whistles and the panic-stricken blasts; they turned just as the *Imo* hit the *Mont Blanc*. They saw the shower of sparks as the vessels pulled apart and the first flames from the exploding benzene. Standing on the bridge over the Richmond railyard gave them an ideal vantage point from which to enjoy the pyrotechnics.

On board the *Mont Blanc*, figures scurried haphazardly about in obvious fear and confusion. Joe grabbed Jim's elbow, "Jesus, look! That guy is on fire!" Jim winced under Joe's crushing grip. Joe's years as ironworker had given him the grip of a steel vice. Jim pointed, "It's okay, Joe, his coat was on fire and he's just thrown it in the drink. Thank God it's on the other side. I'll bet someone is below, scuttling the thing." Joe transferred his grip to the iron railing, "You lose your bet, old man, the crew is getting off right now, see the lifeboats?"

"Yeah, well there could still be someone down below opening sea-cocks." Joe chuckled, "Only an Irishman would be daft enough to still be on board that tub, and since she is flying a French flag that seems pretty unlikely. I don't blame those poor sods for deserting; I wouldn't even be waiting for a lifeboat. I'd have jumped off the minute it started. I'd rather drown than burn any day—burning is the one way I don't want to go."

Jim looked at him with amusement, "So, what do you have planned for your grand finale?" Joe didn't even need time to think, "I'd like to be shot by a jealous husband when I'm ninety-five years old." Both men laughed uproariously and Jim said, "You tell that to my sister and your demise may be a lot sooner than that."

More barrels exploded as he spoke, sending sheets of writhing yellow and orange flame through the dense pall of black smoke that now billowed more than a mile above the *Mont Blanc*. The men's banter ended.

Joe pointed at the ship, "James, my lad, that's a cannon on the fore-deck of that tub. Where there is a cannon there must be shells. I think it might be wise if we get the hell out of here. Home is a safer place to be. Besides, Mary Jean gets hostile when I'm late. She worries a lot and won't relax until I walk in the door." Both men walked the rest of the bridge and when they reached Barrington Street they took a last look at the burning ship. As they parted ways, Jim said, "I'll come over after I eat to get that tarp."

They were wrong about one thing, neither home would be a safer place.

The fire on board the Mont Blanc *was out of control from the moment it began. The push from the larger ship and the propeller of the* Mont Blanc, *still churning in reverse, forced the deadly cargo toward the Richmond shore, less than fifteen hundred feet away. Captain LeMedec tried to organize his men to fight the fire, but when an exploding drum of benzol splashed a man's coat, which erupted in flames, it quickly became obvious to both captain and crew that further effort was futile. He ordered the engines stopped and lifeboat stations made ready. LeMedec then commanded the men near him to lower the boats and abandon ship.*

This order was promptly obeyed. Within minutes the boats were being lowered and the crew of the Mont Blanc *were escaping from the inferno.*

The captain could do nothing to save either his ship or the city; his effort must now be directed to saving his crew. In this, with the exception of one man, he would be successful.

As JIM JACKSON made his way home on the east side of Barrington Street, two young girls were among the crowd of people running down the other side of the street toward the waterfront. Florence and Muriel, like many others, had been distracted from their job at hand. Thirteen-year-old Florence had her father's lunch pail clutched tightly to her chest with both arms.

Their uncle's voice boomed from across the street, stopping them in their tracks, "And just where do you think you two are going?" Florence held up the lunch pail, "Mum told us to deliver Daddy's lunch." Jim made a decision, "No, that's too close to the fire—you could get hurt. I think you had better go back home, the pair of you. Your dad can get along without his lunch today. Don't go any closer to the fire. Go right home now—do you hear me?" The sisters nodded and turned to go back along Barrington Street. By the time they reached Kenny Street, their uncle had turned the corner on Duffus and was out of sight.

Florence started running across Barrington toward the pedestrian bridge over the Richmond Railyard, with Muriel in hot pursuit. "Wait up, wait for me," she cried. Florence stopped long enough for her younger sister to catch up. "We can go across here and down the steps and get a good look from Pier Six or by the Lorne Club." Muriel stopped. "I'm not going down there. Uncle James said we were not to go closer to it. And besides, we'll be late for school." With exasperation, Florence exclaimed, "Oh, for heaven's sake, Muriel, what Uncle James doesn't know will never hurt him. Come on, don't be such a scaredy-cat. We'll be able to tell the kids at school how close we were."

Muriel backed up a few steps, "I don't care, I am scared, I'm going to school and afterwards I'm going to tell Mum what you did and you'll get it for sure when you get home." She started to cry. Florence threw her hands up in disgust, "Go on home then you little cry-baby, I'm going down on the wharf." As Muriel turned to run toward St. Joseph's School, Florence started down the steps from the pedestrian bridge, no longer quite so brave, but committed to her defiance.

THE EDMONDS BROTHERS had reached Isaac Creighton's store, on the corner of Barrington Street and Roome. Mr. Creighton, his wife, and more than a dozen people were standing outside the store watching the burning ship. Isaac Creighton, at age eighty-eight and his wife Annie, aged seventy-three, were two of the most well-liked and respected people in Richmond; their store was a popular meeting place for many of the locals. Overhearing young Arthur urging Henry to go with him to the wharf, Mr. Creighton intervened. "You boys had better stop right where you are. There is no way of knowing what's on that ship—could be dynamite or anything—and you could get blown to pieces or burnt to a crisp. Just stay here now, young fellows." Arthur hesitated, but decided to obey. He reached in his pocket to make sure the dollar his mother had given him to buy a scribbler was safe and then looked in the store window. He saw one of the clerks, Laura Perry, and waved to her before turning to watch the burning ship from the safety of the storefront.

The Stella Maris *was just leaving the Narrows into Bedford Basin when the frantic activity caught the crew's attention. They saw the first flames shooting skyward. Moments later an urgent message from Naval Command ordered them to render immediate assistance. They were not told about the explosives; their instructions were simply to secure a line and tow the burning vessel outside the harbour. They cast off the towline to the barges, made a U-turn and steamed at top speed toward the flaming ship, now almost in the middle of the Narrows, about a thousand feet from either shore.*

Their task was hopeless. Within five minutes of the fire's start there was no place on the Mont Blanc's *deck to stand without being burned to death and they could see no means of securing a line without being on board.*

CLOSETED WITH INVOICES, in the small room on the back of his store that he used as an office, Constant Upham wasn't aware of the furore in the Narrows until he noticed the reflection of flames on the wall. After watching from his office window for a few minutes he determined that the burning ship was going to drift over to either the Sugar Refinery or Pier Six. He walked rapidly to the front of the store and saw the flames reflected in the windows of the Protestant Orphanage and Hillis Foundry on the other side of Barrington Street. His wife, Jenny, was at the front window when Constant told her, "I'm going out to have a look and see how bad it is. You stay here. I'll be back in a few minutes."

The alarm box was within a hundred feet of his store. He reached it, broke the glass with a stone, opened the door and pulled the lever down. The alarm would sound in the West Street Fire Station. The *Patricia* was about to undergo baptism by fire.

Within minutes of leaving the doomed ship the crew of the Mont Blanc *landed on the shore at Tuft's Cove. Mrs. Agnes Marsh watched them scramble from the boats and start to race toward her, away from the water's edge. She had finished bathing her one-month-old daughter, Lenora, just minutes before and had left her home on Fernhill Road, trailing two-year-old Florence, to see what all the yelling and excitement was about. With the baby securely in her arms, bundled against the cold, and Flo by her side she watched the antics of the crew.*

The French mariners tried to alert the bystanders of the impending danger. They didn't speak English and their wild gesticulations were greeted with amusement and treated as an added fillip to what was already turning out to be an exciting day. Even the harbour pilot, Francis Mackey, was having little success in moving people out of danger. One crew member solved the problem by grabbing Lenora from her mother's arms and racing for the protection of the woods. Another sailor picked up Flo and followed after him. Agnes gave a scream and ran after both sailors, intent on rescuing her children.

Two more ships joined the Stella Maris *in her crew's effort to get the* Mont Blanc *out of the Narrows. Fourteen seamen aboard a whaleboat from the* Highflyer *attempted to secure a towline, while a launch from the* Niobe, *carrying one officer and several seamen, stood by in case of need. The four vessels were now within a few feet of Pier Six at Richmond. As the* Mont Blanc *came to rest against the wooden pier the line was finally secured and Tom Triggs, acting-captain of the* Highflyer, *ordered the whaler and its crew back to the ship.*

JOE HINCH CAME through the kitchen door to be pounced upon by the twins. He scooped one squealing little girl under each arm, and gave Mary Jean a peck on the cheek. "You're missing all the excitement, old girl. There's a ship on fire in the harbour." His wife put his breakfast on the table, saying, "So, that's why you're late coming home. What kind of a ship?" Joe shrugged, put Annie and Margaret down, and sat at the kitchen table, "I've no idea, but it could be an oil tanker, judging by the black smoke. The thing is almost touching Pier Six. Whatever it is it's going to burn right down to the water. The fire department just showed up, but they haven't a hope. Me and your brother Jim were watching from the bridge when the sailors got off into lifeboats. Soon as I finish eating, I'm goin' back out, I don't want to miss anything."

Mary Jean put the frypan on the top of the warming oven and wiped her hands on her apron. "I think I'll just pop out and see for myself. The dishes can wait until I come back." She folded her apron neatly, placed it by the sink and walked to the hall stand. Joe was watching her as she put on her hat and pinned it in place, put on her new coat and wrapped a scarf around her neck, then examined herself in the mirror. By the time she finished he was laughing uproariously. "Pay close attention ladies, your mother is showing you how to dress for a fire. It's exactly the same as if she were going for tea and crumpets with the mayor or some other high muckety-muck."

As she reached the front door he became serious. "Now listen, Mary, my love, don't get too close. That ship has a cannon and there's got to be gunpowder on board. Go across the street and peek around the Matthew's house, but don't go any closer than that. I'll come out in a few minutes and watch with you."

He turned back to Annie and Margaret who had been trying to quiz him about Christmas. In a serious tone he reassured two wide-eyed little girls. "Sometimes, if there are little twin girls, who have been very, very good, Santa has been known to leave two teddy bears. Not one, mind you, but two teddy bears, one for each." Neither girl knew that, at this very moment, two, large, very cuddly teddy bears were quietly hiding behind a box on the top shelf of the closet in their mother's closet, also impatiently waiting for Christmas day.

WILLIAM EDMONDS WAS also thinking of Christmas. At age eleven he was too "grown up" to believe in Santa Claus, but maybe someone else would give him enough balsa wood to build his model plane. That'd be more fun than anything—even a tree house—and he wouldn't have to wait until spring to build it. Maybe he could even get his dad to help. He finished his glass of milk and walked over to the kitchen window.

FLORENCE JACKSON WAS no longer having fun. She was almost at the Sugar Refinery and could feel the heat from the fire tightening the skin on her face. She now wished she had gone to school with Muriel. Her father's lunch pail was still clutched in her arms but any thoughts of delivering it had long been abandoned. She decided she'd had enough of being a responsible young lady. It was a frightened little girl who turned her back to the blaze and started to run toward the railway over-pass and the safety of school.

The Patricia *had arrived to fight its first chemical fire. In addition, there was another chemical pumper from the Quinpool Road station, a horse-drawn hosewagon from the Isleville Street station and nine members of the Halifax Fire Department, including Chief Condon and Deputy Chief Brunt. Another engine from the Brunswick Street station was on the way.*

Realizing the futility of trying to control the fire on the ship, Chief

*Condon directed his efforts to saving the wooden pier that was beginning to
smoulder. With the line in place, he was hoping the* Stella Maris *might tow
the* Mont Blanc *to deeper water and somehow scuttle the blazing vessel.
This was a forlorn hope. Scuttling was out of the question; no one would ever
set foot on her deck again. The deck plates were turning red with the heat.*

*The heat below deck had long since passed human tolerance; in a fraction
of a minute it would reach a level beyond the tolerance of the cargo.*

CLARA HINCH ROLLED over in bed and pulled the comforter up under
her chin. Feeling completely miserable she reached under her pillow
for a handkerchief. She had argued with her mother about staying
home from her job but was glad Mary Jean had insisted. Until this cold
was over, this was the best place to be. Besides, the Christmas party and
dance was only a week from Saturday, that gave her nine days to get
back into shape.

Thinking of the party sent a shiver of excitement down her spine.
She was almost positive a certain young man would be putting a ring on
her finger that night; she simply had to be over this cold by then. Sitting
up she blew her nose vigorously and looked across the room. Lena was
still asleep and Mary Mabel's bed was empty. Both had been down with
a cold all week and were still home today. A body hadn't a chance of not
catching a cold with two sisters in the same room hacking and honking
day and night. She should have her own bedroom. The trouble was that
there were too many people and not enough house. She heard her
father, in the kitchen, romping with the twins. Every word was clear as
could be. How could you have any privacy? Never mind, soon she
would be married and maybe she would have a home of her own. She
snuggled down in the warm bed and pulled the comforter over her
head. It was a time to dream. To dream of waltzes and love; a ring on
her finger; marriage and babies; a home of her own with a
pretty little fence and flowers all around, and most of all, endless
happiness with a young man who adored her.

JUST BEHIND THE Hinch home, on Albert Street, their friend and
neighbour, Harriet Bungay, had a problem. This morning she'd promised her husband, Edward, a beef stew for his noon meal. The vegetables were on the stove and she was about to brown the meat when she
realized she had no savory. Damn. Almost everything else in a beef stew
could be left out or substituted with something else, but in Harriet's
book, a stew was not a stew without parsnips and savory. Her mind
raced. The boys, Edward Jr., sixteen, and his brother Howard, eigh-

teen, had already left for work at the nursery and she was alone with ten-year-old Gladys, who was at home from school with a cold. Surely it wouldn't harm the girl to run to the store if she bundled up warm and didn't stay out too long. Besides, Wallace's store was only two doors away and Harriet could leave the stove long enough to watch the girl from the front yard.

"Gladys, I need you to go to the store and get me five cents worth of savory. Put on your blue coat and wear your mittens, you have enough cold now, run both ways to keep yourself warm. Here's a quarter. You can buy five cents worth of candy as long as you promise not to eat it before dinner. I want you to go right there and come straight home, don't you dare dawdle, I'll be watching you from the front yard." Harriet gave the vegetables a stir, put the iron skillet on the back of the stove to stay warm, and glanced at the kitchen clock. Two minutes after nine. She would have plenty of time to make a pan of biscuits to go with the stew. With a final stir of the vegetables she went to the front door.

Harriet gazed in shock at the billowing black cloud of smoke spiralling and spreading from the waterfront. Anxiously she looked for Gladys. The girl was almost to the store but walking slowly, her eyes turned toward the fire. "Gladys, hurry, I told you to run." The girl started to run and reached the door of the shop. Jack, their English Setter, was whining and prancing around the gate, anxious to follow. Stamping her feet to keep warm Harriet patted him briskly. "Stay here, Jack, she's only going to the store—you'll see here again in a minute." With a sense of dread she again stared at the pall of smoke.

For only an instant the tableau was frozen in time. Annie Turner stood in front of the Lorne Club, floodlit by the garish glare of the blazing ship. The firemen began the struggle to save the wooden pier, watched by Constant Upham who had called them to the hopeless task. Ada Moore was in the doorway of her home, waiting for Mabel. Hundreds of school children gazed in awe. Joe Hinch told another improbable tale about Santa Claus to the twins while he ate his breakfast. James Jackson turned toward Margaret to speak as their daughter, Minnie raised the bedroom window to speak to them. Tom Triggs and Richard Woolams watched the towline from the Maris grow taut, but it was far too late. Charlie Mayers had watched the spectacle from the beginning, the burning hulk had moved toward him and was now less than three hundred feet away. The first sense of fear gnawed at him and he turned to retrace his steps to the Middleham Castle; there would only be time for one step. Frank Carew also felt fear. The hatches on the Picton were battened, and the explosives were now safe. His job was done; he ordered his men to run. Some chose to run behind the Sugar Refinery, some ran in front; the first found safety, the latter found death. John Jackson stood straight up on the boxcar; he saw three of his brothers running in front of the Sugar Refinery. His nephew, Lew Jackson tried in vain to get his attention from the tracks below. Clara Hinch was lost in her dreams. From behind the windows of homes people stared. And then the final second ticked into eternity.

MARY JEAN LEFT her warm, comfortable home to the sounds of two little girls shrieking with delight and a husband's booming laughter. She hurried along Veith toward Richmond Street, clutching her coat tightly against the morning chill. As she was passing the Matthews' house she glanced to her right and saw the huge pall of smoke above the roof. With dismay she said aloud, "Lord help us, I just put Clara's good blouse and skirt on the line. They'll be black with soot if I don't get them in soon." In the same glance she could see the reflection of flames in the windows of the north wall of the Hillis Foundry. The whole side of the building glowed an ominous orange.

At that instant there was a blinding flash of light far brighter than a hundred suns. So bright that colour disappeared and the scene would be forever etched in her memory as a silhouette of intense black and hurtful white. The Matthews' home came toward her in thousands of pieces and she tried to throw her hands in front of her face. There was not enough time.

CHAPTER
5

At approximately five minutes past nine, on the morning of December 6th, 1917, close to six million pounds of explosives on board the Mont Blanc *detonated. To understand the almost incomprehensible potential of this amount of explosives, consider the tragedy that occurred on April 19, 1995, in Oklahoma City. On that day a van containing eleven hundred pounds of explosives erupted in front of the Alfred Murrah Federal Building. One hundred and sixty-eight people died, either instantly or within a few days. Many hundreds more received injuries. The nine-storey concrete building was totally destroyed and sixteen other nearby buildings were structurally damaged.*

To equal the magnitude of the Halifax Explosion would have required more than fifty-three hundred vans parked in front of the building. And even this is not a valid comparison. The buildings in Oklahoma City were steel and reinforced concrete; those in Halifax were wood-frame construction.

Heard and felt over two hundred miles away, the Halifax Explosion ranked as the largest man-made explosion in the world until surpassed by the atomic bomb, twenty-eight years later. Even today, eighty years after the event, it is still classed as the most devastating disaster in Canadian history.

To explain the almost unexplainable power released, the explosion must be dissected into the individual facets unleashed at the moment of detonation, for there was far more than just one force. Each force, in its own right, can be classed as a catastrophe; combined and taken in total they become a mind-numbing cataclysm.

The first effect was a fireball with an intensity approaching the temperature on the surface of the sun. It lasted a fraction of a second and did not reach far, probably no more than a few hundred feet. It did, however, last long enough and reach far enough to incinerate many of those who had moved closer for a better view of the burning ship. The cells of the human body are primarily water. When exposed to many thousands of degrees of heat, the water turns instantly to steam. Steam, with an expansion factor two hundred times that of water, will cause human body cells to explode. People within the critical area, not shielded by buildings or objects between them and the ship, vaporized and disappeared as if they had never existed. Within that radius, every combustible surface burst into flames, extinguished a split second later by the rush of wind.

The concussion at the instant of detonation dealt a hammer-like blow to the bodies of those beyond the fireball but still in the immediate area and not shielded by structures. Some would have no outward mark as evidence of the damage done, but internal organs were crushed, eardrums ruptured and brains destroyed.

The Mont Blanc has often been referred to as a floating bomb. It more aptly should be compared to a hand grenade—a hand grenade 300 ft. long, 40 ft. wide and 30 ft. high, powered by an explosive charge tens of millions times more powerful than any grenade that ever existed. The 3,121 tons of metal that had been a ship were now millions of shards of iron and steel spewing outward in a hemisphere of destruction with a muzzle velocity greater than any bullet or shell. Those ejected in a horizontal plane scythed a bloodied path through Richmond, the railyard, the dockyard and the waterfront. People were beheaded, cut in two or slashed so horribly that death was only a matter of moments. Even the pieces that went straight up would arch over and descend with sufficient force to maim or kill. The majority of the shards were small, some as tiny as needles, but the force with which they were flung gave them the capability to cause injury or death. Some of the larger pieces were convoluted into bizarre shapes, much as a dishcloth that has been wrung and left to dry.

Only three pieces of the Mont Blanc were large enough to be recognizable. The shaft of the anchor, five feet nine inches long weighing 1,207 pounds, was hurled westward over the city to imbed itself four feet into the ground on the west side of the Northwest Arm—almost two and one-half miles from the blast centre. The shaft was at an angle of sixty degrees. This angle of inclination indicates that at the height of its trajectory it would have been one and one-half to two miles above the city. The anchor's arms were broken off near the crown, the flukes had been sheared from the shaft; the force necessary to cause this type of fracture has been estimated to be between 3.5 and 4 million foot-pounds of energy.

The barrel of the stern cannon, weighing within pounds of the anchor, travelled in the opposite direction. It came to rest in a wooded area of Dartmouth more than two miles from the waterfront and 280 feet above tide water. The barrel was partially melted and twisted. Also, a three hundred pound piece of the Mont Blanc's stern post, twisted and bent beyond credibility landed on the deck of the Imo, more than a quarter mile away.

The explosion ripped through the bottom of the Mont Blanc *and smashed into the harbour floor, causing a ground shock that rippled the massive rock foundation of the city. It was comparable to a medium-sized earthquake with enough power to crack walls, bring down ceiling plaster and shift some houses off their foundation. Much of the structural damage to homes in the south and west ends of the city was caused by this shock wave. It was felt, as a ground tremor, as far away as Cape Breton and New Brunswick where it smashed windows and knocked items off shelves. However, The major effect of the ground shock, in the Halifax/Dartmouth area, was the weakening of buildings and homes making them more vulnerable to the blast of air now moving away from the explosion centre with the strength of a thousand hurricanes.*

We think of air as a soft and gentle thing, the first warm breezes of spring, the freshening breeze on a hot summer day; but this wind was a diabolical thing. Within the first half mile it was, by far, the most destructive force unleashed by the explosion. After that distance it created an equivalent and opposite force that was equally destructive. In shape, the wall of air moving away from the point of explosion was as an ever-expanding doughnut, the outer surface a rigid wall that smashed everything in its path; the 'hole' of the doughnut being an intense low-pressure system that caused buildings to explode.

The rigidity of any material is determined by the space between the molecules; the only difference between the strength and rigidity of a feather and steel is the density of its molecular composition. This wind was being compressed by the explosion of nearly 3,000 tons of TNT and picric acid. It has been determined the force exploding outward from these materials is moving at 4 mi. per second which translates to an incredible 14,400 mi. per hour. Since it was pushing the air ahead at the same speed, the molecules were compressing into the ones ahead and they, in turn, into others. Within a hundred feet of epicentre the rigidity of the air would have a consistency greater than steel; witness the fact that an iron footbridge over the Richmond Railyard tracks was shorn from its anchorage in a mass of screaming and shattered metal; freight cars and locomotives were lifted off their tracks and tossed like toys; railway tracks were torn from their bed and twisted like pretzels.

This velocity decayed rapidly with distance, the resistance of the undisturbed air in front and the structures being demolished, depleted the energy, but people a half mile from the ship were smashed by the wind before they heard the sound of the blast. The wall of air, even at that distance, was moving faster than the speed of sound, almost certainly in excess of seven hundred miles per hour.

Most people find a hurricane of one hundred miles per hour a frightening experience. It will tear shingles from a roof, do structural damage to houses and uproot trees that have lost their flexibility. If you double that speed to two hundred miles per hour it would destroy everything in its path. The damage would not be just doubled it would be hundreds of times greater. Before the explosion the damage possible with a wind force exceeding seven hundred miles an hour would have been unimaginable. After the explosion there was no need to imagine—the graphic evidence was there in the form of photographs taken in the Richmond area. In a circle with a diameter of one mile, centred where the Mont Blanc had been, not a house was standing; of the trees, only those saplings thin enough to offer little resistance to the wind survived. Richmond was a sea of rubble.

The other force, just behind this battering-ram of compressed air, was the partial vacuum being created. Since the molecules of air were being compressed into a solid ring, smashing outward at an enormous speed, following behind it was an area the air had been blasted from—an intense low pressure system. This would be as damaging as the outer ring that created it. Houses protected by other buildings and not flattened by the battering-ram, erupted microseconds later as this low pressure swept over them. The effect was similar to the eye of a tornado. The air inside the building, at normal pressure exploded outward, destroying the home from within. People in these homes did have a better chance of survival; the debris blew away from instead of toward them. Many were blown out of houses, through windows and doorways, escaping entrapment in the wreckage and the ultimate horror of being burned to death in the flaming ruins of their homes. This force also lessened with distance. Houses and buildings within two thousand feet of epicentre were totally demolished while houses three thousand feet and beyond had roofs blown off or sidewalls driven off the sills. The Richmond area was subject to the unmitigated force of both wind and vacuum.

The explosive wall of wind and the topography of Richmond combined to create an additional, freakish force, that was exclusively confined to this area. Richmond is built on a very steep hill. From mean sea level to the top of Fort Needham and Gottingen Street, a distance of approximately a half mile, there is a vertical rise of over two hundred feet. As the explosive wall of wind hit this hill, the incline and the drag effect of the ground surface caused the wall of air to start rolling under itself. Just as the rotation speed of a windmill's blades are governed by the speed of the wind, so was the rolling motion of the air wall determined by the forward, supersonic speed that propelled it. The super-hurricane was now compounded with attributes of a monstrous tornado. This tornadic effect was confined to the area that created it—the Richmond hill, from Duffus Street south to Russell Street and from Veith Street to Fort Needham.

Pickets were plucked from fences; shingles were ripped from roofs; and pieces of glass, lumber and other debris whirled in the maelstrom; slashing and gouging those in the way. Even people were caught up in this tornadic tumult. Swept up and held suspended, they were spun and twisted about by the tornadic effect, still propelled forward by the leading edge of the air wall. They experienced the feeling of passing and being passed by bits of debris that had been lifted from the wreckage. When the weight of their body balanced the force of the lift and the forward velocity of the air wall lessened, they were deposited back on earth. In some cases they found themselves more than half a mile from where they began—their clothing shredded and torn from their bodies, tightly-laced boots ripped from their feet. But miraculously, most were still alive.

As the southward edge of the air wall reached Citadel Hill it was again deflected upward. Just as Richmond Hill and Fort Needham had protected the West End, Citadel Hill saved the South End from total destruction. Dating back to Halifax's early history as a garrison town, the Citadel finally fulfilled its mandate to protect the city, or at least part of it.

By now, two miles from blast centre, the wall of air had decelerated well below the speed of sound but was still well above the velocity of a violent hurricane.

As the ring of air exited over the ocean and Dartmouth to the south and east, Spryfield, Herring Cove and Saint Margaret's Bay to the west, and Bedford and Sackville to the north, it left behind an area depleted of air. The wind may have waned but it was far from finished. Nature abhors a vacuum. There was an inrush of air to fill the low pressure space. Houses that were weakened by the outgoing wind but still standing, collapsed under this new onslaught from the opposite direction. Evidence of this returning blast of air are trees, uprooted and flat, lying in the opposite direction to those flattened by the outward blasts. This mass of air, racing in from all directions, met with a thunderous clap in the space where moments before a ship had been—and at last grew still.

In addition to the fireball, concussion, the deadly shower of shrapnel, the battering-ram of air and the eruptive damage of the low pressure system, there was another death-dealing phenomena—a wall of water. The explosion of the Mont Blanc *affected the water as well as the air. The concussion split the bottom and sides of the ship, violently pushing the water of the harbour away from the blast centre. As the ship was almost ashore at Pier Six, initially Halifax received little more than a splash. However, on the other side of the* Mont Blanc *there was deep water and room enough to generate a wave estimated to be fifty feet high, which surged across the harbour and smashed into north end Dartmouth.*

Semi-circular in shape, the wave peaked in its centre and tapered gradually on either end to a negligible height. Dartmouth received the main impact of the wave, while its southern tail surged through the harbour, sinking and damaging ships and washing many stevedores from the piers to their death. The north end blast dissipated in Bedford Basin, causing minor damage.

For the next five minutes or more the main section of the wave oscillated back and forth across the Narrows, inundating first one shoreline and then receding and flooding the other. For the Richmond area, the first wall of water coming back from the Dartmouth side was the most damaging. It was twenty feet or more in height and surged through the spot where the Mont Blanc *had been, racing over the rubble that was the Lorne Club, Sugar Refinery and the Barrington Street houses and shops. The torrent streamed over the wreckage of the lower reaches of Richmond all the way to Fort Needham. At the upper reaches, the wave was as surf along a beach; never very deep but with the power of the sea behind it. The wave raced over the rubble but penetration was negligible. In some places it served to extinguish the fires that were starting, but not nearly enough to stop the eventual conflagration that consumed most of the homes and some of the families of Richmond.*

Subsequent waves decreased in height and destruction. In their return to the harbour these waves clutched the bodies of the dead, the mortally wounded and the relatively uninjured. Many of those who survived the explosion would now drown or perish from hypothermia. Massive amounts of debris were scoured into the harbour. The harbour was littered with wreckage and bodies for days, and corpses were still being recovered along the shorelines weeks later. Others were washed out to sea, never to be afforded the dignity of burial.

Richmond suffered a further indignity generated by the explosion of the Mont Blanc. *When explosives detonate not every grain of the substance ignites. Such was the case with the devil's brew on the* Mont Blanc. *Probably hundreds of tons failed to explode. This heated material was propelled upwards and converted by condensation into a sticky, black sludge which rained down upon the victims. Unlike the other forces released, it wasn't fatal, neither did it inflict injury, it was simply another indignity for a people already saturated with indignities. This black rain was confined to an area about three-quarters of a mile in diameter, directly under the centre of the explosion. As with so many effects of the Halifax Explosion, it confined itself to Richmond.*

Ordeal by fire was the final catastrophe. The collapsed houses upset the kitchen and hall stoves, setting fire to the ruins. Richmond would burn for more than a week, fuelled by the winter's load of coal and coke contained in most basement bins. The majority of the bodies recovered from the Richmond area were charred by fire, many to the point of being unrecognizable even as to sex. Those trapped and beyond rescue died screaming as they endured the horror of being burned alive. The frustrated rescuers were forced to confront the trauma of standing by, helplessly, listening to those screams, a sound they would hear and be haunted by for the rest of their lives.

Indian School at Tuft's Cove

Photo courtesy of P.A.N.S. (N-7034)

St. Joseph's Convent

Photo courtesy of P.A.N.S. (N-7035)

These two photographs illustrate the two major forces, the explosive wall of air and the destructive low-pressure system that followed behind. Both buildings were the same distance from the **Mont Blanc**, approximately two thousand feet, and received about one-fourth of the explosive force that hit the lower part of Richmond.

In the top photograph, the Indian School at Tuft's Cove was not shielded by other buildings and the sidewall facing the explosion was punched in by the wall of air.

In the bottom photo, St. Joseph's Convent was shielded from the blast by other buildings and was destroyed by the tornadic effect of the low pressure system. The walls bent outward and the roof was lifted off. The near sidewall has been pushed off the sill. All the damage was caused by the air within the building, at normal pressure, exploding outward into the semi-vacuum.

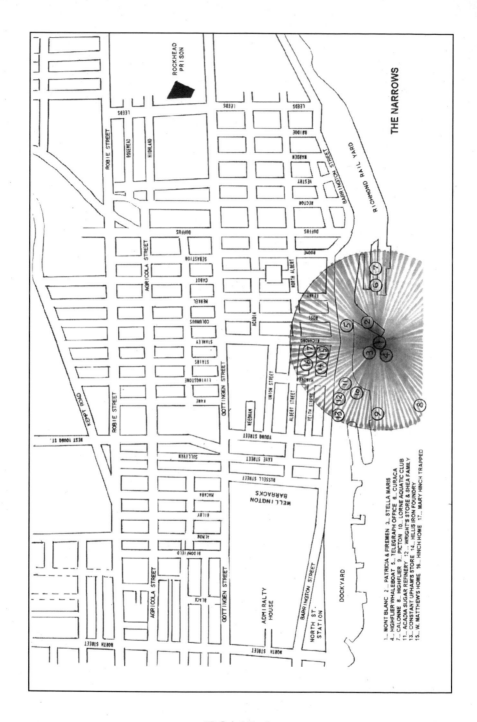

ZONE 1
One thousand feet from explosion site

Map labels and legend:

THE NARROWS

ROCKHEAD PRISON

RICHMOND RAIL YARD

ROBIE STREET
ROSEHEAD
HIGHLAND
LEEDS
LEEDS
BRIDGE
LEEDS
RICHMOND RAIL YARD
BARRINGTON STREET
BARDEN
VESTRY
RECTOR
DUFFUS
SEBASTIAN
AGRICOLA STREET
CABOT
MERKEL
ROSS
COLUMBUS
STANLEY
STAIRS
KANE
LIVINGSTONE
GOTTINGEN STREET
NEEDHAM
YOUNG STREET
FAYE STREET
SULLIVAN
RUSSELL STREET
MACARA
BILBY
ALMON
BLOOMFIELD
BLACK
AGRICOLA STREET
NORTH STREET
KEMPT ROAD
ROBIE STREET
WEST YOUNG ST.
GOTTINGEN STREET
WELLINGTON BARRACKS
ADMIRALTY HOUSE
NORTH ST. STATION
BARRINGTON STREET
DOCKYARD
NORTH STREET
NORTH ALBERT
BOONE
ACADIA
RICHMOND
FERRY
UNION STREET
ALBERT STREET
VEITH STREET
HANOVER

Legend:
1... MONT BLANC 2... PATRICIA & FIREMEN 3. STELLA MARIS
4... HIGHFLIER WHALEBOAT 5... TELEGRAPH OFFICE 6. CURACA.
7... CALONNE 8... HIGHFLIER 9... PICTON 10... LORNE AQUATIC CLUB
11... ACADIA SUGAR REFINERY 12... WRIGHTS STORE & SHEA FAMILY
13... CONSTANT UPHAM'S STORE 14... HILLIS IRON FOUNDRY
15... W. MATTHEWS HOME 16... HINCH HOME 17... MARY HINCH TRAPPED

50

CHAPTER
6

THE FULL FORCE of the explosion smashed into the Richmond water-front area, demolishing everything and killing or injuring almost every-one in its path. The *Mont Blanc*—its boilers, metal plates, wooden structures, furniture and everything on board—was instantly converted into a fearsome bombardment of projectiles hurtling outward at awesome speed. For a moment the Richmond community faced a with-ering volley far more vicious than any battlefield in Flanders Fields. Many, who were within the first few hundred feet, not killed by concussion or seared by the fireball, were skewered by metal and jagged wooden fragments; some were cut in two, others with veins and arteries severed, stood in stunned horror as the life-blood spurted from their bodies. Bones were broken, internal organs pierced, eyes destroyed; only a very few in this group were miraculously untouched.

The firemen were the closest victims. Surely they must have known their lives were in mortal danger, but with disregard for their own safety they began to unroll the hoses. They were the first to exhibit an uncommon heroism that would become common in the next few hours and days. Ten fireman had answered Constant Upham's summons; nine died instantly, including Chief Condon and Deputy Chief Brunt. The only survivor was Billy Wells, who was inside the cab of the new chemical pumper and protected from the fireball and concussion. The Patricia *was flipped end over end and smashed beyond repair. Her maiden battle was destined to be her last, and her rescue record limited to a single life.*

In total, nine ships in the harbour were rendered unseaworthy—either sunk or severely damaged by the blast. Of these, the HMS Highflyer *was the most fortunate. An operational naval vessel, she was built more ruggedly than any cargo ship, designed to withstand the blows of battle. She would never receive a more fearsome blow than this. Also in her favour was the fact* that she was not moored rigidly to a wharf, but at anchor in the harbour—approximately nine hundred feet from the Mont Blanc—allowing her to "go with the blow" much as a prize fighter in the ring will roll with a punch to lessen the shock. Riddled with shrapnel, the Highflyer was pushed and rolled by the wall of air, but was able to right herself quickly. Moments later it lifted and settled again as the growing wall of water pushed away from the exploding ship passed under her hull. Fifteen personnel were injured and three on board died, in addition to the thirteen who were killed in the whaler.

At Pier Nine, the Calonne was shielded from the explosion by the Curaca. Even so, seven of her sailors died and the ship received severe structural damage. The Niobe was also more fortunate than either the Stella Maris or the Curaca. Moored with her bow to Mont Blanc she was spared the massive brutality she would have suffered had she been broadside. The decks were a shambles, the wooden additional quarters were destroyed, the funnel was torn away, leaving a mass of twisted debris. Eleven men were dead.

All three vessels involved in the attempt to save the Mont Blanc suffered complete destruction. The Stella Maris had played a brief and fruitless role as a rescue vessel. Ripped and shattered by the fireball and concussion, perforated by thousands of steel shards, lifted and tossed ashore like a useless, broken toy, her final role was to serve as a coffin for five of her nine-man crew. The four men below deck, escaped death, but suffered punctured eardrums, broken bones, severe lacerations and bruises. The captain, Horatio Brennen, died along with four of his men.

Only one of the fourteen-man crew in the Highflyer's whaleboat, survived the explosion. Blasted into the harbour, he came ashore near the wreck of the Stella Maris, dazed, disoriented and bleeding. None of the crewmen on the Niobe's launch were so fortunate. They all died instantly.

Nothing stood between the Curaca at Pier Eight and the monstrous forces spewing from the Mont Blanc. Utterly unprotected, the ship was struck a mortal blow by the unabated force. Her funnel and everything else above deck simply ripped away from her hull, which was lifted like a toy, by the force of the wind; four-inch mooring lines parted like cotton threads and the hull was perforated by thousands of shards, above and below the waterline. Unfettered, the Curaca now moved away from Pier Eight and drifted to midstream. She would toss helplessly in the waves, oscillating between shorelines, before eventually sinking in Bedford Basin. Her wreckage became a crypt for the bodies of forty-seven crewmen.

At Pier Eight, Lieutenant-Commander James A. Murray, Commander of the Convoys, was killed instantly. He had only recently been appointed to *his position after serving for a time as Captain of the* Empress of Britain. *Nearby, sat the Acadia Sugar Refinery's new tug, the* Ragus; *weighing 100 tons, the tug was lifted bodily out of the water and heaved over Pier Eight killing the captain, John Blakeney, and all four crew members.*

A DISOBEDIENT YOUNG girl, aged thirteen, also died near Pier Eight. Her punishment far in excess of her misdemeanour. Florence Laura Jackson, the daughter of Edward and Ellen Jackson, was the first of forty-six family members to die as a victim of the Halifax Explosion. Her body was never recovered.

A great boulder, weighing in excess of one ton, dropped on the Picton. *It crashed through the upper deck and landed on the deck below, killing thirty-three crew members. The surface of the boulder was worn smooth, which suggests that it came from the harbour bottom. As no water washed over the vessel, the boulder must have been lifted straight up from the harbour floor. Such phenomena shows the air disturbed was now more than an intense compressional wave travelling out in a straight line. There had to be a vortex motion similar to a tornado, a vortex motion capable of lifting a 1-ton rock.*

FRANK CAREW, A gang foreman for the Furness Withy Company, was privy to the nature of the *Mont Blanc's* cargo. In the final twenty minutes before the explosion, he and his crew worked frantically to batten down the hatches of the *Picton*, moored at the Sugar Refinery Wharf. The *Picton* also carried a load of explosives—far less than the amount on board the *Mont Blanc*, but enough to wreak havoc on the immediate vicinity. His gang of stevedores was supplemented by additional men from another Furness Withy gang, bossed by James Mahar. Among the additional hands were three of the Jackson brothers, Edward Bungay and Charles Moore. As the final hatch was covered, Frank ordered his men to run for their lives. Again, what was apparently an innocuous alternative, was really a choice between living and dying. Some of those who chose to run behind the Sugar Refinery lived; the majority of those who ran in front were hit directly by the awesome blast. Of sixty-four stevedores who had risked their lives to prevent a further explosion, thirty-three were killed, including Frank Carew, Edward Bungay, Ada Moore's husband, Charles, and the three Jackson brothers, William, Frederick and Edward. The body of Frederick Jackson was never found; the body of William was cut in two.

The Lorne Amateur Aquatic Club, below the Sugar Refinery, was instantly reduced to rubble. Among the property destroyed was the clubhouse, wharf, boat-slip, boat-sheds, line-racing shells, canoes, thirty-two motor launches and forty to fifty small boats. In addition, many valuable mementos were lost forever, including all the competitive trophies that attested to the proficiency and sportsmanship of the club members. But, material things can be rebuilt. More trophies can be won. A far greater loss, and not replaceable, is human life. The caretakers, Henry and Annie Turner and their son Allan were killed. Her body was also never found.

The Acadia Sugar Refinery, stood within five hundred feet of the Mont Blanc. *Of its sixty employees, almost all were enjoying their ringside seats at the fireworks and the drama unfolding before them. Most had gone outside, some were watching from windows and a few enjoyed a bird's-eye view from the roof. Despite the obvious fact that the fire was beyond control of the fire department, there was no sense of immediate danger and a carnival-like atmosphere prevailed. The initial blast shattered the building and it collapsed in on itself, one floor after another, killing the entire workforce. No one survived. The wreckage spread and blocked Barrington Street, impeding rescue efforts for several days.*

CHARLES MAYERS, THIRD mate on the dry-docked *Middleham Castle* had walked to within three hundred feet of the fire. Hearing the pre-liminary explosion of benzol drums, he started to run back toward his ship. He was overtaken by the blast. He experienced the oddest sensa-tion of flying—of passing, and being passed by, other objects—before blacking out. When he regained consciousness he found himself near the top of Fort Needham, more than a half-mile from where he started. Except for his boots he was stark naked. He watched a badly injured woman give birth to a child in a nearby field.

The westbound arc of the compressed air wall struck Richmond's homes and businesses on Barrington Street from just before the intersection of Hanover to just past the intersection of Kenny Street, a radius of approximately one thousand feet from the explosion centre. The death rate at the waterfront and the railyard was in excess of 90 per cent. On Barrington Street, from civic numbers 1299 to 1416, the death rate was only slightly lower.

The grocery store, owned by Constant Upham and his wife, Jenny, was one of the many buildings on Barrington Street that were within the critical one thousand foot radius of the explosion. It was reduced to a pile of splinters and broken glass that were driven by the outrageous force of the expanding wall of wind to Veith Street and beyond. The wind-force would leave

Barrington Street relatively clear of wreckage. Constant and Jenny Upham were killed; their bodies were never recovered.

In the stretch of Barrington Street, from Constant Upham's store at 1301, opposite Hanover Street, to civic number 1414, the crescent-shaped wall of tightly compressed air hit forty-three homes, killing over 150 of the people within and inflicting horrifying injuries on the few who survived.

The Acadia Sugar Refinery, at fifteen storeys, was the tallest building in Richmond. It employed approximately sixty workers. The brick building shattered and collapsed killing everyone within or near the structure.

Photo courtesy of P.A.N.S. (N-170)

Homes and places of business were torn from their foundations, twisted and ripped into shreds of splintered wood and driven further up the hill. Debris from the Barrington Street buildings landed as far away as Albert Street and even Union Street, hundreds of feet from where they started. In addition to the Upham family, terrible loss of life was suffered by the families Duggan, Fraser, Guess, Heffler, Hill, Shaw and Stratton and other Richmond families. Many of the bodies from this first zone were unrecognizable, they would be delivered to the morgue, listed simply as "Charred Remains."

THE FIRST HOME to be hit on Veith Street was that of William Matthews at number seventy-one. His family of four were killed instantly and their home was driven across the street toward two vacant lots. It was the east side of the Matthews' home that saved Mary Jean Hinch from the deadly shower of shrapnel blasting from the ship. It also protected her from the full force of the air wall. Most of the debris from the shattered homes that lay between her and the *Mont Blanc* passed straight over her head. She was struck by the lower part of the Matthews' home's front wall and driven into a ditch on the west side of Veith Street. Dazed and barely conscious, she lay buried six feet under the wreckage of her neighbours' homes, pinned to the ground by splintered lengths of lumber. Mary Jean rubbed her face with her hand and in the dim light that trickled through the debris saw blood on her hand. She could hear nothing but the ringing in her ears from the concussive blast. Her legs were pinned by a heavy beam and as she tried to roll over, acute pain caused her to scream in agony. She slipped into merciful unconsciousness and was spared from witnessing the destruction of her home and family.

RESIDENTS OF 66 VEITH STREET

Joseph Hinch, 50	....	Killed
Mary Eugenia (Jackson) Hinch, 40	....	Injured
Clara Hinch, 19	....	Killed
Helena Catherine (Lena) Hinch, 17	....	Killed
Thomas William Hinch, 15	....	Killed
Mary Mabel Hinch, 12	....	Killed
Joseph Francis Hinch, 9	....	Killed
James Frederick Hinch, 8	....	Killed
Annie Agnes Hinch, 5	....	Killed
Margaret Cecilia Hinch, 5	....	Killed
Ralph St. Clair Hinch, 3	....	Killed
Helen Eugenia (Jean) Hinch, 2	....	Killed

This was the largest loss of life for one single family in the Halifax Explosion on December 6th, 1917.

The home was within eight hundred feet of the explosion centre. The house and all possessions were destroyed and burned. The bodies were not recovered until December 21st. The charred remains of Joseph Hinch and his ten children were buried in a common grave at Mount Olivet Cemetery on December 22nd, 1917—one day before his 51st birthday.

Prior to the explosion Joseph and Mary (Jackson) Hinch had lost four children to the ravages of childhood disease. She was five months pregnant with their fifteenth child, Hubert, who was born the following April.

Mary was buried under the debris for twenty-four hours, she suffered severe injury to her right hip and massive bruises.

The Hillis Foundry simply blew apart as Frank Hillis and Harry Saunders entered the building. They were killed instantly, almost entirely crushed beneath the fallen cement; only their faces were intact. There were only two survivors out of the seventy-five employees, a death rate higher than 97 per cent.

The home of Mary Jean and Joseph Hinch was shielded from the wall of air by the Hillis Foundry, but a split-second later the sidewalls exploded outward in the following low pressure system. It then collapsed in on itself, pinning Joseph and all ten children under a hopeless tangle of wreckage. Both the hall and kitchen stove overturned and set fire to the rubble. Much of the foundry building collapsed across Veith Street, landing on the Hinch home as well as those of their neighbours'. The crushing weight of heavy beams and concrete made any possibility of immediate extrication of the victims hopeless.

CLARA HINCH WAS pinned between the second-storey floorboards and the roof. Moments before she'd been dancing with her dreams under the warmth of her comforter. She awoke to a nightmare. Now she could not move, not to roll over, not to sit up; all she could do was scream. Lena was dead beside her, crushed beneath the wreckage. Her father, her other sisters and her brothers, were pinned in the debris below, unable to help. And then the first few tendrils of smoke curled upwards from the wreckage below.

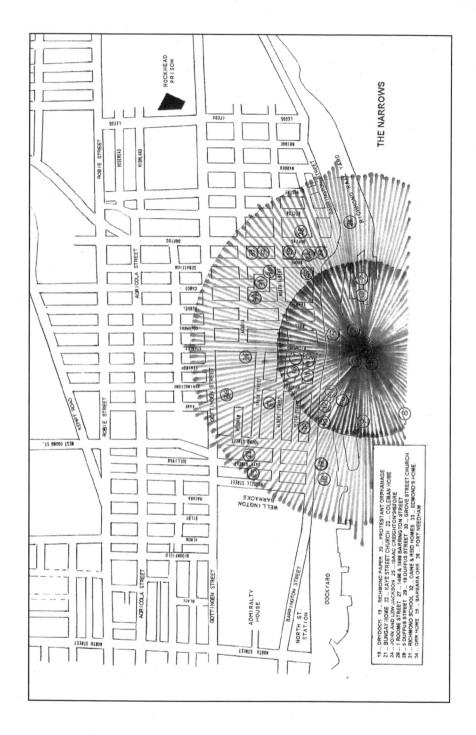

ZONE 2
Two thousand feet from explosion site

CHAPTER

7

If one were to draw a circle around Pier Six, with a radius of two thousand feet, it would encompass almost all of Richmond and certainly its major residential area. To the south it would reach the first block of Russell Street; Vestry Street to the north; Stairs and Stanley Streets just above Gottingen to the west; and its eastern arc would almost touch the Dartmouth shoreline. This circle of destruction we will call "zone two."

The first zone—one thousand feet from the Mont Blanc—*was completely and instantaneously destroyed. The blast was weakening as it reached the second zone. Its victims heard the explosion a split second before they were hit; the wall of compressed air was now moving just slightly below the speed of sound at approximately six hundred miles per hour. The percentage of deaths in zone two was fractionally lower, but this area was more densely populated and the actual number of fatalities recorded was the highest in the whole city. The few who escaped immediate death, would almost certainly be grievously wounded, or trapped in the wreckage to suffer a horrible death in the fires that would rage for days, and even weeks, in the Richmond area.*

The force of the explosion that hit the area from Constant Upham's grocery store on Barrington Street south to Russell Street and the beginning of Wellington Barracks flattened homes and buildings within the smallest fraction of a second. The Richmond Printing Company was totally demolished. Of its thirty-nine employees, only one survived. The rest were crushed to death by either the heavy machinery, the collapsing roof, or the cement blocks of the building's outer walls.

The north block of Veith Street, located in zone one, had simply disappeared into a pile of rubble, killing almost everyone in their homes. Further south, the blow was slightly less. However, excluding the Protestant Orphanage, the death rate on Veith Street was over 95 per cent. Of the 149 people who lived on the ill-fated street, all but 7 died. Many who survived the initial blast, were fatally injured and lay trapped beneath the burning wreckage of their homes. They would welcome the oblivion of death.

HARRIET BUNGAY DID not hear the sound. There was simply a blinding flash of light and a momentary impression of Wallace's store blowing away. She could not see Gladys; her young daughter had disappeared in the devastation and would never be seen again. The picket fence Harriet had been leaning against was hit by the rolling wall of wind. Ripped from the cross pieces, the pickets swirled into the maelstrom to became yet another lethal weapon in the already deadly storm. The blunt force of the blast broke her ribs and flung her body against her home even as it disintegrated. She lay semi-conscious, in blinding pain, amidst the broken boards as Jack, whimpering with shock and fear, nudged her anxiously. The English Setter was the only household member to survive the explosion unscathed.

Some of the children at the Protestant Orphanage on Veith Street before the explosion.

Photo courtesy of P.A.N.S. (N-4840)

The Protestant Orphanage comprised numbers one to thirteen on Veith Street East. A large, rambling, wood-frame building, it flew apart in an instant, parts of it landing as far away as Fort Needham. On the morning of December 6th, there were three adults and thirty-six children on the premises. All three adults and twenty-nine children died; most of the children were under the age of six. There were twenty-one boys, five girls and three bodies unidentifiable as to sex and listed only as "charred remains."

*To a small degree the bulk of the Sugar Refinery had protected the Halifax
Shipyards and the Dockyards from the awesome force of the wall of
compressed air expanding outward from the point of the explosion. The
Drydock, a major ship-repair facility was put out of commission for months as
effectively as if it had been bombarded with a cannonade. The basin and gates
remained intact, but the plant and machine shops were wiped out. More than
half of the 235 employees died in the blast.*

*The north-west quadrant of the expanding air wall slammed into the
Richmond Railyard with barely diminished force. The Yard, which ran
parallel between Barrington Street and the Harbour, was a sorting area for
freight and cargo. Ships laden with goods arrived at the wharves, where they
were unloaded by the stevedores and placed in boxcars by the freight handlers
and then shunted to the Richmond Yard to be consigned to trains heading
west. Conversely, trainloads of supplies arriving in the Rockingham Yard
from Central and Western Canada and the United States, were sorted for
shipment overseas. During these war years, the volume of goods heading
overseas was decidedly greater.*

*The boxcars at the Rockingham Yard were tagged by their serial numbers
and matched against the bill of laden. The engineer coupled his engine to the
designated freight car and sorted them to a siding. When enough cars
heading for the same destination were gathered, they were shunted into the
Richmond Yard where they were guided through a series of switches to the
connecting track for the wharf.*

JOHN JACKSON WAS sitting astride the brake wheel shaft on the front
boxcar as it came around the curve from Fairview Cove. Brakesmen
usually were not aware of the cargo beneath their feet, and mostly they
didn't care—a cargo was a cargo—it was just a job. But John couldn't
help but know, the sides of the cars were slatted to allow air in, and the
same slats allowed the pungent smell of horses out. He could hear them
stamping in mild panic. These cars were destined to be loaded on the
Curaca and *Colonne*, to be shipped to the battlefronts of Europe. "Poor
bloody creatures, if I had my way you'd all be turned free on a nice farm
somewhere."

As they rolled through Africville into the straight-away to Richmond
Yard, this altruistic thought was wiped from his mind. The burning ship
captured John's immediate and full attention. He and the engineer had
seen the smoke earlier from Rockingham and wrongfully assumed the
fire was on the Dartmouth side. Not so. He was now heading straight
for it. The spot he had intended to stop would only be a few hundred

61

feet from the inferno. "Holy Jeez. These poor dumb horses are already panicking—they'll go berserk if we get much closer to that. They'll kick the damn slats out."

He stood up and looked back toward the engine but could see neither the engineer nor the fireman without walking back over the boxcars. There wasn't time. "Are they blind? For God's sake, don't they see the fire? If they don't stop now it'll be too damn late." John glanced to his right, toward his home, and saw the people running along Barrington Street to the pedway, others were on the bridge moving closer to the flames. "The bloody fools." He waved frantically and screamed for them to go back but his voice was lost in the tumult. A few of the people, still in high spirits, waved back. John glanced again at the burning ship and spat in frustration. "Crazy idiots! Are they that bloody stupid that they don't know they could get hurt?" Just then the engineer uncoupled the engine from the cars, thus releasing himself from further responsibility. John Jackson was now on his own.

"The hell with everybody—I'm stopping this bloody thing now." He frantically spun the wheel of the brake mechanism and brought the boxcars to a grinding halt less than twelve hundred feet from the blazing ship. Even from here he could feel the skin on his face tightening from the heat. He stood up straight, his mouth dry, his heart pounding. With legs braced on each side of the wheel shaft John watched the leaping flames and thick black smoke. He was held immobile by a paralysing mixture of awe and dread.

On the tracks below, John's nephew, Lew, was gripped by the same sense of fear. He had long since abandoned his search for the missing boxcar. New to the job of checker, he was uncertain what to do. He looked for one of the older men to give him advice but they were gone. Most had moved closer to the fire. With a feeling of relief he saw his uncle standing on the string of boxcars gliding by, the squeal of its brakes lost in the roar of the flames and the bedlam of bewildered shouts. The cars stopped between Lew and the flaming hulk of the *Mont Blanc*. He yelled to John, but his voice was lost in the din. He could see only his uncle's head and shoulders from this angle, so he ran toward the iron rungs of the boxcar's ladder.

John's last sight on earth was the fireball. A microsecond later he was dead. The blunt force of the blast crushed his chest and destroyed his internal organs. His body was perforated and ripped by hundreds of slivers of steel. This close to the source, the fragments spewing outward were close together, as with shotgun pellets close to the muzzle; only with distance would they fan out enough to allow the target any hope of survival. John's heavy coat was torn from his body and his other clothing shredded. From the perch on the car his now lifeless body was driven diagonally across the railyard to be smashed against the retaining wall below Barrington Street. There it would stay for several minutes until the wall of water, returning from the Dartmouth shore, carried him on his final journey through the streets of Richmond.

The boxcar protected Lew from the full impact of the explosion. They would permit him to live a little longer than his uncle. The wooden casing of the boxcar immediately in front of him was just above his head when it disintegrated. Torn from its iron base, it sailed over him along with the body of his uncle and the carcasses of the animals that were now spared from death on the Western Front. The iron ladder, still attached at the base of the boxcar's frame, twisted around, as if it were no more than paper, and smashed into Lew's knee-cap, crushing bone and cartilage. He was lifted and driven with extreme violence against the body of a dead horse. The mutilated carcass of a second horse crushed against him, pinning his legs between them. In shock, he tried to roll away from the blood and offal pouring over him from the animals. The effort made him scream with pain and pass into unconsciousness.

He was spared from witnessing the nightmarish scene of death and devastation that continued around him. Sixty-five of the railway employees were killed instantly or so badly injured that death was only moments away. Most of the bodies this close to the blast, suffered concussive wounds from a battering-ram of air that had the consistency of steel. Chests were crushed, internal organs shattered; arms, legs and heads were torn from torsos and the intense concentration of shrapnel-like particles ripped bodies to shreds.

Twenty locomotives, that looked so massive and impregnable just seconds before, were utterly destroyed. The ground shock rippling under the road bed lifted the heavy cross ties and twisted the iron rails; the eight-inch spikes that secured them were wrenched from the wooden sleepers. Rails were twisted into bizarre shapes by the rippling force and the wind of a thousand hurricanes. Loaded boxcars, weighing hundreds of tons, were lifted from the tracks and hurled aside like a child's abandoned toys. Three hundred boxcars and their cargoes were pulverized into splintered debris. The pedestrian bridge over the tracks, from where Jim Jackson and Joe Hinch had watched the fireworks just a short while before, was wrenched from its footing in a scream of tortured metal that drowned the mortal screams of those who were standing there.

The irresistible force surged over the low retaining wall on the Barrington Street side of the railyard and slammed into the houses on the east side of Barrington with the same frightful impact with which it was hitting the Richmond Printing and other targets in the southern quadrant. The death rate for these homes also reached nearly 100 per cent. Entire families were wiped out in a fraction of a second. At 1287 Barrington Street, seven members of the Elliott family were killed. At 1329, five members of the Duggan family met a similar fate. Every home on this side of Barrington Street suffered a shocking number of deaths.

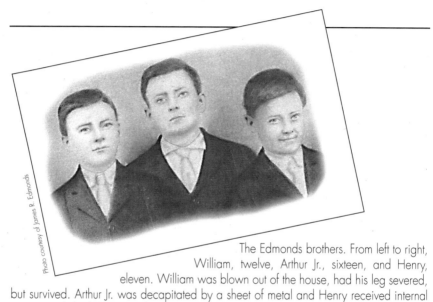

Photo courtesy of James R. Edmonds

The Edmonds brothers. From left to right, William, twelve, Arthur Jr., sixteen, and Henry, eleven. William was blown out of the house, had his leg severed, but survived. Arthur Jr. was decapitated by a sheet of metal and Henry received internal injuries and died near Creighton's store.

ARTHUR EDMONDS PLAYED with the dollar bill in his pocket, wondering if, in the excitement of the fire, it might go unnoticed if he spent just a nickel of it on candy. He took the ship's pennant that the sailor had given him a few days ago, and wrapped the dollar and the pennant into a tight ball. Jamming the two items deep into his pocket helped remove the temptation and he turned his full attention back to the burning ship, dutifully obeying Isaac Creighton's admonishment to remain safely in front of the store. He was beheaded by a swirling fragment of the *Mont Blanc's* metal plate. His younger brother, Henry, was thrown against the building in the split second before it collapsed. The violence of the blow caused massive internal injuries that killed him almost instantly.

Creighton's store, at the corner of Roome and Barrington Streets, was struck with the full force of the expanding ring of compressed air, which flattened the building. Isaac and his wife, Annie, their son, J. William and daughter, Anne, were all killed. Mary Walsh and Laura Perry, their clerks, also died. Their bodies would be consumed by fire with the exception of Laura Perry whose body was never found. Along with the Edmonds brothers, at least a dozen people standing in front of the store were killed, their bodies riddled with shrapnel.

The northern quadrant of the air wall struck the area that Ada Moore humorously referred to as 'Jacksonville.' The home of Elizabeth Jackson and the families of her sons, John and William, and those of Ada and Margaret were clustered together around that short section of Barrington Street that takes a slight jog to the east. Around the corner, on Duffus Street were the homes and families of Edward and James Jackson. All of them were within thirteen hundred feet of the Mont Blanc.

Number one Roome Street was on the Richmond hill, sitting just above the protection of the other houses in the vicinity. It took the full force of the wind's blast and was instantly demolished. John and William Jackson, killed at their places of employment a split second before, were joined in death by their mother, Elizabeth, their respective wives, Louisa and Mary, and

---

RESIDENTS OF 1 ROOME STREET

Elizabeth (Halloran) Jackson, 67 .... Killed
(The matriarch of the Jackson family)

Her son William, his wife and child:
William Jackson, 23 .... Killed
Mary (Mullins) Jackson, 21 .... Killed
James William Jackson, 3 months .... Killed

Her son John, his wife and child:
John Jackson, 34 .... Killed
Louisa (MacDonald) Jackson, 30 .... Killed
Dorothy Jackson, 6 .... Injured

William Jackson was killed at the waterfront. His brother John was killed in the Richmond Railyard. Dorothy Jackson was injured at St. Joseph's School. The charred remains of four bodies: Elizabeth, Mary, Louisa and the infant, James William Jackson, were delivered to the Chebucto Morgue in one box, simply marked: "Charred remains from No. 1 Roome Street."

---

*William's three-month-old son James William Jackson. The only survivor
was John's daughter, Dorothy, who had already left for school.*

ADA OPENED THE front door yet again. She was dressed and ready to
go, coat buttoned, hat and scarf in place, gloves in hand. She could see
straight past the railyard almost to North Street. The tram car Mabel
should have been on was just moving out of sight on its return trip past
the North Street station, and there was still no sign of Mabel. The
homes and warehouses on the east side of Barrington blocked her view
of the burning ship, but the crowds of people and the writhing mass of
smoke laced with flame, left little doubt a major event was taking place
near the Sugar Refinery.

For a moment she debated the wisdom of leaving the children in
Mabel's care with a major fire raging so close to her home. But the new
coat she so coveted pushed the thought from her mind. If she put off
her shopping trip the coat would be snatched up by someone else. Mind
you, if that daughter of hers didn't turn up soon she'd miss it anyway.
She checked her purse for the money. It was all there. The only thing
missing was Mabel.

Ada glanced behind her at the grandfather clock in the hallway. It
said a minute after nine; but the damn thing was always at least three
minutes slow. Her nephew, Gordon McDonald raced past Creighton's
store and she called out to him as he sped by, "Hey, Gordie, where's the
fire?" But the boy either failed to see her or was so excited he didn't
bother to answer. He ran up the steps to his home next door.

Her attention caught once more by the flames licking the sky, Ada
reluctantly started to unbutton her coat, "Damn, damn and double damn,
that coat's gone forever. Oh well, sales are like tram cars, there will be
another one in half an hour. I'd never forgive myself if the kids were
frightened and I wasn't here. But that isn't going to save that girl from a
tongue lashing—if she ever gets here." She turned back into the house.

With her back turned to the waterfront, Ada didn't see the blinding
flash of light. Nor did she hear the ear-splitting sound. The buildings
on the east side of Barrington Street took the full force of the circular
wall of air as well as the shower of shrapnel blasting out from the
doomed ship. The low-pressure system following the air wall caused
Ada's house to explode outwards, driving her into the middle of the
street. Her heavy coat protected her from the worst of the abrasive slide
and she lay stunned in the centre of Barrington Street. The javelins of
wreckage from across the street flew above her, landing in the rubble
that had been her home.

RESIDENTS OF 1496 BARRINGTON STREET

Charles Moore, 43 .... Killed
Ada (Jackson) Moore, 39 .... Survived

Their children:
Morton Robert Moore, 15 .... Killed
Charles James Moore, 12 .... Survived
Vincent Moore, 11 .... Survived
Mary Nellie Moore, 10 .... Survived
Irene Elizabeth Moore, 7 .... Survived
John Moore, 4 .... Killed
Rupert Moore, 1-1/2 .... Killed
Margaret Moore, 1-1/2 .... Killed
Catherine Moore, 1 month .... Killed

Lawrence Boutilier .... Survived
Emma Jackson (Baker) Boutilier, 33 .... Killed

Emma's children from 1st marriage:
Hilda Catherine Baker, 9 .... Injured
John Stanley Baker, 7 .... Injured
William Baker, 5 .... Injured
Clyde Baker, 3 .... Killed

Emma was the youngest of the Jackson girls. Her first husband and father of her children, Leverette Baker, died in 1915. She married Lawrence Boutilier three weeks before the Halifax Explosion and moved to 1496 Barrington Street, renting rooms from her sister Ada.

AFTER HER WEDDING, three weeks before, Emma had left her mother's home on Roome Street to rent the top floor of her sister Ada's home. Emma, was still trying to get the place livable for Lawrence and the four children from her first marriage. She was amazed at how much stuff she had picked up over the years and was beginning to realize the frustration of moving from a large house into three rooms. The living room was still cluttered with unopened boxes and Hilda, her eldest girl was helping to find one of Leverette Junior's favourite toys. Emma gave an exasperated sigh, "It will, without a doubt, be in the very last box we look through." Hilda smiled impishly and said, "That makes it easy, Mum. All we have to do is figure out which one's the last box." A moment later Hilda found the teddy bear but her triumphant cry was cut short as the floor moved out from under them. Emma crashed down through the disintegrating floorboards and was struck by a large beam, which killed her instantly. Three-year-old Leverette landed nearby and was crushed to death under the wreckage. Hilda was sliced by glass, receiving severe cuts and seven-year-old Stanley had his leg broken. The most badly injured was five-year-old William. His head was fractured by the falling debris and he had severe scalp wounds.

RESIDENTS AT 1498 BARRINGTON STREET

Vincent McDonald, 44 .... Survived
Margaret (Jackson) McDonald, 37 .... Killed

Their children:
Mary (McDonald) Boutilier, 21 .... Killed
Ethel McDonald, 17 .... Killed
Emma Ann McDonald, 15 .... Killed
Charles McDonald, 12 .... Killed
Albert William McDonald, 9 .... Killed
Gordon Richard McDonald, 7 .... Injured
Arthur McDonald, 6 .... Killed
Allan McDonald, 3 .... Killed
Carroll McDonald, 1 .... Killed

The grandchildren:
Vincent Boutilier, 2 .... Killed
Carol Boutilier, 4 months .... Killed

Other occupants:
Mary's husband, Carrol Boutilier, 24 .... Killed
Vincent's mother, Mary Squires, 64 .... Killed
Vincent's step-brother, Richard Squires, 47 .... Injured

Vincent McDonald was at work in the Rockingham Railyard.

Of the fifteen people who were in the house at the time of the explosion, thirteen were killed and two were injured. This was the largest loss of life in one residential dwelling.

All the bodies were burned and the body of one grandchild, Vincent Boutilier, was never found.

Gordon McDonald, seven, suffered horrible cuts to his face and scalp. His right eye was damaged, he had a projecting collar bone, there were shell fragments imbedded in his shoulder, he was badly disfigured and suffered extreme shock. There were six operations on his face and eye.

THOROUGHLY EXCITED BY the turn of events on the waterfront, Gordon McDonald ran to tell his mother the news. Always a highly charged bundle of energy, the seven-year-old tripped over his feet and sprawled on the front steps at 1498 Barrington Street. Picking himself up, he dusted his knees with his hands and wiped the dirt on his shirt-tail. He tucked the shirt-tail inside his pants. Now was not the time to have to contend with his mother's "Take care of your clothes; money does not grow on trees you know" lecture.

Gordon took the steps two at a time and threw the front door wide open. His mother, Margaret, was just descending the hall stairs with her one-year-old, Carroll, dozing in her arms. She looked down at Gordon's abrupt entrance with annoyance. Before she could speak he blurted, "Hey, Ma, come on out and see the big fire, there's a ship ..." But before he could finish the sentence his home exploded outward, blowing him back to Barrington Street. His face and scalp were badly cut from flying glass and he was knocked unconscious. The twelve others in his home were dead or dying. Gordon sustained severe lacerations on his face and scalp, damage to his eyes, a projecting collar-bone, and severe shock. His father, Vincent McDonald, was at work in Rockingham Railyard and would survive the explosion uninjured.

Number five Duffus Street was fourteen hundred feet from the explosion centre. Owned by Annie Creighton, the building had been converted to a rooming house. Edward and Ellen Jackson lived there with their six children. This was sufficient reason for Edward's sister, Ada, to consider it part of 'Jacksonville.'

In addition to the Jackson family there were others living in the building. Johanna Chapman, aged sixty-one, lived there with her nineteen-year-old son, William. Mrs. Chapman was a widow and worked as a cleaning lady at the North Street Railway Station. She was at work on the morning of the explosion. Her son-in-law, Robert Simmons, was a corporal in the Nova Scotia 85th Highland Division. Having returned from overseas service one month before, he had been classified as unfit for further military service. He, his wife, Mary, and their two daughters, Frances and Madeline, had an apartment on the top floor of the building. Corporal Simmons was away from home that morning at an army barracks.

Mrs. Georgina Lewis was also a tenant, but she, too, was away that morning. Both she and the corporal had picked the perfect day to be away from Richmond.

Like many houses on Richmond hill, five Duffus Street was too high up to be shielded from the explosion by other buildings.

RESIDENTS OF 5 DUFFUS STREET

Edward Jackson, 32 .... Killed
Ellen (Sidebottom) Jackson, 35 .... Injured

Florence Laura, 13 .... Killed
Muriel Ellen, 10 .... Injured
Edward, 9 .... Killed
Charles F. .... Killed
Gerald, 3 .... Survived
Patricia, 8 months .... Killed

Mrs. Johanna Chapman, 61 .... Injured
William Chapman, 19 .... Killed

Robert Simmons, 23 .... Survived
Mary Simmons, 23 .... Killed
Frances Simmons, 4 .... Injured
Madeline Simmons, 1 .... Injured

Roger Stevenson, 23 .... Survived
Christina Stevenson, 22 .... Killed

Georgina Lewis, 38 .... Away from area
Viola Marie Lewis, 5 .... Away from area

Mabel LePine, 27 .... Survived
Violet Theresa LePine, 9 .... Survived
William Henry LePine, 8 .... Survived

Number 5 Duffus was a three-storey rooming house, housing six families. All of the families were related by marriage.

Johanna Chapman's son was killed. She was buried under debris at North Street Station for three days. She never fully recovered and a guardian was appointed for her, for the rest of her life, by the Halifax Relief Commission.

Robert Simmons had been a corporal in the N.S. Highlanders 85th Regiment, and had been home one month after being declared unfit for further service. His wife, Mary, was killed. Mary was the daughter of Johanna Chapman. Frances, aged four, his daughter, was badly cut about the arms and face and lost both eyes.

Madeline Simmons, his youngest daughter, was cut severely. She lost her left eye.

ELLEN JACKSON WAS blissfully unaware of the ship burning in the harbour. After Florence and Muriel left to take Edward's lunch pail to the waterfront she had busied herself tidying the kitchen and putting away the breakfast dishes. That finished, she walked over to check on three-year-old Gerald. He was awake. As she lifted the little boy from his crib, the house was struck a shattering blow by the wall of compressed wind. The roof blew off and a large fragment of metal plunged down through the crib, where only an instant before, the baby had been. The house swayed and collapsed. Gerald was torn from Ellen's arms as she plunged through the wreckage. Nine-year-old Edward, five-year-old Charles and the baby, eight-month-old Patricia, were all killed.

Richmond School

Photograph taken from near the corner of Duffus and Albert Streets. The automobile is on Albert Street. The building was approximately thirteen hundred feet from the epicentre.

Photo courtesy of P.A.N.S. (N-1263)

Richmond School had recently switched to its winter schedule, this meant that classes began at 9:30. At 9:05, the school was practically deserted. The school was located at the corner of North Albert and Roome Streets. There were seven classrooms with a total of 421 students in grades one through nine. Large classes, sometimes upwards of sixty students, were not unusual. Class attendance had been well below normal since Monday. Many children were kept home because of the cold that was running rampant throughout the city. The majority of the children lived within a short walk from their school and by the time they left their homes the fire in the Narrows had captured their full attention, making 'Reading, Riting and Rithmatic' seem a bit dull by comparison. Only a handful of dedicated students were near the schoolyard on that morning.

One teacher was at her desk correcting papers and a carpenter was repair-

ing desks in the basement. The school janitor was in the playground watching the flame-laced smoke billow from the burning ship. He could not see the actual ship and briefly debated whether he would have time to go closer and return before the bell rang. The next microsecond made a decision academic. The two-storey frame building was blown to pieces, only the lower part of its shattered outside wall still standing. The janitor was instantly killed.

CLASSES AT ST. JOSEPH'S School started a half-hour earlier than those at Richmond School. Muriel Jackson was late. From the railway overpass she had a long hill to climb to reach her school near the top of Russell Street. Still teary-eyed from her argument with her sister Florence, she ran up Richmond Street and along Veith Street past the home of her Aunt Mary Jean and the Protestant Orphanage. Her legs growing weary, she half-walked and half-ran up Young Street to Albert Street and continued along that level road to Russell Street. She paused for a few moments and then, panting with exertion, walked as quickly as she could the final few blocks up Russell Street to the school.

Before entering the front doors, Muriel looked back at the towering flames, visible just past the corner of the Sugar Refinery. It was frightening even from this distance. Her fear of the fire was swallowed by her anxiety about wreaking the wrath of the Sisters; she tiptoed up the stairs to the second floor. But she was too late; she could hear the children in the other classes saying their morning prayers. Two of the girls from her own class were also late. They were standing outside the closed door of the classroom and, as Muriel drew near, one of them put her finger to her lips while the other opened the door a crack and peeked

---

RESIDENTS OF 18 DUFFUS STREET

James Edward Jackson, 48 .... Injured
Margaret (Topping) Jackson, 47 .... Killed

Mary Minnie (Jackson) McGrath, 27 .... Injured
Clifford McGrath, 2 .... Killed

James A. Jackson, 26 .... Away from area
Monica (Mullane) Jackson, 21 .... Away from area
Sophye B. Jackson, 24 .... Away from area
Annie Jackson, 22 .... Killed
Lewis Patrick Jackson, 19 .... Killed

---

in. She motioned silently for the others to follow—Sister's back was turned. The classroom suddenly lit up with a brilliant blueish-white flash and there was a simultaneous, ear-splitting crash of thunder. Muriel was frozen with shock. The floor tilted down and the three of them started to slide toward the windows. Through Muriel's mind streaked the thought, "God is punishing us for being late. He's striking us with thunder and lightning!"

MARGARET JACKSON HAD already called James twice to come in and have his breakfast. She tried a third time, also to no avail. With a sigh of resignation she put her errant husband's plate of bacon, eggs and hash browns in the warming oven above the stove and decided to join him in the front yard. She placed her grandson, Clifford, in his crib near the kitchen stove and yelled to her daughter to come downstairs and look after her son.

Clifford McGrath, two, son of Minnie (Jackson) McGrath, was crushed to death by the kitchen stove at eighteen Duffus Street. His charred remains were not recovered until near the end of January.

But Minnie's attention was completely wrapped up in the fire she was watching from her bedroom window.

James turned to Margaret as she came up behind him, "Joe and I were watching from the bridge. We saw the crew row away in the lifeboats, so you don't need to worry about them." Margaret put her arm around his waist, "I heard the fire engine's bell clanging a little while ago and I wondered where they were going. Lord, I pray no one gets hurt." They watched, with growing apprehension, for a minute. As more drums of benzene added another burst of flame and billow of smoke to the blazing inferno James turned to his wife. "This is getting worse, Maggie, I don't like the look of it one bit. Joe pointed out the cannon on board that thing and said there were cannon shells on board. If they start going off it could be a disaster." Margaret took her arm from around his waist, and started to back toward the house. "Do you think we should go inside where we'd be safe?" James frowned, "I don't think anywhere is too safe if those things blow. Pieces of a shell would go miles. I hope Lew and John are in the Rockingham Yard. You're right, we better go back; if we hear an explosion we'll go down in the cellar, it would be safer there." They heard the squeal as the upstairs bedroom window was opened. James half-turned to his right as Minnie leaned out to say something to him.

The house exploded outward in the low pressure system. Minnie's nightdress was ripped from her body. A piece of metal rod buried itself in her leg above the ankle, she was thrown out the window and her arm was broken when she landed on the wreckage below. Her father, with his left side facing the blast, was struck a monstrous blow. His left eye was destroyed and his left ear almost completely severed. The ribs on the left side of his chest were broken and driven back into his lung, causing haemorrhage. Both of his hands were injured and slivers of glass were embedded into his head, face and back.

Margaret was blasted back into the wreckage and killed instantly. And the pathetically small, crushed remains of two-year-old Clifford would eventually be found under the kitchen stove.

WHILE HIS MOTHER cleared the breakfast dishes, and his father remained in the basement mending the horse's harness, William Edmonds stood at the kitchen window and surveyed the large tree at the back of the yard. It was perfect for a tree house, and despite what his Mum said, he knew his father would help him build it. After all you never knew when you may need additional accommodation. There were some pictures in his book. He would have another look at them; they'd show him where to start. As he turned to pick up *The Swiss Family Robinson*, fifty-seven Duffus Street became yet another victim of the low pressure system. Every pane of glass in the house and both front and back doors were blown out. Jagged spears of glass sliced through Willam's clothes and flesh as he was hurled through the window to land in the back yard. In great shock and bleeding profusely, he looked up. The tree was gone. In its place was a shifting mountain of wood and debris and a rising cloud of dust and dirt.

William looked at the sea of blood around him and realized it was his own. He called for his mother, but she did not answer. He called again, as loud as he could. When she still did not reply he turned toward the place his home had been just moments before and started to crawl painfully back toward the wreckage. Seconds before, a link from the *Mont*

Blanc's anchor chain had been projected high above the city and now was descending with ever-increasing velocity. Red-hot from the intense fire, the metal sliced through William's left leg just above the knee, cauterizing the wound as it passed through, and buried itself in the ground. There would be little loss of blood; the limb had been amputated with surgical precision.

While the northern quadrant of the ring of air was demolishing "Jacksonville," Richmond School and the Grove Presbyterian Church, the western quadrant smashed into what was left of Albert, Union, Acadia, Russell and Young Streets. It was here the rolling wind effect caused by the drag at the bottom of the wall of air and the incline of Richmond hill produced the cyclonic effect. Pickets were ripped off fences, splintered wood and glass was vacuumed into the maelstrom to become lethal javelins.

THE BUNGAY BOYS, on their way to work, became victims of this tornado of death. Howard Bungay, eighteen, was picked up from the ground and spun over and over within the maelstrom. His body was pierced by a picket that entered through his stomach and exited through his back; he died almost instantly. His younger brother, Edward Junior, sixteen, was hurled through the air with great violence and buried under debris.

Within two seconds of the explosion the entire community of Richmond was totally destroyed. At least one thousand people were dead, their bodies brutally battered and mutilated. Hundreds more were severely injured by shrapnel, flying glass, and other debris, and over one hundred were imprisoned in the rubble of their homes.

At the same instant that the blast reached the Wellington Barracks and the rest of the Dockyard to the south, Gottingen Street and the first streets of what is now the Hydrostone area to the west, it also hit the shores of Dartmouth at Tuft's Cove, over two thousand feet from the blast's centre.

THE *IMO* WAS almost ashore at Tuft's cove. The decks were lined with crew members watching the fire. Captain Haakon From and his harbour pilot, William Hayes, were on the forward deck, both concerned about the probability of blame. The problem became academic as the *Mont Blanc* exploded. The captain and the pilot were both instantly killed and blown overboard. Their bodies would be recovered, well up on the shore, near the Oland's Brewery. Four crew members on deck were killed. All those on deck suffered serious injuries.

The smokestack was levelled to the deck; much of the superstructure was twisted and destroyed and below deck there was severe damage. The hull and upper parts of the Imo were riddled with metal fragments and a three hundred pound metal bollard from the Mont Blanc landed on Imo's deck. The wall of compressed air lifted the 5,000-ton ship and deposited her on the shoals. Less than a minute later the great wave of water, nearly fifty feet high, would increase the damage by driving the grounded ship further up on shore. However, the Imo, although severely damaged, would live to sail again, as would most of her crew.

Photo courtesy of P.A.N.S. (N-138)

Belgium Relief ship **Imo**. The **Imo** was pushed by the blast and flung on the Dartmouth shoreline. The captain and harbour pilot were killed and their bodies were blown ashore near Oland's Brewery.

Oland's Brewery at Turtle Grove. The brewery is across the Narrows from Richmond and approximately three thousand feet from the explosion. Based on this distance the force was one-ninth the force that hit Hillis Foundry.

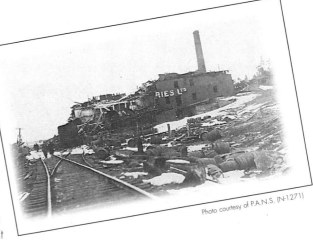

Photo courtesy of P.A.N.S. (N-1271)

THE SAME SHOWER of shrapnel hitting Tuft's Cove peppered the wooded area where the *Mont Blanc*'s crew sought shelter. One seaman was struck by a fragment of metal that severed an artery. He bled to death in minutes. He was the only man of *Mont Blanc*'s forty-one crew members to die in the Halifax Explosion.

Oland's Brewery lay within a few hundred feet of the *Imo*. The entire building was demolished and Dartmouth suffered its first casualties; there were fifteen men working in the brewery, all except one was killed. The children's one-room school at Tuft's Cove had not even one survivor. The thirteen children were all in school awaiting the arrival of their teacher who lay mortally wounded in the streets of Richmond.

With the destruction of Richmond complete, the nearby ships either shattered or sunk, the creation of a massive wall of water surging toward the shores of Dartmouth, the shock waves rippling through the rock formation beneath the city, and the beginning of the carnage of the rest of Halifax and Dartmouth well underway, the strength of the unleashed forces began to wane.

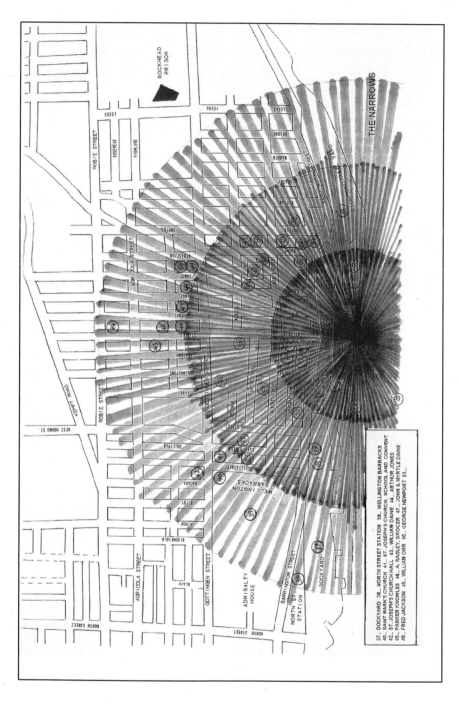

ZONE 3
Three thousand feet from explosion centre

CHAPTER
8

SAYING THE POWER of the explosion had waned may create a misconception. The reader might interpret this to mean the danger was over. Nothing could be further from the truth. While it is true this battering-ram of highly compressed air had lost much of the strength it brought to bear against the lower reaches of Richmond, it was still, by far, the most powerful, destructive, chaotic force ever to invade the city of Halifax and the town of Dartmouth.

The unharnessed energy was still more than abundant to kill, maim, injure and destroy that which stood before it. But, after two thousand feet from the centre, the decelerating wall of wind had dropped below the speed of sound. Now, almost instantly after the fearsome burst of light, came the ear-splitting noise—a mind-numbing crack followed by a rolling, reverberating roar that echoed and rumbled for endless minutes. It was heard at Sable Island, 168 mi. off the coast of Nova Scotia. It was heard in Cape Breton and New Brunswick, more than 200 mi. from the source. It was a sound that would ever live in the memories of the survivors; for many the sound of thunder or any loud noise would trigger a panic attack, an immediate moment of fear and apprehension, years and even decades after the event.

As the wind force weakened, the method of destruction changed. Victims in zone three were not thrown with the extreme violence suffered by those closer to the epicentre of the explosion. Bodies were not torn asunder by the unmerciful blast and the percentage of deaths dropped sharply. The majority of injuries were now inflicted by flying spears of glass and the jagged javelins of wood created in the destruction of their homes. Many who watched the chain of events from behind the assumed safety of their window panes were slashed about the face, neck and shoulders by needle-sharp splinters of glass. Hundreds lost their eyes; their last visual image was an intense ball of white light, fading to an impenetrable darkness. Others watched in shock as their blood spurted from severed veins and arteries; they felt little pain, only bewilderment—merciful death arrived in a matter of minutes.

Also, only slightly lessened, was the intensity of the low pressure system behind the wall of wind; from this point on, it became the major destructive force. In zone three the air inside the homes did not explode outward with the same degree of violence that completely destroyed buildings in the lower reaches of Richmond. Many of the homes affected had roofs blown off, windows and doors blown out or sidewalls moved away from the sill, providing avenues for the air inside to escape. The homes were rendered uninhabitable but, in most cases, they did not collapse, crushing the residents beneath beams, falling ceilings and furniture. The low pressure system was abetted by the ground shock. Foundations and sidewalls, cracked and weakened by the earthquake-like ripple, became easy victims to the low pressure system.

Several factors combined to produce one of the very few good things that happened that morning. First, the bulk of the Sugar Refinery stood between the Mont Blanc *and the army and navy personnel housed respectively at Wellington Barracks and the Admiralty Grounds. The wall of compressed air was reduced in strength, split and diverted to either side of the large building. The buildings were of sturdier construction than the majority of the homes and they were end on to the explosion. They did not present the broadside target offered by the houses in Richmond. The damage was still severe, but the toll of dead and injured was far lower than might have been without these factors. The military facilities, with hospital beds, blankets and clothing plus their complement of doctors, nurses and trained personnel would remain alive and available to help the less fortunate.*

Just above Wellington Barracks, on the corner of Russell and Gottingen Streets, was St. Mark's Anglican Church with St. Mark's Church Hall next door. These buildings were not shielded by the Sugar Refinery. They were struck by the massive force of the wind wall and totally destroyed. There was no loss of life within the buildings but over two hundred members of the congregation were killed at their homes or places of employment.

AS MURIEL JACKSON was making her way up the long hill toward St. Joseph's School, nearly four hundred students from grades one through eight were already seated at their desks waiting for roll-call. The school was a reflection of the loving care bestowed by the Sisters of Charity. There were four statues, created in Paris, three pianos, many beautiful paintings and well-cared-for plants, tastefully arranged.

The basement accommodated the youngest pupils, including Sister Beatrix's and Sister Edwina's grade one pupils. The second- through fifth-graders had their classrooms on the first floor, while the older children, in grades six through eight, were taught on the second floor. The large Assembly Hall also located on the second floor was empty at the time. Almost half a mile from the Narrows, few of the teachers or pupils were aware of the gravity of the burning ship. The first indication that something dreadful was happening was the brilliant flash of light, followed almost instantaneously by the rumble of the ground shock passing beneath the building and the thunderous sound. The least fraction of a second later the building was torn asunder with an appalling shredding sound. Windows shattered, beams and woodwork ripped away from walls, stairways were sheared from their mountings, and desks, statues, plants, pianos and furniture flew through the wreckage. It took only seconds for St. Joseph's School to be transformed from an orderly schoolhouse to a debris-filled shell.

The attic and roof caved in on Sister Mary Cecilia's eighth grade classroom pinning the teacher to her desk platform. The floor gave way and the debris of the second floor classroom plunged to the floor below. All but two of her students made their way to safety through the broken ground-floor windows. Two girls were crushed in the wreckage and killed. Sister Mary Cecilia, cut and bruised but not seriously injured, was freed from the wreckage.

The seventh-grade classroom was totally demolished. Sister Agnes Gerald was knocked unconscious and covered by debris. By the time she recovered, her class had managed to escape, with the exception of one girl who had been killed. Sister Agnes made her way to the school-yard to help the injured.

Part of the school roof above Sister Ethelred's classroom was found on the next street, but the Sister led a charmed life, still seated at her desk, unharmed and flanked on either side by huge beams. One of her pupils was killed and many were lacerated by flying glass.

Two little girls from Sister Rita's class were instantly killed when the ceiling and the second-storey floor landed on them. Sister Rita was temporarily blinded by the torrents of blood gushing from her head wounds. In danger of losing sight in both eyes and unable to find her way over the rubble, she was stranded until several little girls came to her aid. Another small child found her way out of the wreckage but went back again and again to help her schoolmates. There were many instances that displayed the heroism of both the Sisters and their students. Sister Francis had her wrist broken and was pinned under a fallen stairway; she was also rescued by two of the girls from her class. Sister Cecila Lawrence suffered a broken leg and bruising and Sister

John Baptist sustained severe cuts about her head and face. But despite their own injuries, the Sisters of Charity cared for the frightened and injured children until the arrival of ambulances and outside aid.

St. Joseph's Convent was next door to the school building. It housed the Sisters on the top floor, Sister Superior's private room and office on the second floor and a chapel on the first floor. At the time of the explosion a music class of about fifty pupils was in progress in a large music room on the main floor. The building was a victim of the low pressure system. The north-west corner of the building blew outward and a large portion of the floor went through to the Chapel. Sister Superior and the young ladies in the music room were uninjured but, of the four Sisters in the Convent, three were seriously hurt.

THE MOMENT AFTER the flash of "lightning" and the terrible "clap of thunder," Muriel Jackson realized it was not just the latecomers who were feeling the wrath of God. She and her two tardy companions slid across the now tilted floor of the classroom to end up against the outside wall just below the windows—but so did the ones who had been on time. The northern wall of St. Joseph's School had cracked and bent outward as if hinged. The classroom was falling. Every bit of glass was gone from the windows; Violet Hartlen and Muriel both jumped out the window at the same moment. The wall was slanting away from them and they slid down, as if on a slide in the playground, then fell off the edge of the upper section and dropped ten or more feet to the ground. Both girls suffered injuries. Violet had broken her arm and Muriel had cuts on her head, arm and leg. But they were alive. Both sat on the wreckage and gazed in stunned disbelief at the black billowing smoke, shaped like a giant mushroom, spiralling to the sky above them. They gazed at the carnage and devastation that, only a few seconds ago, had been Richmond. But they were alive. Others were not so fortunate. Eight of their classmates lay dead within the shambles.

AFTER DOROTHY JACKSON had made the toast for her grandmother she realized the time and hurried on her way to school. She saw the ship on fire but far from becoming fascinated by the flames she became frightened. Arriving at St. Joseph's just as the nine o'clock bell rang, she made her way to the basement where the girls for Sister Edwina's class were gathering. She had chatted for a few minutes with one of her friends, and just as she turned away the blast came. For a moment she was knocked out. When she regained consciousness there was a terrible roaring sound in her head. Sister Edwina was kneeling over her, her lips

Dorothy Jackson, the orphaned daughter of John Jackson and Louisa (MacDonald) Jackson. This picture was taken in California several years after the explosion.

Photo courtesy of Diane Walker.

were moving but Dorothy could not hear a word above the volume of the roaring sound. Sister's habit was splattered with blood and she was wincing with pain but she led Dorothy and three other girls out of the school, then went back for more.

Dorothy saw her cousin, Muriel Jackson, sitting on a pile of boards and went over and sat beside her. The older girl asked her a question but Dorothy simply put her arms up over her head and rocked back and forth in total misery. One of the sisters came over and told Muriel to take some of the younger children to the clearing near the Convent. Violet was holding her broken arm and crying and Muriel shepherded both her and Dorothy to the bog where they stayed for most of the day. As help arrived, the injured were placed in ambulances and taken to the Camp Hill Hospital or the Halifax Infirmary. All day long parents arrived, frantically searching for their children. Fires were breaking out in the wreckage of many homes and the scene was like a battlefield. A shamble of broken homes extended from the school to the Narrows and north to the hill that shielded Africville. The children were traumatized by the cries and screams of the injured and dying, thrust into a nightmare beyond their ability to comprehend. Surviving parents, some hideously wounded, all with devastated homes, destroyed, searched for what they had left—their children. No one would be searching for Dorothy.

All four churches and both schools in Richmond were destroyed by the explosion. Also demolished were the glebe, manse and church halls; the facilities for Sunday School, recreation, and social gatherings were gone. Richmond was deprived, at least temporarily, of the provisions for religion and education.

St. Joseph's Church, before the explosion. The church was located on the corner of Russell and Gottingen Streets, two thousand feet from the **Mont Blanc.**

Photo courtesy of P.A.N.S.

Photo courtesy of P.A.N.S.

St Joseph's Church, after the explosion. The church was totally destroyed but was rebuilt over the next few years.

In the initial count, Richmond's churches lost a total of 941 parishioners. Two hundred members of St. Mark's Anglican Church were killed; St. Joseph's Catholic Church would suffer the loss of 404 members; Kaye Street Methodist lost 167; and 170 members of the Grove Presbyterian died in the tragedy. Only twenty families in St. Joseph's Parish escaped having at least one death.

This list was compiled in haste during the first week after the explosion, a period of great confusion and stress. Many church members who were killed were not listed. Neither were those who died from injuries days, weeks or months after the explosion. The list is an understatement of the number killed who were members of those four churches.

To determine the total death toll for the community of Richmond, the number of people who were not members of a church must be added to that list. It would increase, yet again, with the addition of those from other areas who were working in Richmond that morning. More than fifteen hundred of the total deaths in the Halifax Explosion occurred at Richmond, an area of one-quarter square mile This figure represented more than three-quarters of the total casualties of the Halifax Explosion.

The sign inside the entrance to St. Joseph's Church Hall said, "EVERYONE WELCOME." It meant exactly that. The hall was one of the most popular social facilities in the entire North End of the city. Many people, Catholic and otherwise, looked forward to the dances and other events held here. The emphasis was not placed on religious beliefs; the emphasis was placed on fun. The building was located diagonally across from the church on Gottingen Street, which saved it from total destruction by a guest that was most UNWELCOME—the Halifax Explosion.

The wall of compressed air split to pass by either side of the church and missed the hall before it could regroup. But the ground shock had weakened the structure, making it vulnerable to the low pressure system following. The roof was lifted and the sidewalls pushed out, making the building unsafe for further use without massive repairs.

The wall of compressed air began to lose its pristine shape. The perfect circle expanding outward was corrupted by the various points of resistance it encountered, creating gaps and bulges that themselves caused freakish effects. It would miss some properties entirely while annihilating others. Its strength was weakened after three thousand feet; no longer were the molecules of air being pushed forward with the same unimaginable force. The battering-ram of steel was softening.

The low pressure system following the wall of compressed air was no longer as intense. The explosive force of the air inside the homes was thereby lessened. The houses, from this point on, received structural damage that made many uninhabitable, but the majority were not beyond repair.

The largest change to the amount of destruction was caused by topography. At the lower reaches of Richmond the irresistible force had met the immovable hill upon which the community was built. It had no choice but to deflect upward. The major portion now blasted over the top of homes in the city's West End and extreme North End, in itself doing little damage. The majority of the destruction from here onward would be accomplished by a combination of the ground shock, now racing ahead of the air wall, freakish blasts of wind and the lesser outward explosion of air within the structures.

Another factor which would soften the blow was the physical layout of the streets. Richmond had been the perfect target. The homes were mainly on streets running north and south, broadside to the explosion. Each street was higher on the hill than the one before; the houses on the west side of each street were higher than their neighbours on the east side of the same street. None of the homes offered protection to the others. They were as targets on shelves in a shooting gallery, each broadside to the blast. But, after Gottingen

Street, the homes and buildings were primarily on the streets running east and west. The terrible strength of the blast was hitting them end-on. The first few houses on the block acted as a bumper, protecting to some degree the homes behind them.

From Young Street to Duffus Street, bounded on the east side by Gottingen and on the west by North Creighton Street (now Isleville St.) is the area we know today as the Hydrostone. In the days and months following the explosion it was simply referred to as the "devastated area." This, despite the advantage of being end-on to the explosion and the protection offered by Richmond hill. Eight residential streets, Kane, Livingstone, Stairs, Columbus, Merkel, Cabot, Sebastian and Duffus, were now hit by the ground shock and the low pressure system.

The ground shock weakened the houses, cracked foundations, broke windows, ruptured water lines, severed phone and electrical wires and toppled furniture. The topography combination of Fort Needham and the rise of the Richmond hill did save many lives in this section of the city. The low pressure system, still well below the normal pressure of fourteen pounds per square inch, caused the air within the homes to explode outward. The air inside the homes exerted an outward pressure of over 1 ton per square foot in its effort to escape.

The interior air pressure blew the roof off many homes, sidewalls off the sills on others. The houses swayed, leaned crazily and settled. Many ignited and burned to the ground. People within the dwellings were thrown about and struck by falling furniture; not crushed beneath falling floors and beams. The death toll dropped sharply from that of the lower reaches of Richmond. There were deaths, but the damage was primarily cuts from shattered glass, broken bones and bruises from falling objects. Of the homes that were spared total destruction, at the moment of disaster, or escaped the ravages of fire, there was hardly one suitable for habitation without massive repairs. The wintry cold and the threat of an imminent major storm would not permit anyone to be without shelter for any length of time.

The majority of people in this "devastated area" would live. The injuries sustained were generally not life threatening; they would be able to rescue themselves from the wreckage of their badly damaged homes. But, like many throughout the city, they would face the problems of caring for the injured and finding shelter, heat and food after the loss of almost everything. By their own ability and ingenuity they must stay alive until aid poured in from the rest of the country and the world. For at least a while they were on their own.

For many the answer was banding together with others in the same predicament. In numbers there is strength. Most of the people in the north *end of the city at least knew each other by sight. They had perhaps attended the same church, passed each other on the street enough times to justify a nod or a greeting, or even perhaps they were distantly related by marriage. In the circumstances facing them, casual acquaintances rapidly became friends.*

The people of the "devastated area" had lost almost everything. The few homes not demolished, or now being consumed by fire, were unsafe for habitation. Some could be repaired but not soon enough to provide relief for the homeless. A few of the items necessary for living were spared—some pots and pans, a few tables and chairs, bedding and clothing—these simple things would be invaluable in the weeks ahead.

For the first few hours they were fully occupied, attending to their own injuries, binding the wounds of others, rescuing family and neighbours imperilled by fire, or trying to find medical attention for those seriously injured. After urgent needs were met they simply sat amidst the ruins, trying to reconcile themselves to the enormity of their loss and waiting for help.

Immediate help was not forthcoming. Some made their way across Gottingen Street and up the steep incline of Fort Needham, the only spot not covered by debris. From here they had a panoramic view of the damage suffered by the rest of the North End. From their vantage point to the harbour, half a mile away, they saw the community of Richmond lying flattened and burning. It was from this they could derive the consolation they were more fortunate than others. Their losses had mainly been the material possessions of life. They and their families still had the most precious gift— they were alive.

Each individual, realizing the futility of trying to fight alone, began to become part of a group. By this there could be a combining of strengths, talents and abilities that would allow all to weather the immediate problems of survival. The families, Newport, Knowles and Daine, neighbours and friends of the Jacksons, were among many North End families to join forces in the aftermath of the disaster. John and Myrtle Daine, Parker Knowles and his children, joined forces with John's father, William, and his children. They would face the immediate future sharing the same abode—boxcar number 305422.

THE HOUSE AT seven Merkel Street was owned by the parents of Fred Jackson's wife, Bessie. Fred and Bessie lived there with their three children, four-year-old William, two-year-old Eileen and two-month-old, Eva Margaret. Her parents, John and Jane Bradley, had nicknamed the home Lucky Seven and on December 6th, 1917 it at least partially lived up to its name. It was not broadside to the blast and it received some protection from two houses that lay between it and the *Mont Blanc*. This slight degree of protection, plus the fact the strength of the air wall was diminished at this distance, saved the occupants from death. The windows were blown in, the chimney toppled and the kitchen stove plunged through to the basement; the house began to burn.

Fred's wife and children were at the kitchen table having breakfast. Bessie's face and head were pierced by small slivers of glass, some would remain embedded under her skin for years. The children, although shaken and in shock, were uninjured. Despite her injuries Bessie was able to guide the children out of the burning house. She made her way to seventeen Merkel Street to the relatively undamaged home of her parents.

A split second before Merkel Street was hit, Fred Jackson was killed at the waterfront. His body was never found. He was close enough to the blast to have been a victim of the fireball, or he might have been carried out to sea by the tidal wave; the first supposition is the more probable. The bodies of his brother Edward, his niece, Florence Jackson, and Annie Turner, caretaker of the Lorne Club, were also never found. All three were an equal distance from the exploding ship. Their home at seven Merkel Street was just over two thousand feet from the epicentre, the furthest that any Jacksons were from the blow.

A three thousand foot radius from the explosion's centre would also encompass the area of Dartmouth from Tuft's Cove to what is now Rosedale Drive, curving back toward the Narrows at Jamieson Street. The eastern quadrant of the wall of compressed air smashed into this small area, striking it with a force equal to that devastating the properties west of Gottingen Street on the Halifax side. Considerably weaker than that which destroyed Richmond, the blow was lethal nevertheless. Dartmouth would count approximately fifty deaths, the majority of these had already occurred. The crew members on the Imo, *the employees at Oland's Brewery, the people at Tuft's Cove Indian Reservation and the Mic Mac school children were already dead.*

This area also saw the most serious injuries and the most properties totally destroyed. The area was sparsely populated; the busier part—downtown near the ferry wharf—was almost a mile away. The hills in this area made up the other side of the bowl that deflected the air wall up and over eastern Dartmouth and would work in conjunction with the Richmond hill to set up an oscillatory movement for the wall of water even now pushing away from where the Mont Blanc *had been.*

CHAPTER
9

RICHMOND PRISON squatted, sturdy and immovable, at the northern end of Gottingen Street, thirty-five hundred feet from Pier Six. Constructed to incarcerate law breakers and prevent their escape from custody, it would serve another function on December 6th, never foreseen by the designer. The strength of the concrete and steel that kept prisoners in prevented the entrance of an unwelcome visitor.

The Warden's son was enjoying a schoolboy's ideal day, too sick to go to school, but not sick enough to stay in bed. After breakfast he started to add some pieces to the Ferris wheel he was making with his erector set. He was thoroughly engrossed in the mechanics of construction when he heard the first exploding barrels of benzene. Now, with his forehead and nose pressed against the window, he was enthralled by the spectacular fireworks in the Narrows. He had an excellent view from more than two hundred feet above the harbour, looking directly over Richmond and the waterfront. This was far more exciting than his Ferris wheel and infinitely more interesting than a boring, stuffy old classroom.

The cold of the glass felt good against the slight fever of his skin. He had watched the small boats jockey for position around the burning ship as it drifted toward the Halifax side; now it had reached Pier Six. He saw the fire engines arrive and the stevedores scurrying about in confusion. He saw the freight cars with the man standing on top roll to a stop just short of Pier Eight and he saw all the people standing on the wharves, watching the fire.

The flash of light almost blinded him and the ungodly sound left him stunned. The prison swayed with the rippling passage of the earth shock, almost knocking him to his knees. The shrapnel, spewed out from the doomed ship, battered against the prison's concrete walls. Every window but one was shattered. The only pane of glass that did not break was the one pressing against his face.

He stared in stunned disbelief. He was one of the first to view the damage caused by Canada's greatest disaster. He remembered his father taking him to a travelling vaudeville show the year before. There had been a magician who made things appear and disappear; doves that came from nowhere and magic scarves that changed colour in the man's hands; a cane that transformed into a bouquet of flowers and the pretty lady locked in a box. When the magician opened the box the lady was gone.

Now the city was gone. All the houses of Richmond had disappeared. The Sugar Refinery was nowhere to be seen. Even the burning ship and those ships around it were gone. They weren't exactly gone—they had been turned into large piles of broken boards, some still showering from the darkened sky. As he watched, a huge wall of water raced to the Dartmouth shore and surged up the hill; it turned and flooded back across the Narrows and surged up the Richmond Hill, flushing some of the wreckage further up the slope. There were people in the water, bobbing and sinking and reappearing just like magic. Then it went back again taking the people and boards and even a freight car with it. All the people were gone. There were no wharves where the people had been. The freight car the man had been standing on had disappeared; so had the man. There was no one left.

The boy held his breath in shock and amazement, waiting for whoever made it disappear to wave the magic wand and bring it back. But the act was over; there was no magic wand. No power on earth could make it reappear. He turned from the horror and ran screaming to find his father.

Gottingen Street ended a few hundred feet north of Rockhead Prison. Here the ground falls away in a steep hill that drops down to Fairview Cove. The level land below the embankment forms the roadbed for the rail lines connecting the Rockingham Yard with the Richmond Yard. There is a long, sweeping curve from Fairview along the shore of Bedford Basin to the Narrows. Nestled on this flat land, with the rail lines running through its centre, is the community of Africville.

Humankind has never taken kindly to the loss of personal freedom. The people of Sierra Leone, Liberia, Nigeria, and the other West African countries bordering the Atlantic Ocean were certainly no exception. They were a proud people, with a rich heritage dating back thousands of years. But they were no match for the guns and brutality of the slave traders of the mid-nineteenth century. Bound and chained they were herded like cattle to the ships deporting them from their homeland and sold to fill the demand for slaves in the United States. Thousands would die from starvation or disease in the deplorable conditions during transportation. More would die at the hands of brutal masters on their arrival.

With the enactment of the American Emancipation Act, many fled to Canada seeking freedom from oppression. They were joined in their exodus by a group, loyal to the British flag, that became part of the United Empire Loyalists. Here they escaped the physical bonds of rope and chains but did not elude the emotional bondage of discrimination and prejudice.

The name itself mirrored pride in their roots and traditions. Africville— African village. Here, in close-knit family groups, they found comfort and kinship. Here, in a community bonded by church and school, they fought the battle for justice and equality, seeking the day when a Black person could be a doctor, lawyer, engineer, teacher or anything they dreamed they could be. In the ensuing years, through courage and determination, significant inroads would be made in this direction. But, this was 1917, the battle had barely begun.

Africville was spared by the topography from terrible death or destruction. The wall of air was diverted high above the homes by Richmond hill. Even the low pressure system behind the wall was elevated to a height that weakened its power of destruction. Only the church and the school, the taller buildings, received severe damage; except for broken windows the homes were largely untouched. Three residents are shown on the official list of the dead, and they are believed to have met their death on the streets of Richmond while walking to work.

THE EARTH SHOCK travelled under the Exhibition Grounds sending a tremor through the Cotton Factory, located near the corner of West Young Street and Kempt Road. This shook the building and loosened the connection each floor had to the sidewalls. A split second later the building was struck by a lobe of the now erratic air wall and this completed the damage. Most of the factory's heavy equipment was on the top floor. When it gave way, the massive weight of machinery and the concrete floor plunged down on the floor below, it in turn was pushed down to the next. All of the employees, except one, was crushed under massive tons of concrete and machinery. One wall stayed intact, the stairwell was attached to this wall and the lone survivor had just started down from the third floor. The building pulled away from her as it collapsed, saving her life.

Immediately the air was rent with the screams of her fellow employees, trapped and dying. Surrounded by pools of blood and severed limbs, for several minutes she remained on the shorn stairs—frozen with shock—and screamed, one piercing scream after another. She screamed one final scream, ran the rest of the way down the steps, now canted at a sharp angle, and ran sobbing with terror until, physically, the factory and the scene of slaughter was far behind. Emotionally, it would be with her until her dying day.

West from Robie Street to Oxford and south from Bloomfield to beyond North Street the land lies level. The north end of Oxford Street is the highest point in the city, a few feet higher even than the top of Citadel Hill. The wall of air that was diverted high over the community of Africville to the north, basically at sea level, barely skimmed over the tops of these homes more than three hundred feet above the harbour's surface. The following low pressure system was also closer to the roofs of the homes and it was this system that caused the major damage. While the death rate here was much lower, the property damage was heavy enough to make the majority of the homes uninhabitable.

Several factors combined to reduce the death toll and the severity of damage for this area and for the rest of the city. First, and most importantly, the force of the wall of air was much reduced. Explosive force diminishes inversely to the square of the distance. At 2,000 feet the strength was 1/4; at 3,000 feet it was 1/9; at 6,000 feet, 1/36. The force that hit the lower reaches of Richmond was approximately thirty-six times greater than the force that would hit Citadel Hill. What started as a fourteen thousand mile-per-hour wind lost momentum with every foot it travelled from the blast centre. The energy expended in smashing through the obstructions in its path and overcoming the resistance of the inert air ahead of it greatly sapped its strength. It still was monstrous, with the strength of many hurricanes rolled into one but, unlike a hurricane, it was not a sustained wind, rather a steel-fisted punch lasting only a fraction of a second. The low pressure system weakened concurrently but still had the strength to rip off the roof or tear a sidewall away from a building. The low pressure system now became the major facet of the destructive force.

Every foot away from the epicentre weakened the ground shock rippling under the city; from this point onward it was not a major concern. By the time it reached the three thousand foot point it no longer posed a major threat; it contributed to the breaking of windows, cracking of foundations and caused trauma to those who experienced the rippling of the otherwise solid surface beneath their feet but was not a prime contributing factor to death or injury.

Finally, the nature of the target had changed. Only Richmond had offered the perfect shooting gallery effect, broadside to and in perfect alignment with the full force. After Richmond the majority of residential streets ran east to west and even those running north and south were being struck an oblique blow. Houses on streets end-on to the blast received a lesser punch from the wind, now at an oblique angle, and were offered a bit of protection by neighbouring homes between them and the source. The houses from here on would receive damage that would necessitate major repairs before they could supply shelter but the majority would not collapse onto stoves that would cause them to burn, the fate of so many in the north end of the city. A combination of these factors reduced the death rate to a small fraction of that in the area already devastated. Of the more than two thousand deaths that occurred in Halifax and Dartmouth in the Explosion of December 6th, 1917, 70 to 75 per cent occurred in Richmond; 15 to 20 per cent took place in the rest of the North End.

ADA'S DAUGHTER, MABEL Shanks climbed to her feet. Both of her knees were scraped and bleeding. Her purse and one shoe were missing, as were her hat and that damned hatpin that had caused her to miss the tram; judging by the pain of her scalp, a large tuft of her hair had gone with her hat. She was completely dazed. As many will do when confronted by a major catastrophe, Mabel occupied her mind with a minor problem—she searched for her shoe. Finding it, with the heel missing, about fifty feet from where she had been standing, she put it on. She took a few tentative steps. It wasn't too bad if she walked on the heel of one foot and the toes of the other. Slowly she looked around her. The houses on Almon Street had all the windows broken and the front doors had blown off the hinges. The street and sidewalk were littered with chimney bricks, shingles and shards of glass and she offered a silent prayer of thanks that none had hit her. The Cotton Factory was gone, the houses further down the street were smashed and twisted, and some had collapsed. When she looked to the east she could see bits and pieces of houses swirling through the air and settling in the north end of the city. In every direction there was chaos and devastation, and the realization broke through that the heart of the devastation was Richmond, the home of her mother and her brothers and sisters. Her mental anguish blocked physical pain. People began emerging from the battered homes, a few were bleeding, some were in shock, all were confused and frightened. Her two children had been left with Mrs. Shanks, a woman not physically strong. For only a few moments Mabel was indecisive, then a mother's instinct prevailed; she limped as fast as she could, back toward home and her babies.

The east side of Oxford School, more than sixty-five hundred feet from the explosion, was broadside to the force of the wind. The second storey of the school building was above the houses on North Street and denied their protection. The flash of light and awesome blast interrupted morning prayers. The east-facing windows shattered, flying straight across the room in a deadly rain of jagged spears and splinters. Kneeling by their desks in prayer, most of the children were below the shower of glass; only a few were tall enough to be hit. None of the children were killed or seriously injured, and they were in good hands; most of the Sisters of Charity, who were teachers, were also well versed in first aid. The children were quickly attended to and then sent home. A few would occasionally have tiny splinters of glass removed from their scalp even decades after that day, unwanted souvenirs of their experience.

Only a few hundred feet further south of Oxford School, Chebucto Road School also jutted above its neighbouring houses, the upper floor exposed to the wind force. The school sustained the same type of damage; every window was blown in and there was some structural damage to the roof and sidewalls. A crew of forty men worked for one and a half days to make the school fit for its temporary new function as the largest morgue in Canada.

St. Patrick's School on Brunswick Street, near Cornwallis, was more fortunate than either Oxford or Chebucto Road School. It too was located about six thousand feet from the centre of the explosion but the classrooms of the building were facing east and west. The glass was cracked by the shock wave travelling under the building but not propelled by the wind to become a lethal weapon. The building was sheltered to a degree by the buildings to the north and the wall of air hit the north end of the school which had few windows. The children, the majority frightened but unhurt, were ordered to go straight home and most of them were only too willing to comply.

JAMES MAHAR'S DAUGHTER, Madeleine, and her best friend ran from St. Patrick's School up to Gottingen Street through a passageway between two buildings and headed north toward home. It was only then that Madeleine noticed that her friend's arm was bleeding; a piece of glass had sliced it open just below the elbow, leaving a large piece of flesh hanging loose. Madeleine, ever the decorous young lady, walked back to the alley to lift her dress and tear a long strip from her slip. Modesty preserved, she returned to her friend and wrapped the make-shift bandage tightly around the wounded arm, fastening it with the safety pin that had been substituting as a button on her blouse. Together, the two young girls walked north on Gottingen Street toward Almon and home. Until they reached North Street they only passed scenes of destruction and they were chatting excitedly, each pointing to damaged houses and people on the street who had also been cut by glass. But, then, they saw houses on fire. They heard the cries and screams of people in terror. Now they had to make their way around wreckage that littered the street and they saw the first bodies of the dead. Instinctively Madeleine and her chum gripped each other's hand for comfort and began to run but the further they ran the worse it became. By the time they reached Almon Street both girls were hysterical with fright.

Gottingen Street and Barrington Street and the areas between, from North Street to Citadel Hill, were struck a glancing blow, at an angle of approximately twenty-five degrees, by the wall of air. This obtuse blow was far less destructive than the perfect right angle that hit the Richmond homes. But it was strong enough to cause massive destruction. The New York Garment Company, on the corner of Gottingen and Cornwallis Streets had opened their door at sharp nine o'clock to begin their sale of women's winter coats; by five after nine the door had been blown off the hinges and lay on the other side of the street. Every plate glass display window had been smashed and the racks of clothing, including the coat so coveted by Ada Moore, lay in disarray on the floor. The building, as many others around it, was a victim of the other destructive facet of the explosion, the intense low-pressure system. It would be past Cornwallis Street before the majority of homes would remain fit to house the victims.

AT THE FOOT of Cornwallis Street Madeleine's father, James William Mahar, was supervising the unloading of a freight car at the open door of a storage shed. The dark and musty shed behind him was lit by a brilliant flash and the ground beneath his feet undulated, throwing him off balance. For a moment he and his men stood frozen in shock. The other end of the shed, jutting out into the harbour, had been struck by the weakening wall of wind. A dozen men were down, writhing in pain, calling for help. One man's arm was severed at the elbow and he was holding the stump with the other, bellowing in shock and terror. The survivors worked feverishly to help those bleeding to death, but their efforts were mostly in vain. They would be among the ninety-eight stevedores who died that day.

When they had done what they could for their comrades, the men of the waterfront started for home. Those who lived in the North End would find terrible tragedy; residents of Richmond would find utter chaos. Many who had lived for years in the same house on the same street could now find neither their home nor their street.

Just a few blocks south of Cornwallis Street lies Citadel Hill. In the early days of the city a fortress was built on this massive feature to protect the city from any enemy. It was never called upon to serve in that capacity—until now. Its sheer bulk offered an unyielding shield to the force of the Halifax Explosion. The steep incline batted the wall of compressed air harmlessly above and beyond the houses and streets that lay behind the hill. The subsequent low pressure system was also diverted, inflicting minimal damage in the south end of Halifax. Windows were shattered, foundations and ceiling plaster cracked, and there were numerous glass injuries, but the majority of the homes and buildings remained intact and habitable. Some of the larger buildings would soon be pressed into service as first aid stations or hospitals.

At approximately the same instant the force was diverting over the top of and around the bulk of Citadel Hill it also struck the populated downtown area of Dartmouth, more than a mile and a half from the epicentre. Even without the protection of a massive hill the strength of the blast was considerably weakened. Nevertheless, it wreaked havoc on the homes, churches and other buildings but without the heavy loss of life and serious injury that had been its forte in the nearer reaches of the epicentre. Many of the homes would be rendered unfit for immediate habitation; almost every pane of glass shattered, but most could and would be repaired.

Now, less than ten seconds after the Mont Blanc *exploded, the catastrophic forces departed the city and the town. It catapulted northwards over Bedford and Sackville, fanned harmlessly south and east over the broad Atlantic, and to the west it dispersed above Spryfield and St. Margaret's Bay. It had taken less than ten seconds to destroy a city and the lives of thousands. For the survivors it had been a hundred lifetimes.*

Nature abhors a vacuum. There was a violent inrush of air, from every point of the compass, to eliminate the semi-vacuum created behind the air wall. It, too, reached hurricane strength. Buildings weakened by the outward blast toppled before this new onslaught. Trees flattened in one direction were joined by others facing the opposite way. The onrush of returning air met with a thunderous clap where, seconds before, the Mont Blanc *had been.*

The last of the buildings swayed and collapsed. Timbers creaked in protest before falling; large building blocks and stones slithered and ground to a halt. There was a last resounding crack of a breaking beam, the final high-pitched tinkle of falling glass, and dust began to rise from the debris.

And then there was silence. A profound, awesome, ominous silence.

CHAPTER
10

Catastrophe begets crisis. With the final tinkle of broken glass, before the first whimper of pain, during the long moments of terrible silence, the city and its people reached a state of crisis. The status quo was shattered. This was the crucial turning point—the place of departure toward progression or regression. The direction would depend upon the courage and will of the people and the quality of leadership by those in charge. Only one thing was certain—things could never return to what had been.

In less time than it takes to draw a deep breath, almost every building in Halifax and Dartmouth was damaged. A preliminary report issued by the Canadian Commission of Conservation several weeks after the disaster listed 794 buildings as totally destroyed, 337 as partially destroyed and 394 as severely damaged, totalling 1,525 homes no longer fit for habitation. In addition, another 5,000 buildings suffered minor to considerable damages. A conservative estimate of absolute property loss was given as $25 million. This was in 1917 dollars.

In the same few seconds all city services ground to a halt. Power lines, telegraph lines and phone lines were knocked down, effectively leaving the city incommunicado. There was no immediate way to notify the world of the urgent need for aid. Transportation was interrupted; the North Street Station was destroyed, while the absence of electricity rendered the tram cars useless.

There is the potential to build a bigger and better city on the ruins of the old. But, human life cannot arise from the ashes. The true tragedy of the Halifax Explosion was the tragedy of the people. Fewer than eight seconds after the blast more than a thousand were dead. In the next days a thousand more would die. By far the largest percentage of those who died were children. At 66 Veith Street, ten of the eleven who died were children. At 1498 Barrington Street, eight of the eleven who died were children. In the area within two thousand feet of the explosion large numbers of parents were left childless. Nearly one hundred children were orphaned.

Within moments of the destruction the wounded and maimed began to emerge from the wreckage of their homes. Many, still trapped beneath the rubble, would have to await rescue by others. Nine thousand sustained injuries, many of them critical—a casualty rate comparable to the most brutal battles in Flanders Fields.

They who, short moments ago, had the normal material possessions of life now came forth homeless and destitute. Their only possession was the clothes they were wearing the instant of the blast. In many cases these had been reduced to tatters or torn altogether from their bodies. Most of the women and children had been indoors at the critical moment and the clothing they were wearing was inadequate for outdoors on a cold December morning. The homeless and destitute numbered almost twenty thousand. The wounded and the homeless would tax the city's facilities far beyond capacity. And two more tragedies were yet to come.

Even as the first of the wounded cried for help, the wall of water, thrust away from the Mont Blanc, *was rolling across the harbour toward Dartmouth, gaining height and strength with every second. It ascended the hills, taking with it both the living and the dead before being flushed back across the Narrows to inundate Richmond hill. Simultaneously, hundreds of stoves were spilling their burning coals upon the wooden wreckage. The trial by water and the trial by fire were only minutes away.*

Photo courtesy of P.A.N.S. (N-7014)

Photograph taken from the North Street Railway Station showing Richmond and the north end area before the Halifax Explosion. The Sugar Refinery is shown in the centre background. This building is about a hundred feet from the explosion centre.

Photograph taken from near the ruins of the Hillis Iron Foundry looking toward where Pier Eight and Pier Nine had been.

Photograph of wrecked homes further south on Barrington Street. The homes at this point were end-on to the blast; one house shielded the next and most of the damage was caused by the air inside the house, at normal pressure, exploding outward. The roof of the house in the foreground has lifted off, the area around the windows on the side away from the blast have blown out and the front wall has been driven away from the sill.

Photo showing the ruins of Hillis Iron Foundry taken from near the drydock. The front of the building is on Barrington Street, the rear entrance is on Veith Street. The single wall standing south of the factory, on the left side of the picture, is the front wall of the Protestant Orphanage, facing on Young Street.

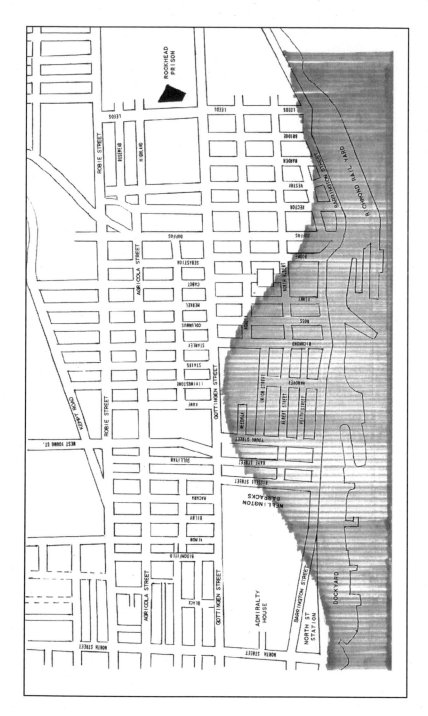

TIDAL WAVE
This is the probable extent of the tidal wave that inundated the Richmond area and the waterfront wharves. It drowned many and flushed bodies and wreckage into the harbour.

CHAPTER
11

GERALD JACKSON HAD fallen from his mother's arms as the house collapsed. He remembered sliding down the floor and landing on his hands and knees amongst the broken boards and plaster. The three-year-old was physically uninjured, he received only a few minor scratches, but he was utterly bewildered. Where was his mother? And Edward and the baby? Where had his house gone? The only familiar thing he recognized was Prince his fox terrier, who bounded toward him with his tail between his legs, equally frightened and distraught. Gerald grabbed him by the collar and hugged him close; boy and dog crouched together, whimpering softly.

A strange man staggered toward them, clutching a baby in his arms. The top of the baby's head was missing and triangles of glass jutted out from its body. There was a jagged cut across the man's throat and another on his forehead; his blood gushed down over the baby. With a terrible sigh the man slowly sank to his knees and fixed unseeing eyes on Gerald. He then fell forward, pinning the baby beneath him.

With a cry of terror, Gerald slithered backwards, under the rubble and away from the sight and smell of blood. He and Prince weaved their way through the wreckage until they came to a near-naked woman splayed across the debris. Blood trickled from her ear and although her eyes were open, she did not seem to see them. For a moment they paused, waiting for the lady to say something. Then, as quietly as they could, they crawled around her and deeper into the pile of broken boards. When they came to the corner of a concrete wall they could go no further. Gerald sat with his back to the wall and took the dog in his arms; at last he began to cry. He pressed his face deep into Prince's shoulder to muffle his sobs, lest they wake the woman and make her angry. There, the two little creatures huddled together, hiding from the horror neither could begin to comprehend.

Hidden beneath the sounds of screams was the sibilant hiss of a wall of water racing back toward Richmond's shore. The centre of the wave passed over the spot where the Mont Blanc had been and flooded through the Richmond Railyard. It was estimated to be twenty to thirty feet high at the centre, tapering to a negligible height at each end. At the centre there was enough power to lift freight cars off their track and roll them over and over like a child's toys. As the wave encountered the hill, its height dissipated rapidly and it became as a wave rolling up a sandy beach. The deepest point rushed straight up Richmond and Ross Streets, diminishing in depth as it progressed, to the top of Fort Needham. The water on each side, less deep than the centre, formed the tidal wave into a lobe, reaching from Fort Needham in the centre to the bottom of North Street on one side and to the bottom of Duffus Street on the other.

In the return journey to the Narrows the centre section surged down the Richmond hill plucking bits and pieces of wreckage and the bodies of the living and dead from the streets. The incline caused the creation of turbulence, similar to the rolling effect of the wind wall that had hit a few minutes before, also creating a lifting force. It picked up speed, depth and power as it passed the lower end of Richmond; sufficient speed, depth and power as it flushed through Barrington Street and the Richmond Railyard to roll the freight cars in the opposite direction, toward the harbour. The bodies of the living and dead within its path were tossed and turned within the turbulent mass on their involuntary journey to the harbour. One of the "living" bodies was that of eleven-year-old Mildred Hale.

ANY CHILD WITH a well-developed sweet tooth—whose mother owns a confectionery store—pretty well has it made. Mildred Hale was so blessed. When her father died in a railway accident five years earlier, her mother, Frances, had moved the family from Truro to Halifax. She purchased the house at sixty-eight Roome Street and converted the downstairs front room into a candy store. Mildred, her sister Thelma, aged nineteen, and fifteen-year-old Ralph all helped their mother in the shop. Mildred's pay was all the candy she could eat. There were old fashioneds, honeymoons, licorice sticks, jelly beans, gum drops and dozens of other penny candies—all there for the taking. Every child in the neighborhood was her friend but her special buddies were Ada's daughter, Nellie, and Mary Jean's daughter, Mary Mabel. Mildred and Nell usually walked to school together but Nell had not shown up this morning.

Mildred and Ralph left for school a few minutes before nine o'clock, their mother was in the front window of the store setting up a display of candy canes and ribbons—seasonal best sellers. Richmond School was hardly more than a block from their home and they had reached it when another of Mildred's best friends, Gertrude Reid, caught up to them. By now all of their attention was riveted on the fire in the Narrows and they moved further down Roome Street so the view was not blocked by the school building.

Caught in the excitement of the moment, Mildred turned to her friend, "Let's go down to the dock and watch from there." Gertie shook her head and held up a fifty-cent piece. "I can't, Mum would kill me. She told me to go to Creighton's and get some things for dinner. I'll have to hurry so I can take it back home before I go to school."

Gertie paused in front of the store and reluctantly waved goodbye to her friend, now running down Barrington Street toward the burning ship. With the money clutched tight in one hand she reached with the other to open the door. The blast drove her through the entrance and into the store. For a short time she remained unconscious, pinned under the wreckage.

Creighton's store was hit by the low end of the giant wave. The water flowed harmlessly over Gertie and the bodies of the Edmonds brothers, the store clerks and Isaac Creighton, among others, but it was not deep enough to lift and flush them back to the harbour. Gertie came to, shivering with the wet and cold, and managed to work her way free of the rubble and back out to the street. She suddenly became aware that her dark blue coat was turning white from the salt water and that her bonnet, which had been knotted tightly beneath her chin was missing. The fifty-cent piece was still clutched firmly in her hand.

MILDRED HALE WAS perhaps a hundred yards further south on Barrington when the blast struck. One hundred yards made a big difference; the wall of water was between twenty and thirty feet high, racing directly at Richmond Street. Mildred had been knocked unconscious by the explosion, her arm was broken and her head injured as she was blown across the wreckage of Barrington Street. Back at the store her mother had been killed instantly by a jagged shard of wood driven through her head. Thelma, already outside the critical area, sustained no injuries. Ralph had left Mildred and Gertie to continue toward school minutes before the explosion and received only minor scrapes and bruises. Their home and shop on Roome Street were completely destroyed.

Photo courtesy of Jane (Hadley) Cocaine, a
daughter of Mildred (Hale) Hadley

Frances Hale was instantly killed by
a shattered board piercing her
head. Her daughter, Mildred, was
flushed into the Narrows by the
wall of water.

Mildred awoke in the
clutches of the giant wave, which pum-
melled and tossed and rolled her without mercy. She was being toyed
with by the rolling, surging force of the water. The wave would drag
her under until she almost drowned, then, with a touch of whimsy, she
was bobbed to the surface to greedily gasp for air. Above the surface she
was assailed by the unearthly screams of the injured and the drowning;
under the surface, the rumbling and screeching of
sliding and rolling equipment and debris was amplified by the water to
an ear-splitting crescendo.

The wave relented as it rolled back to the harbour, losing the rolling
motion and allowing her to float. Her broken arm was useless to her
and only by kicking her legs constantly could she stay afloat. Only now
did she become aware of how icy-cold the water was. The air trapped
in her clothing had given her some buoyancy at first, but now her wool
coat was beginning to drag her down and her strength was waning. A
piece of wood floated near her and she desperately grabbed it with her
good arm. It was not enough to support her completely, but it did coun-
teract the now almost leaden weight of her winter clothing.

Mildred floated and kicked, occasionally sinking beneath the icy
water, where the noise had abated and was no longer frightening. The
water was dirty brown and opaque from the mud churned up from the
harbour floor. Floating around her were hundreds of onions and potatoes from some ravaged warehouse on Barrington Street. The first

drops of filthy black sludge peppered the water around her and when she looked toward Dartmouth she saw another wave, about ten feet high, bearing down on her with the speed of an express train. The wave engulfed her and rolled her under yet again. No longer certain which direction was up, Mildred simply kicked with all she had left and, just in time she surfaced. Coughing and gasping for air, she lost her grip on the plank and it was torn from her grasp. She was within twenty feet of the shore, but it may as well have been twenty miles. Her strength gone, her clothes like lead weights, paralysed by the frigid water, she could fight no more. With a little whimper, Mildred sank beneath the surface without further resistance.

She opened her eyes just as a large hand brushed over her face and grabbed the collar of her coat. She was hauled up without ceremony and her rescuer wrapped one arm around her and held her close. He was standing in waist deep water, seemingly oblivious to the cold. As he turned toward shore the wave returned from Richmond. Bracing his feet on the harbour bottom he resisted the drag as it passed over them on its way back to Dartmouth, and then waded ashore with Mildred Hale in his arms. He put her down gently without a word. He was a big, burly man with a heavy beard. The still bleeding cuts on his face and neck and the speckles of sludge gave him the fierce look of a wounded warrior. He was in as deep a state of shock as she, and they both simply stared at each other. To Mildred, he was the most beautiful man she had ever seen.

ELIZABETH EDMONDS, AGED fourteen was on her way to school when the *Mont Blanc* exploded. She was knocked off her feet and driven up the Richmond Hill but not

Photo courtesy of James R. Edmonds

Elizabeth (Lizzie) Edmonds was instrumental in the rescue of her father, mother and sister.

seriously injured. The same wave that flushed Mildred Hale into the harbour lifted and propelled Elizabeth even further up the hill, but a return journey was thwarted when her coat caught on a spear of wood protruding from some wreckage. After the wave receded she unhooked her clothing and stood in shock in the middle of what had been Richmond and her home. She was surrounded by the bodies of her schoolmates; one girl had been pinned underwater long enough to drown, and several more were casualties of the flying shrapnel that preceded the wall of water. Several minutes passed before she realized she was wet and cold, but this discomfort became negligible as the wounded started to arise from the wreckage. What she witnessed in the next minutes would haunt her for the rest of her life. The terrible lacerations and the resulting massive blood loss doomed many of those unfortunate souls to death within minutes. They were the walking dead.

A rain of black, oily sludge began to splatter the victims with an obscene coating of filth. At her feet lay a man's heavy coat, one sleeve had been ripped off and all the buttons were gone but she threw it over her head and shoulders as a protection from this muck.

Fighting nausea, Elizabeth tried to shrink within herself. She stared at the ground in front of her to avoid eye contact with the outrageous results of the blast and wave, and started instinctively walking toward home and the sanctity of family. The sight of her schoolmates' bodies had filled her with terror.

Reaching home, far from finding succour, she found chaos and confusion. For a moment sheer panic assailed her because she was not sure which pile of burning wreckage was her home. She saw William lying in a pool of blood, his leg severed, but before she could react to that her mother's voice cried out from within the rubble. As she tried to lift some of the boards her father called to her, "Over here, girl, in the basement window." She looked and saw his face, partially blocked by a timber fallen across the frame.

Arthur Edmonds had taken a piece of harness closer to the window for better light when the blast occurred. The house shattered and collapsed into the basement and was now starting to burn. He'd been spared from death by his sturdy work bench which had blocked the wreckage. The window was his only way out but it was blocked by the timber. He could not reach a position, from the inside, to apply his strength and had already cut both hands trying.

Elizabeth ran over to her father. Arthur used a stick to clear away the remaining glass. "Hurry, Lizzie, you will have to move that thing out of the way so I can get out of here. Your mother and sister are trapped and calling for help—we don't have a moment to waste." What was impossible from within was easy from the outside. Elizabeth simply took hold of one end of the timber and swivelled it away from the window, giving her father room to crawl out. Arthur spread a double piece of canvas over the bottom of the window frame and wriggled his way to freedom.

They were lucky. Letitia and Emily were relatively easy to reach. They were pinned beneath the rubble and unable to move, but most of the house had been blown across to the lots next door. Arthur heaved and hauled the wreckage away from his wife and daughter and pulled them away from the burning house. Emily was injured and her mother received burns to her arm and neck, but both would survive.

The massive wave washed over Mary Jean Hinch, imprisoned within the carnage on Veith Street. It rode over the rubble on Duffus Street where a boy and his dog were hiding. It flooded the ruins of hundreds of homes. It flushed the body of Gladys Bungay away from Wallaces' store. The water did not penetrate deep into the wreckage, where it might have extinguished the fires igniting from overturned stoves. It simply rushed quickly over the top— a brief interlude before the next phase of the catastrophe, which saw many suffer the cruellest death of all—burned alive in the shattered remnants of their homes.

A TRICKLE OF water seeped through the wreckage and splashed her face. Mary Jean Hinch regained consciousness as a wave of pain washed over her. She was in a state of total confusion; for a few minutes she didn't know where she was or how she came to be there. Her memory returned in fragments. She recalled the wedding of her sister, Emma, three weeks earlier. After the ceremony, her brother James and his wife had come home with her and Joe. The talk that night had turned to the war and she recalled the men arguing about whether or not the enemy could bomb or shell Halifax. Joe was firmly convinced they could and James was equally sure they couldn't. After company left, Joe turned to her and said, "Mark my words, old girl, one of these days the Jerries will park a couple of battle wagons off the coast and blow the bejeezes outta us. They have guns that can shoot a shell twenty miles or more and they'll be laughing their heads off 'cause we don't have a single gun that can reach them." Joe took the last of the cookies and washed it down with his beer. "If you hear a loud bang—and I'm not here—I want you to take the kids and head for the cellar."

The conversation had filled her with unease and now she became even more frightened as she realized the unthinkable had actually happened. The shell must have hit the Matthews'; she remembered the awful flash of light and the house coming toward her in bits and pieces. Thank God it missed her own home—Joe and the children would be okay—they would be here any minute to find her. Everything would be all right.

A piece of lumber gave way above her with a loud crack and the pile of debris groaned and swayed. Her body moved with it and the pain in her hip made her scream the one word, "Joe!" before she again descended into merciful oblivion.

The first of the hideously wounded clawed their way from the wreckage of their homes. No experience in their life had prepared them for this. Instantly they were plunged into Armageddon, subjected to horrors not witnessed even by those in the battlefields of Europe. And these were not soldiers, not even those fresh-faced boys sent to the front; these were civilians—men, women and children—unprepared for violence and mayhem. In a monstrous moment innocent victims had been plucked from the norm and submerged in the insanity of war.

The first few minutes and hours saw the most horrible of sights. These victims were subject to the most gruesome injuries, blessed death, for many, was only moments away. Richmond was a charnel house of horror. The streets running north and south, broadside to the blast—Union, North Albert, Veith, Acadia and the stretch of Barrington from Duffus to Young— received the full force. Each street was higher on the hill than the one before it—there was no place to hide. Human flesh standing before it was simultaneously lacerated by the slicing slivers of steel and hammered by the wall of intensely compressed air. Arms and legs were torn from torsos; people were beheaded or sliced in two; stomachs were ripped open and vain was the attempt to hold viscera in place with bare hands. Chests were crushed, ribs broken and lungs punctured by the jagged edges. Blood was everywhere. It spurted from severed arteries, flowed from multiple cuts and abrasions, seeped ominously from ears and noses. Some spent their final seconds of life walking as zombies, their eyeballs hanging by sinews. Parents, bleeding to death, cradled decapitated babies. Corpses were sprawled without dignity, faces frozen in a rictus of agony. And everywhere there were the wounded. Their heart-wrenching screams and cries for help would forever echo in the minds of those who survived. Hundreds were beyond help and would die within minutes or hours. More than nine thousand people were injured, many needing immediate medical attention. For the first hour or more those who were injured, and the very few who were not, suffered a state of catatonic shock. They sat or walked, slowly and silently in a stupor, unable to take in the immensity of the disaster. Parents stood before the ruins of their homes, screaming the names of children who would never again come to their call; children sat in the rubble, crying for parents who would never again arrive to comfort them.

ADA MOORE SAT in the middle of the street. Her home and the homes of her sisters and brothers were gone. The homes of her neighbours were gone. Isaac Creighton's store, the Hillis Foundry and all the homes from Barrington Street to Gottingen Street were gone. The ground around her was littered with bodies that were coated with black sludge and unrecognizable. There were injured standing silently in a comatose state, quietly bleeding

Photo from the author's private collection.

Ada was the only member of the immediate Jackson family who was not killed or seriously injured in the Halifax Explosion.

to death. Others were simply frozen in place by shock. With a tremendous effort of will, Ada stood up, instinctively brushing the dirt from her coat, unaware of the tarlike muck that splattered her from head to foot. She walked reluctantly to the nearest body, but it was no one she recognized. She passed by several more strangers before coming to the body of her youngest sister. She knelt beside her. Emma's eyes were wide open, staring sightlessly at the sky. Ada ran her hand gently over her sister's face to close her eyelids and then, with the first of many tears streaming down her cheeks, she cradled the body in her arms. "Oh, Emma, Emma." For long minutes she held her sister and rocked to and fro and silently started to pray. She was interrupted by the wailing of a young boy. Gordon McDonald was sitting on the front steps, the only thing left of his home. His face was horribly slashed by glass and he was bleeding profusely. Ada gently lowered Emma's body to the ground and hurried to him.

"IT'S ALRIGHT, GORDY, I'm here. Thank God you're alive." She picked a few pieces of glass from his face and the bleeding increased. Ada took his hands in hers and pressed one to each side of his face over the gaping wounds. "Gordy, I want you to press as hard as you can, we have to stop the bleeding until we can get you to a doctor, do you hear me?" The boy did as his aunt told him while she looked around the wreckage for something to use as a bandage. She found a tea towel she recognized as one of her own and wrapped this tightly around his face. The bleeding slowed. She said, "Now listen to me, I've stopped the bleeding and you are going to be okay, do you hear?" Gordy was in too much pain and

Gordon McDonald, ten, son of Margaret (Jackson) McDonald. Only Gordon and his father, Vincent McDonald, survived from a family of fifteen at 1498 Barrington Street. Gordon received massive injuries to his face and would bear some of the scars for the rest of his life. This photo was taken approximately four years after the Halifax Explosion.

Photo courtesy of John Versteege
Impact Videographic Services, Dartmouth, N.S.

shock to speak but he nodded his head. Ada tightened the towel even more, "Your dad's probably up around Rockingham and I'll bet he's on his way here as fast as he can go. You sit tight and keep that towel tight against your face for a few minutes, I have to see if there are any others hurt. Okay?" The boy nodded again.

Ada went next door to the wreckage of her own home. One by one she called the names of the five children who should have been there. When no one answered, she called them again, louder. There was still no answer. Tears coursed down her cheeks, washing a path through the black.

The first blue tendrils of wood smoke curled and drifted through the wreckage. Kitchen and hall stoves, upturned from the force of the explosion, ignited the wreckage on top of and around them. Fuelled by the winter's supply of coal and coke, stored in cellars and basements, the ruins of Richmond would burn for a week.

A hundred or more people in the Richmond area would burn to death that day. Many bodies, first crushed to death by rubble, would be rendered unrecognizable by the heat and flames. The morgue designation "charred remains" was applied frequently over the next days and weeks. Despite his strength, Joseph Hinch could not free himself from the burning wreckage of his home on Veith Street. He died the death he dreaded.

VINCE MCDONALD SLAMMED the boiler door shut and was turning to speak to the engineer when the flash of light and thunderous roar occurred. Both men jumped and looked out the engine window toward the Dartmouth shore on the far side of Bedford Basin. But from Rockingham there was little to see. At once they realized the explosion had come from the direction of Richmond, where both of their families lived. The engineer pulled the brake and reversed the engine before it had even stopped its forward motion; the drive wheels screamed against the rails until they found purchase. Neither man spoke, each too terrified to voice his thoughts. The engine picked up speed, careening wildly around the curve of Fairview Cove. It roared through Africville with whistle screaming to warn those who, in dazed disbelief, were emerging from their homes onto the tracks. The school and church were close to the track, they glanced with apprehension at the damage to both buildings and for the first time since the blast, Vince spoke. "Dear God, if it's that bad here where it's sheltered, what's happened to the North End!" He had his answer seconds later when the engine, with a screech of protest, rounded the curve into the beginning of the Richmond yard. Cursing desperately, the engineer slammed on the brake; two hundred yards ahead the track was torn from the sleepers. The train lurched to a halt, but both men had already dropped to the ground and were running toward their homes and families.

They saw the utter devastation at the Sugar Refinery Wharf, and Piers Eight and Nine. The pedway above the tracks had disappeared. The retaining wall below Barrington Street blocked their view of Richmond, but they could see the homes, warehouses and buildings on the east side of Barrington were gone as if they had never existed. They clambered over the rubble piled against the wall to street level. The engineer took off at a run toward his home on Russell Street; Vince had to but cross the street.

His steps slowed. Part of him wanted to rush forward, but he was held back by a desire to run and hide. His home was smashed into a senseless heap of splinters. So was Charlie Moore's. So was every home within sight. Richmond was nothing more than a pile of rubble. He screamed his wife's name. There was no answer. Two people walked toward him, a woman and a child. The child was black with a red cloth around his face; the woman was also black, but with two white streaks running down her cheeks. Her knees were covered in blood. The woman spoke and the child came running to him. It was only then he recognized Ada and his son.

He fell to his knees and clutched Gordon to him, "What in the name of God happened?" Ada gave a long, weary sigh and sat down on some boards. "The bloody ship that was burning blew up. I don't know why and I don't know how, I just know the bloody thing blew. Everything's gone. I can't find my kids. Charlie's not here. I found Emma. She's dead. Gordy has some real bad cuts on his face. Mr. Shea says there's a train making up at Fairview to take the hurt up to Truro, I don't know how he knows but that's what he said. You better take Gordy to the train. I have to rest a minute and then I'll start looking through this stuff till I find everybody." Vince stood up, holding his son to his chest. With the full force of his lungs he screamed, "Margaret! Margaret! Again and again he called her name. Ada got to her feet, "Pull yourself together, man, you're not helping a bloody thing! Get Gordy on that train. He's lost a lot of blood he'll die right here if you don't get him to a doctor. Do you hear me? Now for God's sake move! I'll stay here and look for the others."

With his son in his arms, Vince reluctantly retraced his steps across Barrington, over the embankment, along the railyard and through Africville. As the blood seeped through Gordon's bandage on to his own chest and arms, a sense of urgency finally prevailed and he began to run toward Fairview.

Ada faced the ruins of her home once more. Softly, gently, lovingly, she called the names of each of her children one last time. There was still no answer.

Minnie McGrath sat on the wreckage of her parent's home. She stared in amazement at a round rod of metal imbedded in her leg. She tried to grasp it to pull it out and realized her arm was broken. Her body was badly bruised and blood trickled from the cuts on her hands. Shock precluded pain and she simply sat quietly, waiting for this strange phenomenon to cease. She heard screams from the wreckage behind her, but the horror did not register. Only a moment ago she was leaning out the upstairs bedroom window to speak to her parents. She had a shadowy memory of a blinding flash and then falling, ever so slowly. She remembered the compassionate look Mr. Ryan had given her and the gentleness with which he had covered her with his overcoat. Now she simply sat, fascinated by the rivulet of blood oozing around the shiny metal rod and dribbling down her leg. Her feet were bare but did not feel cold. She put her hand in the large, side pocket of Mr. Ryan's coat. Feeling a bundle of papers, she drew them out. She was holding at least a dozen Bearer Bonds in hundred dollar denominations. It took several minutes before she realized what they were, and then she murmured, "Mr. Ryan left his money behind. I'd better find him and give it back." But she could not will herself to stand up and move. She simply sat.

Several hours later she would be found by rescuers and put on a train bound for the Truro hospitals. There were many others on the train. She would be in good company; almost everyone was a friend or neighbour.

THE GATE OF Harriet Bungay's fence became her stretcher. Only semi-conscious, the pain washed over her in waves as the men tried to lift her. The English setter was whining with distress and as they transferred Harriet from the ground, he shoved his nose against her face and whimpered piteously. Harriet reached out and patted his head, whispering, "It's okay, Jack, they're taking me to the hospital. You be a good boy

Gladys Bungay, ten, and her dog Jack, taken a few years before the explosion. She was sent on an errand from which she never returned.

Photo courtesy of Lorraine (Daine) Rozee.

and stay here. Try to find the others—go to the store and find Gladys." There was no time for more. The men started toward the South End, carrying their burden. Gingerly they climbed over the wreckage of homes, avoiding those that were beginning to burn. Bewildered, Jack watched until they were out of sight.

CLARA HINCH DRIFTED into and out of consciousness. At times she thought she was dreaming and tried to wake up and end the nightmare. The beam was pressed down on her right arm and side, pinning her into the mattress so that she could not move. Her left arm was free but there was nothing she could grip to haul herself off the bed and, in any case, she lacked the strength. In the beginning she had screamed as hard as she could to try to attract attention, but no one came. She heard calls for help from somewhere beneath her; at first she could hear her father and the other children, but their voices had silenced an hour ago. She felt terribly alone. The ceiling was within inches of her face and there was a hole she could reach through and wave her hand, but her voice was weak now from the yelling.

There had been smoke drifting up from below for the past half-hour. It was enough to start her coughing and now it was beginning to get hot. Terrified by the prospect of being burned alive, once again she began to yell as loud as her strained voice would permit.

Miraculously, amid all the other screaming, shouting and tumult around the area, she was heard. Two soldiers who had joined the search for the injured heard her voice and saw her hand. They crawled over the monstrous pile of rubble and one of them gripped her wrist. He pulled without budging her an inch until she screamed with pain. He stopped to assess the situation. The one who had been pulling on Clara's arm said, "She is pinned on the bed by the ceiling and some beams, we'll have to move them." The other pointed to the rubble, "It can't be done. The wreckage itself is held down by those blocks of stone. They must weigh a couple of tons, there is no way we can move them without a crane." Frustrated, his partner replied, "You're stronger than me, you try hauling her out." The larger soldier changed places with his buddy and tried to lift Clara from the bed. It was hopeless. By now the flames were flicking up through cracks in the debris. The stronger of the two braced his feet against a beam, reached in and gripped her arm at the elbow. With every ounce of his strength he pulled until she screamed again and fainted. "She's out cold. Help me. We can pull now without hurting her." Both men took hold of her arm and strained with a steady pull that did nothing. Flames licked through the debris and set fire to one man's jacket. He hastily withdrew his arm to beat out the fire, "It's no use she's wedged tight." Not willing to give up, they both reached in one more time but the flames burned their hands. They let go with shouts of pain. Clara's left hand, which would never bear the ring of which she dreamed, fell limply back into the fire.

THE FOOTSTEPS WERE coming closer; Gerald Jackson and Prince pressed themselves closer against the concrete wall. A gruff voice said, "Here's another one, a man with his throat cut. Cripes! There's a baby under him." A gentler voice, answered, "Poor sod was probably looking out the window with the baby in his arms. We'll have a job getting him over this garbage to the cart." Gruff voice said, "I'll take the kid first and see if I can find a decent path over the trash. You wait here till I get back." "Okay, while you're gone I'll see if there are any more in there." The gruff voice faded as he moved away, "For God's sake don't do any digging. We have enough to do picking up those in the open—leave the digging to somebody else. With the kid from further up the street, the one with the leg off, we have almost a full load for the morgue. Just sit tight a minute, I'll be right back."

The little boy and the dog were both terrified. Gerald wrapped his arms around Prince and hugged him tight; it was difficult to determine who was comforting whom. After a few very long minutes, Gruff Voice was back. "We have to go straight over that way, for a hundred feet or so, and then turn uphill. You take his feet and let me know if you need a rest. C'mon let's go." Gerald heard the men climbing over the wreckage, slipping and cursing until the sounds faded. The danger past, Prince bared his teeth and growled as viciously as only a little fox terrier can growl. Obviously it was effective, the footsteps didn't come back. In fact, no one would come near them again for another thirty hours.

Both men had fallen a dozen times before they reached the morgue wagon. The horse whinnied and shied away from the smell of blood. "Whoa there, Nellie, you damn-fool horse." Gruff Voice tried to grab the reins without letting go of his hold on the body. They finally managed to place the corpse on top of the others near the boy with the severed leg. Between the trauma of the task and the problem with the skittish horse, neither man noticed the limp body of William Edmonds was the only one whose face was not locked in the rictus of death, nor was his body stiffening with the onset of rigor mortis. In fact, a slim trickle of blood still oozed from the stump of his severed leg.

CHAPTER
12

Order began to emerge from chaos. The civic authorities, with the cooperation of military leaders, organized hasty plans to provide relief to the victims even before the full extent of the disaster was known. Within hours of the explosion telegraph lines were temporarily restored and a message describing the unbelievable was heard around the world. The aid that poured in was beyond all expectations, but it would be hours before it arrived from around the province, days from the United States and the rest of Canada and weeks from other countries of the world. The critically injured could not wait.

The immediate priority was locating hospital facilities. The Victoria General Hospital was far enough south of the blast to receive relatively little damage. Although already filled to capacity, beds were found for those requiring immediate surgery. Limbs were amputated; eyes, skewered by glass, and internal organs, irreparably shattered by concussion, were removed. Post-operative patients were transferred to other facilities, including private homes, to make room for more urgent cases.

The new Camp Hill Hospital was not yet officially open. Construction was complete but the finishing touches were still being put in place. These details were now relegated to the back burner in response to the immediate need for beds. This hospital, originally planned for 280 patients, served 1,400 injured the first day, an awesome baptism by fire for the new facility. To augment its capacity and provide for the overflow, the army erected a tent hospital with an additional 250 beds on the adjacent Halifax Common. The majority of the patients at Camp Hill Hospital were from Richmond and included James Jackson, Harriet Bungay and William Edmonds.

Cogswell Street Hospital, on the south end of Gottingen, sustained some damage. Many of its plaster ceilings collapsed and windows and doors had been blown out by the low pressure system. Despite this, the hospital treated over four thousand patients immediately following the explosion. Almost any large building that had been passed over by the blast was pressed into

*emergency service. The YMCA, Bellevue Ladies College, Waegwaltic Club,
and St. Mary's College supplied 494 beds between them.*

*First aid stations, staffed by anyone with medical training or knowledge,
sprung up all over the city. For most of that first terrible day medical aid
was the sole responsibility of local doctors, nurses and volunteer helpers. All
of the hospitals and treatment centres were overcrowded, medical personnel
were overworked and taxed by inadequate conditions and severe shortages
of surgical supplies and equipment. Operations were performed amid heaps
of broken plaster and shattered glass. Instruments could not be sterilized.
By late evening most facilities had run out of anaesthetics, and minor
surgery was being performed on semi-conscious patients. Wounds were
stitched with ordinary needles and thread. Despite the impossible conditions,
almost 90 per cent of those requiring medical aid had been treated before the
day was over.*

*The chaotic nature of initial rescue efforts meant that families were
frequently separated. Children were sent to different hospitals than their
parents, spouses ended up across town from one another. Rescuers sent those
needing medical attention to whichever hospital came first to mind.
Separation caused additional trauma for those who lay helpless, not knowing
if their families had survived the explosion. It was especially terrifying for
children, who were unable to comprehend the circumstances. Many were too
young to tell authorities their names or where they lived. Surviving parents
spent endless hours searching for their little ones. And those whose children
were never found or identified spent heart-breaking years in search of them,
sustained by the slim hope they may have survived and were being cared for
by others.*

HAVING LOST THEIR father the previous year to a railway accident and
their mother to the explosion that very morning, the three Baker
children—the youngest, Leverette Junior, had been killed alongside
their mother—lost one another in the aftermath of the blast. Hilda,
aged nine, suffered cuts and was taken to the Cogswell Street Hospital.
Seven-year-old Stanley, was taken to the Victoria General Hospital to
have his broken leg set, while little William, aged five, had suffered horrible head injuries and was placed on the Truro-bound hospital train.
Despite the best efforts of their aunt Ada and their new stepfather,
Lawrence Boutilier, it would be four months before the three Baker
children were found and reunited, and then only temporarily.

*There is a strong bond between Nova Scotians and their American neighbours
to the south that stems from the eighteenth century. Movement north and*

south has peppered the history of the Eastern Seaboard, beginning with the flood of Loyalists into Nova Scotia during the American Revolution. Many northerners have since sought their fortunes in the New England states and it would have been difficult to find a Nova Scotian family without at least one close relative living in the north-eastern United States. This kinship spurred a mammoth drive to assist the victims of the Halifax Explosion.

The people of the United States of America have the reputation of being the most generous people in the world. This evaluation was never more evident than in the aftermath of the Halifax Explosion of 1917. Their help began immediately. The Old Colony, *an American hospital ship, happened to be in Halifax Harbour at the time. It was fully staffed with doctors, nurses, an operating theatre, medical equipment and supplies which were immediately made available to the injured. The navy personnel of this ship started within minutes of the blast to assist in the rescue attempts and were undoubtedly responsible for saving lives by their prompt response. Over 150 of the more seriously wounded were treated within a few hours. Another American navy ship, several hours steaming time away, heard the explosion and saw the cloud of smoke. Realizing a disaster had occurred they contacted American naval command and requested permission to make port and donate their medical facilities to the service of the city. The request was granted at once, without question.*

Before the day drew to a close, trains from Boston and New York were making their way north with massive supplies and medical volunteers for the stricken city.

SOPHYE JACKSON BARRELLED down the train platform like the line-backer on a pro-league football team. The mammoth suitcases swinging from either arm assumed the status of deadly weapon for any who foolishly blocked her way. The suitcases appeared far too heavy for the slightly built young woman, but what she lacked in size was more than made up by her dogged determination. The train sounded a final warning whistle; most of the steps had been folded and the doors closed, and she ran frantically for the last open carriage. Seeing her plight, a Red Cross officer jumped down from the train and grabbed one of the cases. "It's okay. No need to panic, we've got a minute or so before she moves." The two clambered up with her luggage just before the conductor raised the steps and slammed the door unceremoniously. Sophye dropped her case and leaned back against the carriage wall, flushed and breathless. The engineer gave another blast on the whistle and the huge driving wheels screeched as the train lurched forward on its journey to Halifax.

Sophye B. Jackson, age twenty-four. Photo taken on her graduation as a nurse in 1916.

Photo courtesy of Diane Walker.

Her rescuer had ample time to observe Sophye while she tried to compose herself, seemingly unaware of his presence. He was pleased with what he saw. The young lady was very pretty. Around twenty-five, he guessed, her mass of jet-black hair was topped with a jaunty nurses cap, slightly askew, that came level with his chin. Below the curls a pair of thick black eyebrows framed large hazel eyes; her features were tiny and her complexion, once it lost the flush of over-exertion, was flawless. She wore a dark blue, heavy wool coat, unbuttoned, and beneath it was a spotless, starched, nurse's uniform. Her generous red lips parted in a smile, displaying even white teeth. "Thank you so much for helping me."

The man grinned in return. "You're more than welcome, I make it my life's work to come to the aid of pretty damsels in distress." Both their smiles widened. "My name's Bob Johnson, I don't remember seeing you before—and I certainly would remember seeing you—are you new to the outfit?" Sophye gave a long sigh as she recalled her frantic morning, "Yes, I'm new to the Red Cross. When I heard the news about the explosion this morning I tried to book a ticket to Halifax, but they told me the only people allowed into the city were relief workers. They said the only trains going were with medical supplies, there was no room for sightseers." For a moment her temper flared, "I'm not exactly a bloody sightseer. I'm from Halifax. My parents, brothers and sisters and all my family live there. I've got to get home. I took a leave of absence from my hospital and signed up with the Red Cross. I've been rushing all over New York trying to get on this train." She gave him a pleading look, "Have you heard any more than I have about the explosion?"

Bob's smile quickly faded. "Gee, I'm sorry. I didn't know it was your home. Don't fret, mostly these things are exaggerated in the beginning. All I heard was that maybe about eight hundred people were killed, but that doesn't sound right. It's probably a lot less. But several hundred are injured, which is why we're going." Still seeking a comforting answer, Sophye asked, "Do you know where it happened at least? What part of the city?" Bob shrugged, "I don't know the city so it wouldn't mean much to me even if I knew."

They lapsed into an uneasy silence for a few moments. Bob looked at the two suitcases. In an effort to lighten the atmosphere, he said, "I know guys who served three years overseas with less equipment than that lot, which one is the kitchen sink in?"

Sophye wrinkled her nose, "It's not as bad as it looks. One has my clothes and spare uniforms, the other's loaded with Christmas presents for my family. I was planning on coming home in a couple of weeks anyway and these were already packed. My oldest sister, Minnie, has a little boy named Clifford and I bought a toy train that winds up and it runs on a little track. He's only two but he's really bright, he'll love it. He's so cute. In her last letter Minnie said she is trying to teach him to say his name, but instead of saying 'my name is Cliffie McGrath' it comes out, 'my name is Tippy Daw,' isn't that cute?" Talking about her nephew brought a smile to her lips and a twinkle to her eyes.

By the early afternoon, trains full of the injured had left for Truro and New Glasgow to offer some relief to the overburdened local medical facilities. Three hundred beds were provided by the emergency hospitals in these two towns. This was only the beginning of aid that poured into Halifax from across the province and would eventually arrive from around the world.

JAMES RYAN WAS slightly hurt but still able to help his next-door neighbour, who was lying helpless in the rubble. James Jackson had suffered severe injuries. His left eye was irreparably damaged, he would never again have sight on that side, his left arm was hanging limp and he was coughing blood from his left lung which had been punctured by broken ribs. Ryan lifted his friend's head and cushioned it with his own jacket. "Jim, you're hurt pretty bad. I can't do much for you, you're bleeding inside, but I'm going to get help. Just you lie still till I get back. Minnie is okay, she's in shock but she'll be all right. Just you lie still, okay? I'll be back in a few minutes with a stretcher and some help and we'll get you to a hospital." Sophye's father had no alternative but to lie still.

Also at that moment Sophye's brother, Lew, was being carried to the Victoria General Hospital, his leg strapped to a board. Their sister, Minnie, was on the train to the hospital at Truro. Annie was dead, killed on her way to work. James Junior was searching through the wreckage on Duffus Street searching for survivors. The body of their mother was buried in the basement of their burning home and nearby, crushed beneath the kitchen stove, was two-year-old "Tippy Daw." Neither would be found until late January.

There was hardly a pane of glass left intact in the entire city. Over fifteen hundred homes were rendered unfit for habitation and thousands of survivors were homeless. After the demand for hospitals and emergency medical attention, the greatest dilemma in the aftermath of the explosion was the shortage of shelter.

There was no danger of starvation. The food supplies were plentiful and were quickly made available. If anything, the generosity of thousands of people far and wide created a glut of food. Most survivors were able to find suitable clothing in the wreckage of their own homes, or were supplied by friends, relatives or neighbours. By the end of the first day the problem of food and clothing had been largely solved. But there were thousands with no home to return to when night fell. The solution to this problem was frequently found by the survivors themselves. Many simply moved in with relatives or friends whose homes had survived the explosion. Hundreds left the city to stay with families around the province. The Army erected a tent city on the Halifax Common; any public building, church, church hall, or recreational facility large enough to house the needy was pressed into service. Meanwhile, others simply used their own ingenuity to find shelter from the wintry weather.

IT WAS ALREADY growing dark when Arthur Edmonds returned to Duffus Street. The short December day, the looming overcast of the approaching storm, and the smoke from the fires in the North End laid a pall of gloom over the city. Letitia was badly injured; in addition to severe burns to her neck and arms, she had been generally battered by their collapsing house and it was probable she had internal injuries. Emily and Elizabeth had also been injured and all three were being treated at the Victoria General Hospital. Arthur had returned to the house to see if there was any sign of Annie or Alice—both had left for work before the explosion and could be presumed to have survived—and also to find out if anything could be salvaged from the wreckage of their home or stable. Nothing in the house survived the fire and the stable had been equally devastated. The horses were dead. Both wagons and sleds had been burned beyond repair. Nor was there any sign of either Annie or Alice. William was gone, presumably picked up by the people delivering the dead to the morgue. Arthur sat down on the rubble. For the moment there was no one to share his grief.

The first relief train left Boston on the night of the explosion. In addition to a massive amount of medical supplies, it carried 13 surgeons, 20 nurses, and 6 American Red Cross representatives who would assess the situation and direct more aid as needed. On the following day, a second train left with every item necessary to equip a 500-bed hospital, including 25 doctors, 2 obstetricians, 68 nurses and 8 orderlies.

A relief train also left New York within hours of receiving word of the disaster. It was loaded with 500 cots, 18,000 coats and other garments, 10,000 blankets, 20 cases of disinfectants, 160 cases of surgical supplies, a carload of food, and additional nurses and doctors. The Massachusetts Eye and Ear Infirmary sent four nurses trained in treating eye and ear injuries to help with the hundreds of victims who were deafened by the blast or blinded by flying glass. In all, 222 doctors and 459 nurses would arrive within days of the explosion and stay until the situation was stabilized.

The earliest any of the relief trains would arrive in Halifax was the early morning hours of December 8th. Until then the local medical personnel, supplemented by a few doctors and nurses from provincial centres, would fight the overwhelming battle alone.

Even homes a considerable distance from the epicentre had been sufficiently damaged to be unfit or unsafe for habitation. Now, with nighttime settling in, the wind beginning to rise and the rapid approach of a storm, it was urgent to determine if your battered building still had the resources to provide you and your family a safe haven. Jim Mahar had reluctantly come to the conclusion theirs didn't. The rented house on Almon Street had received a considerable thrashing and he decided to send the girls, Beatrice, Geraldine and Madeline, along with their younger brother, Arthur, to lodge at Rockingham with their married sister, Mary.

EDWARD, JIM'S ELDEST son, stayed behind with his father. It was very cold and they were afraid to start a fire in the furnace, the damaged chimney had already filled the house with smoke and they were reluctant to risk burning down what was left of their home. Since all the windows were blown out, they chose a bedroom in the back with only one gaping hole to cover. This would be their home until repairs could get underway. There was no running water or electricity. Huddled under blankets, they tried to sleep. Edward's voice came out of the darkness. "We'd be a lot better off if we were in one of those tents the army put up on the Common." He had no idea how wrong he was.

James William Mahar's home on Almon Street was almost a mile from the epicentre. At that distance it received approximately one-twenty-fifth the force that struck the lower reaches of Richmond, but this was still enough to make the house and others an equal distance from the blast uninhabitable without major repairs.

Photo from the author's private collection.

For many, still alive but trapped in the wreckage of their homes, it would be the longest night of their lives. Many, seriously injured, would not be rescued for days. They suffered the physical pain of their injuries and the mental anguish of not knowing the fate of their loved ones. Pinned by wreckage, unable to change position, they could only wait. Many would die before help arrived; others would escape, at least for awhile, to the euphoria of hallucination.

MARY JEAN FELT as if she were floating. If Joe didn't have her clasped firmly in his arms she was sure she would drift right up to the ceiling. Her afternoon spent decorating with the Sheas and Ada had been well worth it. They'd transformed the church hall into a fairyland of garlands, ribbons and bows. In the corner beside the stage the manger scene glowed under a spotlight. The band was playing one of her favourite waltzes and she was in the arms of the best dancer in all of Richmond. Her heart was full to overflowing.

"After the ball is over, after the break of morn,
After the dancers leaving, after the stars are gone,
Many a heart is aching, if you could read them all;
Many the hopes that have vanished, after the ball."

They whirled round and round, unconscious of the admiring eyes following them around the floor. Saint Joseph's Hall was crowded with their friends and neighbours. There was Charlie, laughing at Ada's wild gesticulations; at the next table, Margaret and Vince were holding hands. They were all young, happy and free from care. Her babies, Clara and Lena were safe at home being looked after by Harriet Bungay. At twenty-six, motherhood had infused Mary Jean with an ethereal beauty that caught the gaze of everyone in the room. With perfect timing they moved as one, sway and dip, whirl and spin, to the rhythm of the waltz. She closed her eyes as she leaned back in Joe's arms and gave herself up to the music.

This Christmas Dance of 1903 was the fabric from which memories were woven. The waltz seemed like it would never end, but she wasn't growing tired, despite a twinge of pain in her hip. Yet, it was getting cold. Someone must have opened the windows. And the pain was getting worse. She was shivering. In distress she tried to tell Joe, but when she opened her eyes he was gone. The band was faltering ...

"Many a heart is aching, if you could read them all,
Many the hopes that have vanished, after the ball."

The ball was over. The brutal pain in her hip dragged her into consciousness. Her teeth were chattering ceaselessly. She put her finger between her teeth to ease the pain and realized that her teeth were loose in her gums. In the darkness, her trapped body was bathed in a faint, flickering glow of orange. Richmond was on fire. She must have been here all day. She was hurt, cold and alone. Why didn't they find her? Where was Joe? Where were the children?

VINCENT MCDONALD WAS also suffering alone. Though his body was not marked by a single bruise, he was gripped with the pain of shock. Bullied into action by Ada, he had taken Gordon to the Truro-bound train and stayed with him until the doctors took charge. His immediate assignment had filled his mind and insulated him against the emotional shock of his losses. Assured by the hospital that Gordon would live and would be under sedation until sometime the following day, Vincent returned on the Halifax train just after dark.

But it was not dark in Richmond. The flames from dozens of burning homes illuminated the disaster scene with an eerie, orange glow. Vincent pushed his way through the hundreds of volunteers and rubberneckers lining the cleared section of Barrington Street until he came upon the burning wreckage of his own home. He had wakened this morning to a bustling house of fifteen; his mother, wife, children and grandchildren. Now everyone but himself and his nine-year-old son were dead and gone.

Vincent was one of many that night, who stood before the ruins of their home, waiting in vain for a loved one to appear. Even now, almost twelve hours after the explosion, none of the survivors could grasp the reality; almost all held on to straws of hope—perhaps they were in a hospital, only injured; or perhaps someone had found them and taken them somewhere. Most could not allow themselves to believe the fires they watched were the crematorium for those they loved. Most could not accept this unbelievable finality.

Hours later he still stood before the burnt debris of 1498 Barrington Street. He grasped no straws—they were dead and burning. The crowds had moved further south on Barrington and he moved over to allow a solitary horse and cart to go by. It was piled high with corpses, the wheels squealed a high-pitched lament for the dead. He stood and watched until it was out of sight.

Drawing his hand from his pocket, Vince looked at the change in his hand—a silver dollar; three quarters; three large pennies and a small penny. With a tortured scream of defiance he hurled the coins into the wreckage, "Here, damn you, take it all!"

"What in the name of heaven are you doing? Why aren't you in Truro with Gordon?" Ada came up suddenly behind him. Startled, Vince wheeled around and grabbed her in his arms, "Oh, Ada, Ada! They're all dead. There's five ton of coal in the basement. The fire'll burn for a week before we can get them out of there, there won't be anything left to bury. I wish to God I was with them."

Ada pried herself out of his grasp. "What happened to Gordon?" Vincent stood, trembling with grief, tears running down his cheeks. "They're gone, Ada. Margaret and the kids are gone, they're all gone!" Ada swore under her breath. "Did Gordie die? For God's sake, man, make some sense. Is Gordon dead?" Vincent wiped his face with his arm and said brokenly, "No, Gordon is all cut to hell but he'll live. It took them hundreds of stitches. His face and head are going to be horribly scarred for the rest of his life, but he'll live."

Ada sighed with relief, "That's one then. There'll be others, there just has to be others. We've got to find them. You have to help. Oh God, I wish Charlie was here. He'd know what to do, you can always count on Charlie. You have to pull yourself together now Vince. We need a level head here. Don't be thinking the worst; maybe some of the older ones were on their way to school. I know mine were. Nellie and young Charlie, Mort, Vince and Irene all left the house before the blast. I'll bet they are safe and sound somewhere, and I'll bet some of yours are too." But she may as well have been talking to a stone wall. Vincent McDonald was drowning in a sea of grief.

Ada realized that her brother-in-law was too deeply in shock to be capable of helping himself, let alone anyone else. She paused for a long moment to compose her thoughts. They stood together silently and watched the crackling flames consume their homes and families. A burnt beam cracked loudly, sending a shower of sparks skyward and more debris shuddered and slid down into the basement of Vincent's home. The asphalt shingles on a section of the collapsed roof ignited and for a moment the scene was brilliantly lit by its flare.

She turned toward him and gripped his arm, "Here's what we have to do." In the reflected glare of the burning roof his eyes were glazed catatonicly. She shook his arm impatiently and squeezed it tightly until he looked at her. "Vince, pay attention, we haven't got time for tears, here's what you're going you to do. Go back to Rockingham and find the first train going to Truro. It may not go tonight but get in the cab and stay there. If the boiler is not fired up already, start it. It'll keep you warm and out of the weather. As soon as the train gets to Truro, go to the hospital and see your son. The poor kid'll be scared stiff. Give him a hug, kiss him, make damn sure he knows you love him and are there to protect him. Then when he's asleep, find Minnie. Jim Ryan says she has some of his bearer bonds in the pocket of the coat he gave her. He said for us to use some of the money if we need it, we can straighten out with him when this is all over. Take the bonds to a bank in Truro and cash them. Keep some money for yourself, give some to Minnie and bring about fifty dollars back to me. Then, go back and stay with Gordon. During the times when he's asleep, search that hospital for any of the family."

Vincent seemed to wander in and out of Ada's words. She shook his shoulder hard and spoke loudly to penetrate through his shock. "Vince, for God's sake pay attention, I can't do everything myself. I need you.

Ask everyone you know from Richmond if they have seen any of the Jacksons or Dude's bunch, or your kids or mine. There was a soldier here a little while ago that said they'd put tents up on the Common and a lot of people will be sleeping there tonight. I'm going there now. I'll search every bloody inch of the place. Then I'm going to the Chebucto Road School; they said they're taking dead people there. I'm also going to check all the hospitals, but you look after Gordon. He really needs you to be with him right now."

Finally Vincent seemed to understand. He nodded his head, "Okay, I'll do whatever you say. I'm heading back to Truro. But I'm coming back as soon as I can and dig in there and find Margaret and the children. My mother is in there too." He walked away, with the slow unsteady steps of a very old man.

Alone again, Ada continued to watch the flames eat away at everything she had. She gazed slowly around Richmond; the homes of her friends, neighbours and relatives, were also bowing to the invincibility of the fires. "Jacksonville" was gone. Richmond was gone. An overwhelming sense of loss flooded through her and she cried bitter tears. Later, near midnight, she wearily started south on Barrington toward the central part of the city and the Halifax Common. If only Charlie was here, he would know what to do and she could lean on his strength.

At that moment, as she was walking south on Barrington, the decapitated and mangled body of Charles Moore was drifting gently north, just below the surface of the Narrows. His remains would be found on the shore at Tuft's Cove, within a hundred feet of where the two ships collided. Ada's husband would be identifiable only by some papers in his pocket.

The wind had shifted to the northeast, heralding the approaching storm, and a few light flurries of snow were drifting over the destruction. The smoke was blowing away from Barrington Street toward the South and West Ends; since early afternoon, the choking odour of sulphur and the sweet, sickly smell of incinerated flesh had added to the scent of burning pine and spruce.

MARY JEAN WAS only semi-conscious. She drifted effortlessly between her dreams and her pain, confusing the burning glow from the fires with the flickering flame of altar candles. Her mind left the torture of what is and visited a memory of what was on a beautiful, warm and wonderful Sunday in early June. St. Joseph's Church was resplendent with the flowers of spring, forsythia, daffodils crocus and hyacinth. The organist was playing her favourite hymn and Joe was smiling down at her. She returned his smile then glanced at the children to make sure they were all behaving themselves. Six children required a lot of watching. Clara, Lena and Thomas, the older children, had been to an earlier mass; for some reason they found it slightly embarrassing to be part of a group of ten children. They were now home looking after the youngest, Helen, who was not even two.

Joe always sat flanked by his wife and one of the twins. Today it was Margaret. Annie, sat on her mother's other side. Each Sunday the twins took turns sitting beside their father. It was wise to keep a considerable distance between the twins. Joe often said, "Putting those two together is like striking a match in a fireworks factory." The other four were divided beside either parent. Young Joseph, aged nine, and three-year-old Ralph were next to their mother, while Mary Mabel, aged twelve, and James, aged eight, sat on their father's end of the pew.

But it was the five-year-old twins who were the feature attraction. The priest had a hard time keeping the attention of the congregation when the Hinch twins were there. Often dressed identically, today they wore wide-brimmed, straw hats, with blue satin ribbon hanging down their backs and navy-blue pinafores over crisp white blouses tied with matching ribbons. Alike as two peas in a pod in both looks and temperament, with a mutual streak of mischief a mile wide, most people could not tell them apart and the two little girls played on this failing. While their parents never mistook one for the other, Joe liked to tease them a little. With a sigh of pretended exasperation after he had called Annie, Margaret, he would clap his hand to his forehead and exclaim, "I don't know what we are going to do about these two girls, mother. Perhaps when we figure out which is which, I'll take one of them down to that tattoo parlour on Water Street and have them put a great big "X" on her forehead. Then they won't be tricking us again, will they?" Annie and Margaret would both scream in mock-terror and end up in a pile of giggles on the floor. However, at the moment they were sitting demurely, like two little angels in white knee-socks and shiny, new patent leather shoes.

The altar candles seemed to be giving off a lot of smoke and Mary Jean stared to cough. This shook her awake and the pain in her hip brought her back to reality. That wasn't the smell of tallow or wax; it was the smell of burning wood, cloth and flesh. With a whimper of pain she passed once more into the blessed oblivion of unconsciousness.

The Chebucto Road School was rechristened the Chebucto Road Morgue. It took a crew of forty men a day and a half to repair the windows and structural damage to the building in preparation to house the bodies. The largest morgue ever organized in Canada received a steady stream of bodies, pieces of bodies, and charred remains to be identified, ticketed with available information and exhibited for grieving relatives to claim. Too often the ticket simply read "remains," describing the unidentifiable fragments of charred limbs or torsos by where they had been found.

Bodies were being delivered even as repairs to the building were in progress. The morgue was under the command of Mr. A. S. Barnstead. His large staff of soldiers washed the bodies, identified them when possible, attached numbered tickets with the available information, placed them on raised wooden platforms in the school's basement and covered the corpses with a sheet or blanket. Clothing and possessions were placed in bags and identified with the same number as the body. Their final duty was to assist the surviving relatives in the heart-wrenching duty of claiming family and friends.

Once the makeshift morgue was ready, private mortuaries were directed to send all unidentified bodies to this one location in order to expedite the families' search. From December 6th until the day after Christmas 1,122 corpses passed through the Chebucto Morgue.

A few days after the tragedy, Mr. R. N. Stone and fifteen of his employees from the Stone Embalming Company would arrive from Toronto to take charge of preparing the bodies for burial. Four thousand coffins were ordered. Gravediggers were in short supply and advertisements were placed in local and out-of-town newspapers. Many were forced to dig the graves of their families. The situation was just too massive to deal with. Funeral services were often abrupt and meagre; friends and relatives were either dead, recovering in hospital, or were simply unaware of the tragedy. There were not enough hearses so trucks or wagons were used to transport the coffins; clergy were few and overtaxed, and many of the explosion's victims were buried without a formal service. Nearly three hundred bodies were never identified. They were buried in a common grave in Potter's Field.

ADA WAS HAVING the longest day of her life. It had flashed by in an instant, yet seemed as though it would never end. Early this morning she was hankering after a new coat and that seemed the only problem in the world. Then the awful blast had turned the day into a kaleidoscope of nightmares. Horror had been piled on top of horror, draining away her normal, pragmatic approach to life. Ada had never been so weary, never so heart-sick, never so reluctant to simply stay awake. She stood, now, in the tent city on the Halifax Common. For a moment she closed her eyes and her mind, a brief respite from reality. Summoning an inner strength she looked around at the tents and the groups of people around the fires. Despite the orders of the military there were dozens of fires burning. In the late afternoon, just before dark, army lorries had unloaded huge piles of splintered wood from the destroyed homes to fuel the fires warming the soldiers erecting the tents. There was no shortage of wood. Then the army commanders had ordered the fires extinguished to prevent the possibility of sparks setting fire to the canvas tents. Against those orders the fires had now been reignited to provide warmth to those freezing from the cold. Most of the tents were translucent, illuminated from the interior by light from alcohol and kerosene lamps. The exterior canvas was lit by the flickering flames of the bonfires. This macabre effect was accented by the gory glow of the burning North End reflected from the gathering clouds of the approaching storm and the low-hanging haze of smoke. An occasional flurry of snow mixed with ice pellets beat a tattoo on the stretched canvas.

Of those gathered around the fires, most were garbed in torn clothing; a few were wrapped in army blankets; some were wearing army greatcoats, all were huddled against the cold and against their monstrous sense of loss. Some were a family group, intact, that had survived but lost their home. Some of the young had lost their parents. Some were the only survivors of a large family. All had suffered severe shock. All were suffering severe grief. Many were facing feelings of guilt, simply because they were still alive when so many others were dead. A few were keening and sobbing in anguish; but the majority were in a catatonic state. They simply stood, unseeing, unhearing, unfeeling, in silence.

Ada walked wearily from group to group. She knew almost everyone by sight, they were mostly from the North End. Many of the Richmond people she knew by name. "Have you seen any of the Jacksons? Did you see Charlie Moore? Do you know anything about the Hinches? The McDonalds? Have you seen the Baker children?" Most stared at her blankly. A few shook their heads sorrowfully; they had been asked the same questions a dozen times that day, only the names had changed. Others before her had asked about the Sheas, the Duggans, the Uphams, the Vaughans, the Murphys, the Myetts, the LeForts.

With little hope remaining, Ada approached a final group at the far end of the Common. Her questions awoke recognition in one man. "Yeah, I saw Jim Jackson and Joe Hinch on Barrington a few minutes before it happened. Joe was on his way up Richmond going home and Jim was talking to Ed Jackson's kids near Kenny Street. I didn't see them after that. I'm sorry."

Ada's face mirrored her thoughts. If they were that close they were probably killed. The man saw the look, "Now don't fret, my dear. They had time to make it home and even if they didn't they may only be hurt. They could be anywhere. Tomorrow why don't you go to the Chebucto Road School, they are having the bodies of people killed brought there. Just make sure they are not there and then check the hospitals. The chances are you'll find them alive and well—they may even be out looking for you." The words were well intentioned but of small comfort.

She could go no further. Ada entered one of the tents, the alcohol lamp gave off a paltry heat that was immediately swallowed by the cold air entering through the tent flap. She found a couple of blankets and doubled one to put beneath her on the wooden floor. She wrapped the other around herself and lay down to sleep. Between that and her coat she might survive. But when she closed her eyes a wave of nausea washed over her, so she fixed her gaze on the canvas wall. Her mind ticked over unceasingly. Charlie, her brother Jim and Joe Hinch were dead. They had to be. She'd seen the wreckage on Veith Street. Dude and her kids were probably dead too. She shivered uncontrollably. Gordie was alive, so was his father, but Vince wouldn't be much help, he was in a terrible state. Emma's body had been lying alone, Hilda and the other kids weren't there, so maybe they were alive. She'd start early tomorrow morning to try and find them. Surely there would be someone, some of the kids going to school might have survived. Dear God let there be someone. Ada at last fell into an exhausted, restless sleep. For twelve of her fellow occupants at "tent city" there would be no tomorrow—they froze to death during the long, bitterly cold night.

Photo courtesy of P.A.N.S.

Bodies in the Chebucto Road Mortuary. The Chebucto Road School was converted to the largest morgue ever set up in Canada. Many of the bodies were burned or mangled beyond recognition and buried as "unidentified dead."

It was almost midnight—the "witching hour." Two army men bent over a makeshift desk trying to compile and match the list of body numbers to the description of the corpses entrusted to their care. The sergeant had ordered them to organize the upcoming search for victims by relatives and friends. For each body number they were writing a brief description of the corpse, its clothing and any identifying marks or jewellery. It was a gruesome job because these victims were the ones closest to the exploding ship. Many were mangled beyond any hope of identification; the strength of the blow had decapitated some, many had limbs blown off or severed by flying debris. The faces of many had been ripped and torn by shrapnel and glass and only raw flesh existed where features had been. A good many were naked, their clothing ripped from their bodies by the blast, their skin coated with the black slime of unexploded TNT.

But cataloguing them as best they could meant only those bodies that fitted the description of a loved one would be shown to the searcher, eliminating the trauma of viewing all the dead. Those seeking the remains of a daughter in her early teens would not face the trauma of viewing the shattered form of a six-foot stevedore. Those seeking the body of a stevedore killed near the Sugar Refinery would not have to view the charred remains of a housewife who met her death on Duffus Street.

Here, in the basement it was cold, deliberately so, to retard the onset of decomposition. The room was dark and gloomy, lit feebly by widely spaced bulbs set near the ceiling. The wind of the approaching storm whistled eerily through the cracks of the boarded windows; the building's sighs and groans were punctuated by the occasional sharp snap of a board contracting with the frost. Behind the men, who were grimly cataloguing the corpses, dim islands of light weakly bathed the orderly rows of cotton sheets that covered the bodies of the dead. Tomorrow better lighting would be installed to aid the morticians in their macabre task, but for now the dimness created the ghostly atmosphere of an eerie gothic novel. But a novel is fiction; this was fact.

It was quiet. Since early afternoon, carts, cars and trucks had arrived bearing bodies and pieces of bodies. Some were wheeled in by barrows, others were carried by stricken friends or relatives. The burnt remains of a few were in cardboard boxes marked only with the location found. The parade of corpses had continued until just before midnight. And now it was quiet.

WILLIAM EDMONDS FLOATED near the level of consciousness. He opened his eyes and could see only a hazy, dim light shining through the cotton sheet that covered his face. For only a moment he thought he was home, in his own bed, but the searing, burning pain in his leg awakened him to reality. The flash of light, the terrible noise, the oak tree gone, the death and dirt raining from the sky returned to him in one horrible moment of recollection. As he hovered on the brink of coma he gave a keening wail of terror and pain.

The three soldiers were not seasoned veterans of the Western Front. They were young; at twenty-one, the sergeant was the eldest. They had been picked for this duty by the simple army expedient of "we need three volunteers—you, you and you." Since coming on duty they had been subjected to sights of carnage nothing in their training had prepared them for. Their nerves were on edge. By now, near midnight, they had become used to the ghostly whistle of the wind; the spooky snaps and pops of an old building, and their eyes had adjusted to the lacklustre lighting that cloaked the basement morgue with a supernatural aura. The keening wail from one of the "corpses" shattered the thin veneer of composure.

The soldier writing descriptions broke the lead in the pencil he was using. His partner froze where he stood. Their sergeant wheeled around in fright. All three felt the hair on the back of their necks stand on end. For a long moment they remained immobile, then cautiously began to move down the row of sheets, gingerly lifting each one away from the face of the corpse. William was tossing his head from side to side and gnashing his teeth in pain. The three soldiers were galvanized into action. They gently placed the boy on a stretcher and as the two soldiers carried him out of the morgue, the sergeant ran ahead to start the truck parked outside. William was taken directly to Camp Hill Hospital.

The young sergeant returned to the basement after his two subordinates left for the hospital. He sat down at the desk, waited for his heart to slow down and then searched through the pile of papers until he found the card he was looking for:

BODY #:   366
DATE: December 6th, 1917 about 4 P.M.
NAME: unknown male child
ADDRESS: body found on Duffus Street

DESCRIPTION: young boy, approximately ten or twelve years old, found on Duffus Street, left leg cut off above knee, wearing black pants, white shirt, grey knee-length stockings and black shoes.

The sergeant examined the card for a moment before he picked up a pencil and marked it "VOID." He whistled softly and said aloud, "I don't know what your name is, sonny, but God was on your side today. If I was your father I'd change your name to Lazarus—you surely arose from the dead. I hope t'hell you make it all the way back." He stood silently in the cold, dim basement, staring at the rows of the dead. He listened carefully for the slightest sound, and watched closely for the slightest movement.

With the arrival of midnight the terrible day was over. But, the horror had hardly begun. Fires were raging in Richmond and the north end of the city. People still roamed the streets locked in terror and uncertainty, not sure where to go, not sure what to do. The hospitals and medical facilities had exhausted the supplies of aneasthesias and pain killers. Doctors had reached a state of fatigue that precluded the delicate surgery called for in many cases. Nurses and volunteers called upon reserves of energy they didn't know they possessed. And still the injured and maimed came forward. By some miracle, as that day passed into history, 90 per cent of the nine thousand injured had received at least some medical attention. One hundred ninety-nine people had both eyes removed; many more had lost one eye. Massive help was on the way, but for that day the citizens of Halifax and Dartmouth could only call upon their own reserves and their own courage.

By midnight the death toll was probably between twelve hundred and fifteen hundred and many more were still dying in the fires or from mortal wounds. Death would come to others over the next days, weeks and months. Many survivors of the immediate blast had their lives shortened by injuries or trauma. They would die within a few years despite a normal life expectancy of decades.

The official list of the dead, prepared in early 1918, lists 1,963 names; this is an understatement. Many near the Mont Blanc *simply vaporized, leaving no remains to count. Some bodies were swept out to sea or remained on the bottom of the harbour, never to be recovered. In the wreckage of the homes that burned in the North End, most corpses were completely consumed by the coal and coke fires that raged for over a week. And other deaths were never officially recorded simply because the family death toll reached 100 per cent and there was no one left to list their names. Many believe that an accurate figure is closer to 2,500.*

CHAPTER
13

Midnight came and went with no pause in activity for the doctors, nurses, first-aiders and the volunteers trying to alleviate the suffering of their fellow Haligonians. For fifteen solid, exhausting hours they had ministered to the victims, giving unstintingly of their time, knowledge and compassion. They did everything they could do—but it was not enough. The ranks of the local practitioners had been fortified by as many doctors and nurses the provincial cities, towns and villages could spare—but it was still not enough. The point had been reached where many of the doctors did not trust their exhausted bodies to perform other than basic care; delicate surgery would have to wait for hands that did not tremble, eyes that were clear, a brain that was functioning with flawless perfection.

One amazing thing became apparent to the staff of the hospitals long before this time. The people they were treating had a positive mental attitude. There was little whining or complaining; few tried to push ahead of others for treatment. All seemed cognizant of the overwhelming task being tackled by the doctors, nurses and volunteers and they seemed appreciative of the superhuman effort being made on their behalf. The attitude of the victim to the doctors was one of extreme politeness; the attitude of victim to victim was, strange as it may seem, almost jocular. They were as veterans in a war. To those who had not been there—no explanation was possible; to those who had equally suffered—no explanation was necessary. There was a universal attitude of gratitude—they were still alive.

THE CLOCK ON the night-stand by her bed read five minutes past three. It was still dark, so it must be morning. Minnie McGrath looked slowly around the room, which was dimly lit by a small bulb in the corner near the floor. The injection the nurse had given her a few hours ago, when the pain had once again flooded over her, was working wonderfully well. She felt no pain in her injured arm or leg; she was aware of everything around her and she even felt happiness. It was so nice to lie here, warm and comfortable after the horrible, frightening morning and the pain. The people in the other three beds were asleep and she hummed very softly, not to awake them:

"Bringing in the sheaves, bringing in the sheaves,
We shall come rejoicing, bringing in the sheaves."

Oh! How she loved hearing the choir in Africville singing that beautiful old hymn. On warm Sundays she would walk to the hill over-looking Africville, with Clifford in her arms, and listen to the glorious voices pouring forth from the church. The door and windows were always left open and she could usually hear every word, even the preacher's sermon. She was far too timid to walk down the hill and join them, but sitting on the sun-warmed grass, soaking in the music, she was with them in spirit. She too believed in a loving God who was waiting to welcome her home.

The rattle of a nurse's cart outside the open door of her room shook her from her reverie. She frowned as she realized Clifford was not beside her. Where was he? Closing her eyes in concentration, she recalled the blast and the confusion afterwards. She saw her father lying on the ground with blood coming from his mouth. She remembered Mr. Ryan giving her his coat, but her memory was foggy after that. Something about a train? Yes, she remembered now, there was a train. But where was Clifford? Had he been on the train with her? Where did the train go? A creeping sense of horror came over her as images began to trace themselves on her mind. People had been killed. She saw their bodies strewn around the wreckage of her home. Clifford was in the wreckage! Her heart pounded. No! Nothing could harm Clifford! A loving God would never harm her adorable little boy! She had better go home. When the nurse came by again she must ask for Mr. Ryan's coat. Everything would be fine once she got home and found Clifford. But, now she was tired; she would just rest for a few minutes longer. As she drifted away from reality the fear gnawing at the corner of her mind disappeared. It was lovely and warm, here on the hill. A fat robin landed in the bush not ten feet from where she and Clifford sat. She turned him in her arms to let him see. He became excited and reached his arms toward the bird; clear as a bell he said "bird." Why, he would be talking a mile a minute by the time Sophye came home again. The choir in Africville burst once more into the song that filled her heart: "We will come rejoicing, bringing in the sheaves."

The fires that lit the Richmond and north end area of the city with a ruddy glow had been burning since minutes after the explosion. They would burn for more than a week. The "tidal" wave of water had done little to curtail it; the storms to come would have negligible effect. By late afternoon the majority of the people, still alive in the wreckage, could only watch in helpless terror as the flames and super-heated air approached the place where they were trapped. They would die in agony, welcoming the release of death. But that was hours ago; all the screams had ceased.

A few hours before dawn the flames were spread by the north-east wind heralding the approaching storm. On Veith Street this wind fanned the flames away from the pile of combustible material that imprisoned Mary Jean Hinch.

ALL DAY LONG she had listened to anguished screams and cries. The wailing of a small child near her had stopped abruptly hours before; she said a prayer for the young soul she knew had left its tortured body. Mary Jean had listened to the frantic yelling of rescuers. Sometimes they seemed quite close by and she tried to respond but the pain in her face prevented her from yelling. No one was aware that she was under the wreckage. She was alone now in silence.

She could hear the crackle of fire. The flicker of the flames filtered through the debris and cast a crimson glow over her. There was a pervading smell of burning wood, a choking, sulphurous odour of coal mixed with the sickly sweet smell of burning flesh. Her hip had grown numb and as long as she remained absolutely still the pain was bearable. However, she sensed the dried blood caked on her cheeks and she longed to wipe it clean. Her scarf was gone but perhaps if she could find a handkerchief and cleaned her face she might feel better. The coat pocket on the right side was empty but there should be one of the hankies given her last Christmas by Mary Mabel on the other side. She managed to lift her body enough to squeeze her hand under to the pocket and there she found not only the handkerchief but her rosary.

The cool beads brought back a rush of memories. Father Walsh had given her the rosary the night she was married to Joe. Theirs had not been a grand, church wedding—they were married in the glebe—but it certainly had been the most wonderful night of her life. Her father gave her away, and James and his wife, Margaret had witnessed the marriage. Her brother had been grim-faced throughout the service. Because she was only sixteen and Joe ten years older, James had been opposed to the marriage from the very beginning. Trying to hold his temper in check for the sake of his baby sister and his mother, he had been unable to refrain from muttering, "cradle-robber," and casting ominous glances at his new brother-in-law. Joe, in turn, held his in check for the sake of Mary Jean. They all laughed about it now, for over the years the two men had become the best of friends.

When the ceremony was over Father Walsh approached her with a mischievous gleam in his eye. "I have a very special wedding present for you, Mrs. Hinch." She blushed with pleasure as she heard her married name for the first time and gently opened the small box he handed her. On a bed of white cotton wool was a rosary. Black onyx beads were threaded on a thin silver chain; the crucifix was pure silver with a beautifully sculptured body of Christ in bas-relief. "This is a very special gift, my dear. One of our priests visited the Vatican last year and had an audience with the Pope, who personally blessed this rosary. You're such a religious and lovely young woman I can't think of anyone else in the Parish more worthy of it. May you be blessed with a large, loving family and always find happiness. In those hours you experience sorrow and pain, find comfort in prayer. Always remember, child, when you pray you are never alone."

Mary Jean remembered his words as she pressed the crucifix to her lips and began to say her prayers. The familiar ritual enveloped her with serenity amidst the pain and fright. Her heart found the strength to accept the truth her mind already knew. Joe was dead. If he were alive he would have been here long ago. No power on earth would stop him. This was not the shelling of a single home; this was some monstrous catastrophe. It was not just the Matthew's house; it was all of Richmond. And, if Joe was dead, so were the children. Tears ran down her cheeks as she said the prayers, and now the prayers were for them. "When you pray you are never alone," Father Walsh had said, and she felt their presence with her, under the wreckage, and she found comfort.

Every bed in Camp Hill Hospital was occupied. From not being open for business in the early morning it was now working at capacity. The situation was just a little bit more stressful here than at the other medical facilities. Small glitches that had been worked out in hospitals operating for years added minor problems for the doctors, nurses and staff at the new facility. Many of the helpers were young ladies from the colleges. They had never been exposed to the trauma of caring for grossly injured patients. But they learned quickly and earned the respect of the professionals with whom they worked.

WILLIAM EDMONDS DRIFTED effortlessly between consciousness and coma. The doctor who'd examined his severed leg decided to leave it alone until the boy was stronger and had manufactured enough blood to help him withstand an operation required to smooth the jagged stump of bone and prepare the limb for an artificial leg. For the moment they had stabilized the wound, removing shreds of dead flesh and staunching further blood loss. His body was surrounded by warm bricks to keep his temperature constant. Enough morphine had been set aside for his use until more supplies arrived.

The last time he had been conscious he almost felt as if he were drifting through space. The room was tilting and swaying and he fought nausea. William had no idea where he was; but it was a strange place and he did not want to be there. There were hot things pressing against him. He had tried to tell the nurse but she seemed so busy and in such a hurry that he lapsed into silence, closed his eyes, and pretended to be asleep. The nurse had frightened William with her blood-spattered uniform and the rough way she had thrust the hot things around him. The previous nurse was much nicer. She had used her elbow to check how hot the things were and waited for them to cool a little before placing them gently against him.

His leg was numb, but this was a lot better than the agonizing pain he'd felt before. He tried to move it but nothing happened; maybe his foot had fallen asleep. He tried to curl his toes but nothing happened then either. Losing interest in his leg, he traced the outline of the hot things she had placed around him. They felt like bricks; through the towels wrapped around them he felt the rough surface. They were bricks. Why would they do that? And they were too hot, he felt like he was roasting. Squirming and twisting to get away from the heat, he escaped once more to the more kindly world of the comatose.

Dad was asking him to pass the nails again. The sun was beating down on the big oak tree with almost unbearable heat and William really only wanted to go into the house and have a nice cold glass of milk and maybe a cookie. He looked down longingly at the kitchen window where his mother was standing. He was sorry now that he'd asked his dad to help him with his tree house. His father's original reluctance to help had quickly turned to enthusiasm and William was soon relegated to the role of observer. He handed his father the box of nails and tried to think of some way to convince him it was too hot to work. Maybe if he helped a bit it would be done sooner. No, that was no good, it was just too hot to work. Maybe he could sneak down and go visit Molly in the stable. He could give her an apple. It was always cool in the stable.

William was unaware that this hospital was the major one he and the other Richmond residents were taken to when they were found. James Jackson was only a few rooms away, as was Harriet Bungay. It had been fortunate the hospital was completed in time to be of service during the greatest crisis the city had ever seen. Tents had been added outside the main building to take the overflow of patients less seriously injured but most were reluctant to use them because of the weather. In the early morning hours before dawn, the place was as busy as it had been at any time through the day.

IN ANOTHER TENT, not far from Camp Hill, Ada had been lying awake for more than an hour. Despite her exhaustion, the cold and discomfort of sleeping in the tent city had made sleep impossible. Frustrated she threw back the blanket and slowly pulled herself to her feet. The bruises and scrapes she had suffered the previous morning had been easy to ignore in the midst of the trauma; now they demanded to be acknowledged. She hobbled painfully from the tent and stood in the darkness of pre-dawn. It was far colder outside and the wind was springing up from the north-east. She hugged her coat tightly around herself and turned the collar up to cover her ears. The early morning silence was broken by a woman's sobs and the gruff voice of the man attempting to console her. Ada shivered as her teeth began to chatter, and gratefully she made her way back inside the tent. Once more she tried to find a comfortable position; there wasn't one. She pulled the blanket over her head, cupped her hands in front of her face and her own breath eventually added enough warmth to stop her shivering.

Ada was denied the comfort of deep religious conviction. It was many years since she had abandoned the Catholic faith and her marriage to Charlie, a non-Catholic, had further separated her from most of the Jacksons, at least in this one respect. Her children went to Richmond School; while her nieces and nephews went to St. Joseph's. For a moment she thought back to her own childhood. Even then her sister, only a year older, had been firm in her religious belief and a source of exasperation to Ada. Mary Jean possessed an unshakable faith that Ada could envy but never emulate. Cold and distraught, she tried now to find some comfort from a faith rusty with disuse. Thank God Mabel was late yesterday. If she had been there when she was supposed to, she would probably have been killed too. But she squirmed as she recalled her anger when Mabel failed to be on time. Her mind raced on. *What a bloody hypocrite I am. How can I possibly thank a God who would let a thing like this happen? What about the others, are they dead too? What about Dude, did her marvellous God save her? I have to* think. I've got to plan. As soon as it is light I'll have to find everyone. I'll have to check that Chebucto Road School and the hospitals. I'll have to keep asking everyone I see. Dear God, let them be alive. Cripes, there I go again, asking God's help. What the hell is wrong with me.

Ada closed her eyes tightly, she tried to will herself to sleep. This day, as yet undawned, was going to be a terrible day and she needed as much rest as she could manage. She couldn't count on any help from God, or anyone else for that matter; she was on her own. Beyond her vision, to the north-east, the storm clouds were thickening and rolling toward the stricken city in a race with dawn.

For twenty-two hours every doctor and nurse in the city, supplemented by their peers from Truro, New Glasgow, Sydney and other parts of the province, had been on constant demand. Long before this time they had reached and passed the point of exhaustion and were now performing by the sheer power of will. There was so much to be done and so few to do it. A few had dropped from fatigue and managed a rest of a few minutes or a half-hour and then climbed wearily to their feet to press on with the job. They were faced with another day without relief; it would be twenty more hours before outside relief would come to their aid, an impossibly long time.

At City Hall another group, the mayor, his deputy and the councillors comprising the various hastily formed committees had also burned the midnight oil. Some semblance of order was beginning to evolve from the chaos of calamity. The urgent needs of the citizens were mostly being met. But at a tremendous toll, paid in the coin of fatigue. Help was on the way, but this day would pass without relief for the dedicated people trying to solve the problems of hospitalizing, feeding, clothing and providing shelter for the homeless. They too were on their own.

Rescue workers had laboured all night trying to free those still trapped in the wreckage. They too, were staggering from loss of sleep. Much of the devastated area was in flames and could not be approached. Husbands, returning from job locations in other parts of the city, had dug all day and night, until their hands were bleeding, trying to rescue wives and children from collapsed homes. Wives, now widows, pitted their strength against the same foe. All were equally frustrated; more was needed than mere hands. All had reached the limit of endurance. With the approaching dawn, another day would grind by with agonizing endlessness before help would arrive.

Dawn was slow in arriving. Partially due to the now massive clouds heralding the approach of the storm, partly as if reluctant to throw light on the wretched remains of the city. There would be contrasts between this dawn and the dawn of yesterday. Today, no whistles or horns would call employees to the factories and places of employment. There were no cheerful voices raised in laughter as the workers hurried to their jobs. The factories were gone. Except for a few, the employees were dead. The Hillis Iron Foundry, the Sugar Refinery, the Cotton Factory, Richmond Printing and dozens of smaller businesses were totally destroyed. The squeal of iron wheels on iron tracks and the huffing and puffing of locomotives would not be heard in the Richmond Yard. Pier Six was gone as if it had never been and the wreckage of the Stella Maris, so recently designated as a rescue vessel, lay in a deplorable, discarded heap on the shore. From the water's edge west to Robie Street, from North Street north to the curve before Africville, the north end of the city was a vast sea of rubble. Within that rubble, dozens of people still were trapped.

On the other side of the harbour, from Tuft's Cove to the beginning of downtown Dartmouth, there was equal devastation. The legend "BELGIUM RELIEF" had not saved the Imo. The Halifax Explosion was not nearly as selective about its victims as the German Navy might have been. The battered and beaten hulk was grounded on the shore of Tuft's Cove. Nearby lay the bodies of the captain, the harbour pilot and the spectators who had been so captivated by the antics of the Mont Blanc crew. Because of prevailing winds, ocean current and the tides, this cove would become a landing point for many of the bodies flushed into the harbour by the giant wave that followed the explosion.

And so dawn arrived. It held little hope that this would be a good day for the city of Halifax and the town of Dartmouth. Even as it arrived, a few flakes of fine snow began to splatter against the ruins and the already battered bodies of the bewildered victims.

CHAPTER

14

Within twenty-four hours of the explosion help had arrived from other provincial centres. Doctors, nurses and volunteers augmented the local medical facilities. People from the relatively undamaged areas of Halifax and Dartmouth made their way to the devastated section and pitched in to help those who were so greatly in need. In addition to the help provided by the Canadian military personnel and the American forces that were already in the city, massive help was on the way from the Eastern United States. A search was on by the American Red Cross to find every ounce of pneumonia serum in the United States. It would be collected and delivered in time to prevent an anticipated outbreak of that disease. Many people from outside the city originally came as sightseers to gape at the destruction, but most pitched in to help. They were all welcome visitors.

Almost twenty-four hours after the explosion another visitor arrived. It crept silently, and at first gently, on wings of white from the north-east. In the beginning the tiny flakes of snow spread a pristine blanket of purity over the blackened and ugly ruins, much as a sheet, for aesthetic purpose, is thrown over the bodies of the dead. Its beauty was short-lived. This visitor did not arrive with the intention of relieving suffering and pain; it brought none of the necessities of life to the victims of a disaster. Far from bringing succour to the dreadfully wounded city it added more misery to a populace saturated in tragedy and desperate with despair. It was a visitor that quickly outlived its welcome in a city famous for hospitality.

HUGH MILLS HAD walked the streets of Richmond a thousand times, but now he was lost. A sea of rubble stretched from the waterfront west to Gottingen Street and as far as he could see in either direction on Barrington Street. Nothing in his nineteen years had prepared him for the horrors he had seen yesterday and last night. He had been in Dartmouth when the *Mont Blanc* exploded and was not hurt in the blast. By noon he had made his way to Richmond on a boat with other able-bodied men who were answering the call for help from the other side of the harbour.

He had spent that first day working, with a crew of men, along Barrington Street, locating and rescuing the living from the splintered remains of their homes and businesses. It was abhorrent, back-breaking work. There was little to work with. They needed cranes; all they had was human muscle. They needed tools; all they had were human hands, and these were already sprained, lacerated and bleeding. The only thing that never faltered was their indomitable will and the desire to help others.

In the next days there would be literally thousands engaged in the search for those still alive in the wreckage. It would be more than a week before the last living victim was found. But, for now, there were far too few trying to do far too much, with far too little. They did make a difference. Many were rescued in time for medical assistance to save their lives. Hugh, and his comrades, worked long through the night and well into the early hours of the next day. They only stopped when they reached the point of utter exhaustion.

He emerged from the wreckage of a Barrington Street home. He had grabbed two or three hours of restless sleep and now it was daybreak of the first day after the blast. A few hundred feet away a group of men huddled around a fire in the middle of the street. Suspended over the flame was a huge pot of water which they were using to make tea. As he approached, one man poured a fresh mug. Handing it to him he said, "Sorry mate, but we're fresh out of cream and sugar. We're lucky to have found some tea leaves, the pot, and a few mugs." Hugh accepted it gratefully. Looking him over the man continued, "Two of us are staying here to set up a soup kitchen for the workers—we've been promised some food. If you come back in about an hour we may have something for you. The rest of these guys are going up to look over the Protestant Orphanage, somebody said there may be as many as fifty kids there; some might have survived." Hugh shook his head, "I doubt we'll find many more alive. The whole place's been burning since yesterday before noon. Anyone the blast didn't get, died in the fires. It's still burning now. I'm going up to Veith Street—I know some families there." He placed the mug on the ground, "Thanks for that, it hit the spot."

He walked to the foot of Young Street, or at least where Young Street had been. The centre of the road was piled high with broken timbers and torn sidewalls from homes. Gingerly he climbed over the barrier until he reached Veith Street. Here he stopped for a minute and grimly took in the scene. The only thing left standing was the shattered wall of the Hillis Foundry. Everywhere there was smoke billowing up from the fires. He felt like just going home. The chance of anyone being alive in this mess was remote. He climbed over the wreckage of the orphanage toward Richmond Street, jumping cautiously from one broken beam to another and everywhere skirting around flames and broken glass.

Hugh was almost ready to quit. It was starting to snow, he had lost his gloves the previous night and his hands were numb with the cold and throbbing from the cuts and splinters. He hadn't eaten in twenty-four hours and he felt miserable, physically and mentally. The pile he was walking over shifted under his weight; he almost fell, and then he heard a muffled scream. Falling to his knees, he scrabbled at the debris, but was stymied by a large piece of lumber, wedged firm. "Who is it? Where are you? There was no answer. Either the person had just died or was unconscious. He straightened up and looked for help. There was a group of men on Barrington Street and he yelled as loud as he could. "There's one alive here! I need help!" Two American Navy personnel detached themselves from the others and started over the wreckage toward him. As they approached he cautioned them, "Be careful, this pile is moving and there's someone underneath it. I think it's a woman." The older of the two took charge. "Okay, young fella, don't worry. I'm Al and this here's Harry. We'll move back a mite and tunnel in to her. You come down from there real easy." Hugh did as he was told.

The two Americans were bigger and stronger than Hugh. They tore apart the tangle of lumber and heaved the timbers out of the way. When they reached ground level they peered in through the wreckage that imprisoned Mary Jean. "Okay, I see her. She's out cold." The older man turned once again to Hugh. "Son, this could be tricky. There's a big piece of lumber pinned across her hip and I can't see the other end of it so I don't know how long it is. If we can lift it a little we can drag her out through here. You lie down and reach in, get a hold of her coat collar. I'll lever the beam up with a piece of lumber. When I say 'pull' you drag her out. Don't worry about hurting her, we'll have her out before she comes to."

Hugh gladly climbed down into the clear space the men had made. The snow that had started so gently an hour ago had turned into a vicious blizzard, coming at them horizontally from the direction of Tuft's Cove and there was no shelter other than this hole in the debris. He stretched out on the ground and reached in to grab hold of her coat. For the first time he saw who it was they were trying to rescue. He turned to the Americans. "This lady is Mrs. Hinch. She lives here on this street, behind that factory, with her husband. They have ten kids;

I know the family well." Al looked at the shattered Hillis Foundry wall that Hugh pointed to, and then at the smouldering wreckage behind it. "You mean she did have a husband and ten children. If they were in that mess—they're gone." All three looked down at Mary Jean and the younger American said, "Poor soul, let's be very gentle."

Hugh took a firm grip on her collar and Al pressed down on the makeshift lever while Harry tried to prevent the pile of wood from shifting. He pulled her toward himself a foot or more, then slithered backward and hauled again. Once her hip was free of the beam it was easy and she was hauled into the clear area. All three relaxed for a moment. "We need a stretcher," said Hugh. "Buddy, we need a lot of things we don't have, a stretcher is only one of them. We can make something to carry her on; where you were standing up there a minute ago there is a small piece of a roof with shingles. If you fetch that we can put her on it—the shingles will stop her from sliding." Hugh climbed back up to the top of the pile and dragged the roof section over to the hole. The Americans lifted it down and placed it on the ground beside Mary Jean. "Let's work together now. Son, you put your hand under her knees, I'll get hold of her coat on each side and Harry, you take her shoulders. When I say 'lift' we all lift together and move her onto the shingles. That way, if she has broken bones we won't do too much damage, okay?" At his command Mary Jean was transferred to the makeshift stretcher.

A glint of silver caught Hugh's eye. He bent over and picked the rosary out of the slush and brushed it off, he held it up to show the two men, "She was praying." Al looked at the beads and said, "A fat lot of good that did in a mess like this." Hugh thought about it for a moment, "Well, it might not have helped you, and it probably wouldn't help me either, but I have a pretty good feeling it helped her. She's a very devout lady and, after all, we did find her, didn't we?" Hugh cupped the rosary in his hand and carefully placed it in the pocket of her coat.

They gently lifted Mary Jean to the top of the pile. The cold, wet snow blowing in her face brought her back to consciousness. Recognition crossed her face and she tried several times before she could speak. When she did, it was with her usual calm and gracious tone. "Bless you, Hughie. I won't forget that you helped me. You're a fine young man." She tried to turn her head to look along Veith Street, but couldn't make it. "Hughie, can you turn me around? I need to see." They turned the litter and for a long, silent moment Mary Jean Hinch looked at the ruins of her life. Harry broke into the strained silence, "They might've just been hurt and taken to the hospital. Lots of people were cut with glass, nothing serious. We helped take dozens to the hospital yesterday, didn't we Al." The older man nodded firmly. "Yes, Ma'am. There must be hundreds of people now in the hospital getting real good treatment. In fact, the hospitals are pretty crowded, so we're going to take you to our ship. It has a great sick bay and the best doctors in the world."

The words provided little comfort. "They're gone, Hughie. Thank you for trying, but they're gone." Tears were flowing down her cheeks, "I'm ready when you are gentlemen." Al knelt by her side, "Ma'am, this might hurt a bit. Once we get to the bottom of the hill it'll be a piece of cake. But to get to the bottom we have to climb over all this stuff and it won't be easy. Harry and I are going to take the front end of this and drag it over the mess, we can't carry you because we'll be slipping and sliding in this damn snow. Your friend Hughie can stay by your side and if it hurts too much just say so and we'll stop for awhile." The problem was solved quickly, Mary Jean moaned and lapsed into unconsciousness at the first jolt.

Service boots with leather soles were never made for climbing up and down over rough terrain covered with three or four inches of wet snow. The Americans slipped and fell a dozen times before they reached the cleared section of Barrington Street. Hugh Mills fared only slightly better. He was wearing lumberman's rubbers and was more used to snowy conditions. Even so, at one point his right leg thrust down through two splintered beams and he scraped the skin off his shin bone.

The two men on Barrington Street still had the pot of water boiling. They were sheltered from the storm behind a section of wall that was braced with scraps of lumber. "Who'd ya find?" Hugh answered him, "Mrs. Hinch from Veith Street." The man said, "Fine, I'll enter her name on our list, somebody will probably be looking for her. Is she hurt bad?" Al spoke up, "She may have a broken hip, we're taking her to our ship, the *Old Colony*, she'll be well looked after there."

Hugh did not understand why, but he felt better than he had since the tragedy started. Perhaps it was the thought that he had robbed the explosion of at least one more victim. Al and Harry each took an end of the litter and started south on Barrington toward their ship. Al stopped and looked behind him. "Your friend is in good hands now Hughie, and she owes a lot to you. You did a fine job; I'm proud to have met you."

Hugh turned and started to walk north on Barrington; he decided to go as far as Roome or Duffus and then work his way south. The blizzard would be at his back. Somewhere in that sea of debris, someone else could be waiting for him. As he walked away one of the tea-makers yelled to him, "Hey son. Try to join up with a group; the soldiers are patrolling for looters, if you're with a group they won't bother you." Hugh waved in acknowledgement and then turned for a last look at the American sailors and Mary Jean Hinch, but they had vanished into the blizzard.

The snow was a vicious enemy now. By late afternoon over sixteen inches would have fallen and drifts would be as high as a man's waist. Where the snow met the heat from the burning wreckage it turned to water, which quickly became ice as it ran down the beams and boards away from the heat. Before long, most of the ruins were sculptured in ice, making rescue work even more difficult. Conditions became intolerable. Misery had been added to misery.

AT ALMOST THE same moment Hugh Mills discovered Mary Jean Hinch, Ada Moore was descending the stairs to the basement of the Chebucto Road Morgue. The snow had started as she walked across the Halifax Common. In the short length of time it had taken her to walk the two blocks of Cunard Street to Windsor, it had intensified and by the time she turned into Chebucto Road it deserved the designation blizzard. Ada had run the last few hundred feet with her scarf pressed tightly to her face. Inside the basement door, sheltered from the wind and driving snow, she sighed with relief and paused to get her breath. The relief was short-lived.

She looked with horror at the sheet-covered bodies arrayed in rows. In one corner of the basement several men were cleaning a corpse in preparation for embalmment. One of them noticed her and quickly drew a sheet over the body. The door behind her banged open and three men came down the steps, forcing her to move aside. Two were carrying the bodies of young girls, no more than four-years-old, and the third had a dead baby in his arms. She fought nausea and the urge to scream. For a moment Ada wanted to run outside and face the vicious whiteness of the storm rather than face the bleak ugliness of death.

One of the soldiers, seeing her distress, took her by the arm and led her to a chair. "Ma'am, you just sit for a moment, I'll get you a glass of water." Ada drank deeply, closed her eyes to the sights around her and took several deep breaths. When he saw Ada was a bit more composed he said, "Can you describe the person you are looking for?" Ada was afraid to stand up, there was the probability she would faint. "Son, I'll have to look at all of them. My whole family may be here. But let me sit for a few more minutes, I don't feel too good." She leaned forward in the chair and covered her eyes to hide the horrible scenes around her. The basement was cold and clammy and even with her eyes shut she could not avoid the smells of scorched flesh, blood and the beginning of decomposition. A shiver ran through her that was not attributable to the cold of the basement morgue.

Reluctantly she left the solace of the chair and walked over to the soldier and the row of bodies. "I'm ready now. Do you have a list of names of those who are here?" The young man turned to her, "Only a few have been identified, Ma'am. It would help if you can give us the names of some of them so we can try to find relatives."

Ada walked slowly down the first row of corpses, glancing quickly but firmly each time the soldier lifted back a sheet. These were the most horribly mangled. Their bodies had been picked up from the streets closest to the explosion. In addition to the full force of the blast they had been struck by metal fragments, flying glass and other debris. Almost all were missing limbs or had been decapitated by the obscene forces. The force within the first five hundred feet was more than sufficient to decapitate a body or rip of arms and legs just by its sheer power. Chests were caved in. Empty eye sockets stared blankly and some faces were obliterated entirely, the flesh peeled back from the bones. At a glance, many bodies were indistinguishable as male or female.

Many of those in that proximity were naked or almost naked; every stitch of clothing had been ripped from them. In days to come, relatives would raise the spectre that this was a result of looting by, presumably, subhuman ghouls. It is far more likely the bodies were stripped by the incredible force of the wall of air moving outward from the epicentre, compressing the atoms ahead of it into the density of steel and striking the victim with an almost inconceivable force. The ghoul was the Halifax Explosion.

This was the first and, therefore the most horrifying trip that Ada would make to the Chebucto Road Morgue. She was an unwilling observer to the most appalling carnage. From December 7th until the end of January she would have the onerous task of identifying the Jackson dead, including five of her own children. Of the sixty-six members of the extended Jackson family who were in the Richmond area at the moment the ship exploded, forty-six were killed. A few of their bodies would never be found; most of them were burned beyond recognition. They were identified only by the location where they'd been found.

By midafternoon the two American sailors from the Old Colony *hospital ship, Al and Harry, who had helped Hugh Mills rescue Mary Jean Hinch, were joined by four Canadian sailors. A team of six was far more effective than only two or three. There was little they could do with the homes that were burning furiously, but others, where coal reserves in the basement had not ignited, could be torn apart to rescue the injured or find the dead. In most cases, debris that had been blasted into the middle of the streets did not burn, it was not landing on overturned kitchen or hall stoves. But these heaps of broken beams, parts of roofs, and shattered walls had became the prison for many who happened to be passing by when the explosion occurred.*

HOWARD AND EDWARD Bungay Jr. were in this group. On their way to work from their home on Albert Street, they had been unable to resist detouring to watch the burning ship. Both were smashed by the wall of compressed air and driven further up Richmond hill. They were picked up by the tornadic effect, whirled over and over in the maelstrom, and dumped some distance away from where they started. Eighteen-year-old Howard was dead, his body skewered by a flying fence picket. His younger brother, Edward, aged sixteen, was seriously injured by the sledgehammer blow and buried under a massive amount of debris.

The six sailors had split up to cover more territory and it was one of the Canadians who heard Edward's cry. He called the others and they

Photo courtesy of Lorraine (Daine) Rozee

Howard Bungay, left, and his brother Edward Jr. became victims of the freakish rolling motion of the wall of air. Howard's body was pierced by a fence picket, killing him instantly, and Edward was pummelled and seriously injured. He died seven days later from pneumonia.

began casting boards and beams to one side. They found the body of Howard first. As they pulled him from the debris they gazed in shock at the picket driven through his torso. In hushed tones Harry said, "My God, I only saw something like this once in my life, and that was after one hell of a tornado near my home in Texas. There was a tree with a big piece of iron pipe driven in one side and sticking out the other." Al shook his head slowly, in wonderment. "The only thing you can say about it is the guy never felt a thing. He was dead the second it hit him—look, there's hardly any blood." One of the Canadian sailors said, "That won't be much consolation to his folks. What do we do with him? There's not much point taking him to a hospital—they have enough problems."

Harry took control. "Put him over here where the guys picking up the bodies will see him. They'll take him to the morgue. But there has to be another here somewhere, this one sure as hell wasn't doing any groaning." It was another ten minutes before they found Edward. This time the Americans had come prepared, each carrying a rolled up stretcher. They carefully placed Edward, now unconscious, on one of them and moved him gently to level ground. Harry looked the boy over and said "I can't see any fresh bleeding. He's out cold, so he isn't feeling any pain. Let's cover him over and leave him where he is for a few minutes. Maybe we can find some others and then take them all back to the ship."

The six sailors continued to search and comb through the wreckage until the afternoon darkness made the task impossible. Harry and Al each took an end of the stretcher and started the trip back to their ship. The *Old Colony* would be instrumental in saving the life of many of the explosion's victims. Unfortunately, Edward Bungay would not be one of them.

AFTER HER INITIAL trip to the morgue Ada was in the grip of severe depression. She had recognized many of the bodies, at least those that were recognizable, as friends and neighbours. Some of the bodies would never be identified even by members of their own family; their faces had been obliterated and unless they had papers or articles in their pockets, they would remain part of the unidentified dead. There would be about three hundred of them.

Although she had not yet found any of her own family, she nevertheless recognized the horror as the shape of things to come. She was filled with dread about making further trips to that sorrowful place. Ada had always despised weakness; she was proud of her own strength and ability to lead, but she realized now that she, too, had a breaking point. The hour spent in the morgue had been the most stressful sixty minutes of her life.

Ada left the morgue at the height of the storm. For a few moments she braced herself against the blizzard and allowed the pelting snow to scour the smell of death from her. Then she turned and hurried along Chebucto Road and through Dublin Street to Willow. The rooms Mabel rented on Willow Street were an oasis after the shock of the morgue and the fierceness of the storm. The house had been damaged. All the windows were either cracked or completely blown out, there was some structural damage to the roof and chimney and much of the ceiling plaster had fallen. To Ada, comfortable in a wing-back chair with a cup of hot tea on the table beside her, it was as cosy as could be.

Mabel, however, had a problem. She could not call her mother-in-law "mother," as she usually did, because her own mother was sitting beside her. Nor did she feel comfortable using her first name, Catherine, and addressing her as Mrs. Shanks seemed awkwardly formal. So she said nothing unless one or the other of them caught her eye. It didn't really matter because the two older ladies did all the talking.

Catherine asked Ada if she knew what she should do or who she should see to get her house fixed. Ada, of course, knew the answer, "You have to go to City Hall and see the person in charge of the Committee for Housing and Repairs. They'll jump right to it and by early 1923 everything should be fixed as good as new."

Recognizing her mother's trend toward sarcasm when she felt people were getting steamed up over nothing, Mabel attempted to intervene. "I'll look after it for you. I'll go to City Hall, and don't worry, Mum is only kidding. I'm sure they will look after it right away."

Ada glowered at Mabel, "While you're at it see if they can gather my house together and put it back on Barrington Street. Right now it is spread over about three blocks." Catherine decided it would be a good time to sweep up the plaster on the kitchen floor. She excused herself and left the room. As soon as she was out of earshot Ada turned to Mabel, "Silly old biddy, she's lost no one and her house is still livable and she doesn't even know how lucky she is." Mabel sprung to her mother-in-law's defence. "Stop it. She is a very nice lady and treats me real good. She's old and frightened and doesn't have anyone to lean on. Try to be a bit more charitable." Ada was silent for a moment, "Fine. But what she really needs is a few beautiful, fun-filled nights in a tent on the Common, or take a nostalgic trip through the basement of

Chebucto Road School; this place would look like Buckingham Palace to her."

Mother and daughter sat silently for a few minutes, each lost in their own thoughts. Ada finished her tea and put the empty cup on the table. "We have to get organized—there are a million things to do. First of all we have to find the family and the best place to start is the morgue. I'm afraid now that most of them have been killed. I don't want you going there, it's too gruesome. I'll look after that and I'll check out Camp Hill too. You check the other hospitals. We have to try and get Vince and Larry to help us, but they've both gone to pieces and are in a terrible state. I sent Vince back up to Truro to look after Gordon. The big thing is to ask questions. Ask everyone you meet if they have seen any of ours."

Mabel nodded. "Okay. But where can I get in touch with you when I need you?" Ada smiled grimly. "You won't have any problem finding me. I'll be where I was last night, in one of the hundred or more tents on the Common. If I haven't frozen to death we will have a nice long chat." With a sharp intake of breath, Mabel said, "Oh! Mum! You can't stay there. You must stay with me tonight and until you find something better." With a deep sigh, Ada kicked off her shoes and snuggled back into the chair, "Well, thank you dear child, I must admit, I thought you'd never ask."

By late afternoon on the day after the explosion the doctors, nurses and volunteer workers finally received a respite from their frantic battle. The majority of the critically injured had been treated. The raging storm had slowed the arrival of new patients; many would die before they could reach the hospitals. Those awaiting operations were made as comfortable and pain-free as possible until the necessary facilities and supplies became available. Now they could only wait. The caretakers were at last able to snatch a few moments rest and recoup their energy. Few, if any, had ever worked under such stressful conditions.

THE TWO SOLDIERS had waded through knee deep snow down Duffus Street from Gottingen. Their orders were to take up a position at the foot of Duffus and stand guard against looters. Neither was enthused about the assignment. Both carried powerful flashlights but they weren't needed; the scene was bathed theatrically in an orange-red glare from the fires raging in over a hundred homes. The reeking sulphur from the burning coal and coke saturated the air and made them cough continuously. The taller man spat in the soot-blackened snow. "You know, Charlie, if I do see a looter I'm not even going to bother warning him. I'm just going to shoot the son of a bitch. Anyone trying to steal the few things these people might have left isn't fit to live." Charlie quickly cautioned him. "Don't get trigger happy, Bob, it could be people looking for their wife or kids, give them a break. Keep the safety on until we're sure."

Both soldiers stopped as they heard the low growl of a dog. "It's coming from that pile of rubbish there," Charlie said. He moved closer and shone his flashlight over the pile of debris, but could see nothing. The dog growled again. Charlie knelt down in the dirty snow and aimed the flashlight under some of the beams. "There's the body of a woman in there." Bob shrugged, "Well leave her there. It's not our job. Remember, we're supposed to be after looters. She's not going anywhere, they'll find her tomorrow when it's light." Charlie hesitated, "I still hear the dog, maybe we could dig him out." Exasperated, Bob snapped "Look, rescuing dogs is also not our job. Shoot the bloody thing and put it out of its misery."

But Charlie had a dog of his own back home, he wouldn't want anyone to shoot it and he had no intention of shooting someone else's. He moved the light around until it rested in the corner of the basement. There, caught in the glare, was a boy and his dog.

"Hey! There's a kid in there!" Bob jumped down beside him. "Is he dead?" "No," said Charlie, "He's alive and I don't think he's even hurt. But, man he sure looks scared."

Neither of them could squeeze through the rubble to where Gerald was hiding, and the boy had no intention of coming out. After cajoling for half an hour they finally coaxed him out with the offer of a drink of water. He had been without water for almost thirty-six hours.

Charlie picked him up and hugged him, "There, little fella, you're safe now. We'll get you back to your mama. Bob, see if you can find a blanket or a cloth of some kind, the poor kid's shaking like a leaf." There were several blankets in the wreckage and they wrapped them tightly around the boy. He still shook with fear. "I'm going to take him up to Gottingen Street and find the Captain. Look after my rifle till I get back, and for God's sake don't shoot nobody!" He turned and started retracing his steps toward Gottingen Street with Gerald Jackson held firmly, yet gently, to his chest. Prince was right at his heels.

GERALD JACKSON'S FATHER had died at the waterfront along with his sister, Florence. His brother, nine-year-old Edward and his baby-sister,

Patricia, did not survive the collapse of their home. His sister, Muriel was found at St. Joseph's School and taken to the hospital. It would be many days before Ellen Jackson would be reunited with her surviving children. Despite their terrible loss, they would rejoice at the reunion. For the rest of their lives they would share a special closeness. Gerald, Muriel and Ellen Jackson were survivors of Canada's worst disaster.

Lew Jackson, Gerald and Muriel's cousin, was not as fortunate. At almost the same moment that Gerald was being found, Lew was on an operating table in the Victoria General Hospital. The trauma of his terrible injury was too severe. The best efforts of the doctors was futile. He died while they were attempting to amputate his leg, the loss of blood and severe shock had simply been too much.

WILLIAM EDMONDS AWOKE to a cool, damp cloth soothing his fevered forehead. It was the 'nice' nurse. She smiled at him, "We were only supposed to keep you warm, son, nobody was supposed to bake you, is that better?" Still dazed with the confusion of delirium the boy nodded. The bricks had been moved back enough to keep him warm and comfortable and his leg was only a dull ache. If only he could have a glass of cold milk—but he fell asleep before he could ask.

There was no respite for the workers at City Hall. The temporary shelter provided by the army's tent city on Halifax Common had been a disaster. Word spread quickly about the deaths from freezing and now those who had been sheltered there needed and demanded other accommodation. There was little to be offered to them. Many had solved the problem for themselves by moving out of the city to relatives throughout the province; some had moved in with relatives or friends in the South or West Ends. Hundreds of people whose homes had been spared threw open their doors to those less fortunate. It was not enough. By late afternoon the vicious blizzard had abated but the conditions underfoot were almost impossible. In the midst of this the army was working frantically to improve the tents. Extra blankets and some sleeping bags were provided and kerosene heaters had been installed. This presented two new dangers—fire or asphyxiation. Many of the people in need did not want to risk either.

CHAPTER
15

SOPHYE JACKSON WAS able to curb her impatience during the trip through the north-eastern states. She occupied herself by sorting through the relief supplies with her new-found friends from the Red Cross. But by the time the train reached Truro she was more than eager for the journey to end. Now, as the engine seemed to be inching its way through the Rockingham Railyard, her face was pressed against the window to catch her first glimpse of Richmond and home. She was due for disappointment. The engine lurched through a series of switches that guided it to the track leading to the South End. "Oh Damn!" Bob Johnson slid into the seat beside her. "What's the matter? We're here, aren't we?" Sophye turned to him briefly. "Yes, but we're not going through Richmond. The train is heading toward the south end of the city. We should be going to the North Street Station, but this way will take us through Armdale and the West End along the Northwest Arm."

Bob suspected that the train might be rerouted around the damaged area, but he hesitated telling Sophye his thoughts. Instead he said, "Well, it might be busy over there, I know there were a couple of trains leaving Boston with medical supplies and they may be unloading now. We're probably going to the other place so we don't have to wait." Sophye's brow creased with worry; she too was beginning to suspect the truth. "Well if this thing doesn't put on a little more speed we won't get there today." She stared back out the window as they moved south through the Fairview switches. The high rock walls on either side blocked her view of anything else.

These walls gave way to open space as they reached the head of the Northwest Arm. She could see the buildings on the other side of the water and everything appeared normal. There was deep snow everywhere. A few windows were boarded up but it was not the mass destruction she had dreaded. When the train reached Quinpool Road she moved to the other side of the isle, but again there was not that much damage to see. Other than a few people clearing away snow, there was very little activity. In another minute the train was again going between the high rock walls of the railway cut to the South End and there was nothing to see.

Sophye turned to Bob. "As soon as I get off this thing I'm heading up to Richmond and find my family." Bob put his hand gently on her arm, as if to restrain her. "My dear young lady, you can't do that. You signed up with the Red Cross to come here and help the injured, now that's a contract, they won't let you just look after one family. If you do that you'll probably never get work in any hospital again. It's up to you to honour your contract. Besides, if your people were hurt they quite likely are already being looked after. They might well be in the hospital where you will be working." His words made sense, Sophye gave it a few minutes' consideration before nodding her head in agreement. "But that doesn't stop me from finding them on my own time after work, and that is what I intend doing. I'll go up to Richmond tonight."

Almost before the train came to a full halt, army men swarmed in to unload the urgently needed supplies. Sophye stepped off the car to the platform and joined the group of doctors, nurses and Red Cross workers waiting for instructions. In contrast to their crisp, clean appearance the man who greeted them was clearly in need of rest. His face was haggard and unshaven, his posture bespoke exhaustion and his voice, when he spoke, was weak and wan. "Are there any surgeons among you? We desperately need someone who can do amputations—we were dead on our feet long ago and we urgently need help." For the first time since leaving New York, Sophye felt a chill of fear run through her. The seriousness of the situation had been expressed by the doctor in that short speech.

Four surgeons stepped forward and were quickly whisked away in a car heading for the Victoria General Hospital. The doctor was talking to the head of the Red Cross contingent who pointed to Sophye. He came to her and said, "They say you are a nurse and not really with the Red Cross; we also need post-operative nurses. Do you think you could manage that?" Sophye nodded, "That's what I was doing in the hospital in New York." The doctor pointed, "If you get on that first truck in line it'll take you to the Camp Hill Hospital. You'll find all the work there you can handle and then some."

The truck drove up South Street and turned north on Robie. Again, outside of the now familiar broken and boarded up windows there was little damage to see. With the arrival at Camp Hill the picture changed dramatically. The hospital was a beehive of frantic energy. With barely time to hang up her coat, Sophye was pressed into service.

With a sense of growing horror she realized the majority of the first group of patients she saw were from Richmond. Many she knew by name, most by sight, and the realization that Richmond must have been at the heart of the blast exploded in her brain. The rooms assigned her did not contain any of her family, but it was a large hospital. Sophye decided that as soon as she was free, this would be the place to start. Before going to Richmond she would check each and every bed in the other rooms as well as the mattresses that had been spread in the hallways.

The confusion following the explosion would last for months. Those who lost loved ones, and had no definite evidence the ones they were seeking were dead, would spend countless hours searching. Besides visitations to the various hospitals and the morgues there were two main sources that might provide information. Many would simply ask for information from everyone they met, hoping against hope that the next person they asked would have some knowledge of the victims whereabouts. In addition, ads were placed in newspapers in the expectation that a reader might remember seeing the person sought. By Saturday there were many ads desperately seeking information. Many would be answered with the joyous news that the loved one was safe and being cared for.

ON SATURDAY, THE body of Edward Bungay washed ashore on the Dartmouth side of the harbour. He had been near the Sugar Refinery, along with the three Jackson brothers and Frank Carew at the moment of the explosion. He was instantly killed; minutes later the wall of water pushed along the waterfront by the blast plucked him from the wreckage and flushed him into the harbour.

The body of his daughter, Gladys, was probably in the same waters with him. After the blast she had simply disappeared and her body was never found. Gladys had been about to enter Wallace's store at the corner of Hanover and North Albert Streets, in fact she had her hand on the door latch. At one thousand feet from the epicentre, she was too far away to be incinerated by the fireball, but there was nothing between her and the *Mont Blanc* to soften the strength of the steel-like blow. In the most likely scenario she would have been smashed against the building a split second before it was demolished, crushing and killing her instantly. The wave that invaded the Richmond hill would have been the deepest at that point, lifting her from the debris and floating her down over the ruins to the harbour. A few days later the following advertisement was placed in the Halifax paper:

"Ten-year-old, light brown hair, brown eyes,
slender build, may have worn thick velvet cap,
blue coat, ring on third finger with one stone.
Missing since the explosion; her mother, who is
in hospital, very anxious for any information."

The ad had been placed by her brother Charles and would be repeated many, many times over the next few months. It would never be answered.

SOPHYE WAS HUSTLING down the hall pushing a gurney loaded with warm bricks for the Edmonds boy. She turned the corner sharply and almost ran her into her brother, James Junior. Both stood in shock at seeing the other. "For God's sake, Sophye, how did you get here?" With a little cry Sophye threw herself into her brother's arms, "Oh! My God, what happened? Where's Mum and Dad? Was any of our bunch hurt? Tell me where they are!" Jim took her by the shoulders and moved her back to arm's length, "Steady on old girl, we don't know a lot yet, things are really messed up. Richmond took the full blast. Dad was hurt real bad, but they say he'll be okay. He's in the last room on the right down this corridor. I just saw him, but don't go down, he's asleep. Minnie was hurt too but they put her on a train to Truro and she'll be okay. The rest we don't know for sure. Mum, Annie and little Clifford were in the house and they haven't been found yet. They may be okay. Lew was in the railyard—if he was in Rockingham he'll be all right but we haven't found him yet either. It's going to take days to settle everything so try to stay calm, don't think the worst. There's hope yet." He handed Sophye his handkerchief, "Dry your eyes and blow your nose like a good girl." He smiled as she did as she was told. "Hey, this is like the time when you fell off the swing and skinned both knees on those cinders—you messed up one of my handkerchiefs then too." Sophye managed a weak smile as he continued. "You haven't answered my first question, how on earth did you get here?"

Sophye's smile widened innocently. "Well, the other day I was working away in the hospital in New York, minding my own business of course, when this little leprechaun came along and said, 'you'd better go home girlie, your silly people have got themselves in a mess again.'" Jim smiled in return, "Well, girlie, that is the understatement of a lifetime.

Lord, are we in trouble." Their smiles faded. "Dad will be overjoyed to see you, it will do him a world of good. But don't go down for awhile, let him get some sleep."

Sophye pointed to the loaded trolley. "You know the young Edmonds boy, don't you? Young Willie?" "No, I know the family, but I don't remember who's who. Is he in here then?" "He's in the third last room down there. The poor kid lost a leg and a lot of blood. We've got him packed with warm bricks to keep his body temperature up. As soon as he is fit they have to trim the bone and prepare him for an artificial leg." Jim leaned his back against the wall. "There are enough sad stories in here to keep you crying for the rest of your life." Sophye nodded and sighed, "I better go, these bricks don't stay hot very long. I'll go in and see Dad later, tonight I'm going up to Richmond." Jim straightened up, "Oh look, I wouldn't do that if I were you, Sis. There's nothing you can do up there. The place is a shambles and you won't find anybody— they've all been taken to hospitals. You'll just get yourself upset. Besides, Aunt Ada is looking after everything. She treats me like I'm five years old and she'll do the same with you. She is one determined lady, so don't get in her way. She is going around to all the hospitals and dressing stations looking for family." Tactfully, he left out mention of the morgues. "If anyone can find anyone in this unholy mess it'll be Ada."

Sophye started to push the trolley down the hall, "I have to get going, these bricks are important. I'll go see Dad in another few hours and I don't care what you or Aunt Ada or anyone else says, tonight I'm going to Richmond." Sophye had her share of the stubborn streak that ran through the Jackson family.

The crew of the Old Colony *showed many kindnesses to the injured civilians who were brought to their ship for medical treatment. All received gestures of sympathy and compassion from the sailors as well as excellent care from the medical personnel. But Mary Jean Hinch was treated with particular tenderness and compassion. Her two rescuers, Harry and Al, had told her story to everyone on board and, from the Captain to the stokers they were all shocked at her loss. She received a constant stream of visitors who did their utmost to distract her from the tragedy. Every possible delicacy produced in the ship's cookhouse arrived at her bedside. Overwhelmed by the flood of generosity, she quickly developed a system whereby her current visitor would eat the delicious offering left by the visitor before him. By tacit agreement, the crewmen avoided the subject of the explosion and spoke only about their hometowns and their families back home. Mary Jean heard tales of states near and far; a stoker was from the Blue Ridge Mountains of Virginia, a place she had only heard about in song. Everyone sensed the tranquillity of her spirit and the gentleness of her manner and each outdid the other to distract her with their stories. The extent of her loss, and the quiet courage with which she faced it, lay beyond the power of their imagination.*

IT WAS MIDAFTERNOON before Sophye was allowed a break. One thing after another conspired to frustrate her attempts to visit her father. She had finally been able to peek into his room the previous hour, but he was still sound asleep and she knew it was better to let him rest. Later she arranged with one of the other nurses to cover for her for a half-hour and made her way to her father's room.

He was still asleep. She tiptoed to his bedside and looked down at him. His left eye was covered with a large cotton pad that concealed half his head, and his left arm was immobilized with plaster from the shoulder to the end of his fingers. Surgical tape bound his broken ribs. A surge of pity swept over her. This was a man so proud of his strength. She remembered as a little girl how she would rush at him and be caught up in his arms. He would toss her high in the air and laugh as she shrieked when he caught her. How sure she felt in his strong grip, how secure and protected. Tears coursed her cheek as she gazed at his face, drawn with pain. He seemed so much smaller now, as if he had shrunk under the weight of his injuries. He moaned and the eyelid of his good eye fluttered with wakefulness. Sophye barely had time to wipe the tears and concern from her face and replace them with a wide smile. "Well now sleepy-head. Would you be so kind as to be telling me why you are lolling around in bed in the very middle of the day like this? Should you not be on top of one of your silly boxcars trying to do an honest day's work?"

James stared at her without recognition. Then slowly his face lightened with a wan grin. In an exaggerated Irish brogue he said, "Why, sure an' begorra, if it is not me beautiful little Irish colleen, Sophye." Matching his tone, Sophye replied, "Kind sir, I want ye to know that phoney Irish blarney of yours will get you anywhere with me." She squeezed his good hand, leaned over and kissed him. Still holding his hand she sat by the side of the bed. Her father looked at her for a minute in silence, the smile growing broader on his face. "What in the name of heavens are you doing here, girl?" Sophye sighed, "Why does everyone ask me that same question? Why, not an hour ago your silly son and namesake, James the Junior, demanded to know the very same thing. Why, it's getting to the point where a poor girl's beginning to feel no one's happy to see her, even this being Christmas-time and all."

James squeezed his daughter's hand tightly. "Nothing could be further from the truth, dear child. You're as welcome as the flowers in May, a breath of fresh air, a sight for tired old eyes, indeed—or at least one tired old eye." It tugged at her heart to hear him make light of his injury, but she played along, "Mr. Jackson if you don't stop with this wild Irish blarney I'll have to leave; sure and you are making my heart beat wildly and my temperature to rise."

They sat in silence for awhile, each content to be with the other, and then James tugged on her hand. "Bend a little closer, girl, I can't talk very loud. I want you to go up to Richmond and look for your mother. I'm very worried about her. She was standing beside me when it happened and I don't know where she went. Check everywhere around the house, she could have been blown a good distance away. She might be hurt and need help. Promise me you'll do that." Sophye nodded her head, "I intend to go tonight. If she's there I'll find her, but Jim said most everyone has been taken to hospital already. There are at least a dozen places being used as hospitals and Aunt Ada is searching them all."

James shook his head. "Ada's a remarkable woman and I'm sure she's doing her best, but she is doing the job I should be doing and I can't get out of this damn bed. We have to help her, so you go look as well." Sophye stood up, "I have to get back to work but you just concentrate on getting well. Between us, Ada, Jim and I will find Mum and the others. You just rest now, and don't be frettin'."

Once she left her father's room and was away from his scrutiny, tears welled once again in her eyes. To shield her tear-streaked face from others she walked to a window and looked out at the storm. The snow was blasting horizontally past the window and visibility was down to a few yards. "Oh great. Just what we need, by the time tonight gets here the drifts will be to my shoulders and it'll be impossible to find anything. But I don't care; I'm still going to Richmond."

An offshoot of catastrophe is disease. The probable lack of clean water and inadequate sanitary facilities leads to outbreaks of typhoid, dysentery and pneumonia. Quick action by the authorities prevented the first two from becoming a problem, but exposure to the elements led to an outbreak of pneumonia. Many were soaked by the wall of water, then trapped in wreckage for hours or days. Some, in addition to other injuries, developed pneumonia. The American Red Cross had, almost immediately after the blast, notified every Red Cross Centre in the United States requesting serum to combat a disease that was almost inevitable under the circumstances. Their prompt action would save many lives, but it would come too late for others.

EDWARD BUNGAY JR. was on the same hospital ship as Mary Jean Hinch. The wall of water had been deepest where he and his brother had been. Howard was already dead before it hit but Edward had survived being struck by the wall of air, albeit with massive injuries, and was unconscious when the wave of water struck. He had inhaled water into his lungs and then was trapped within the wreckage for more than a day before being discovered. All the factors were right for the development of pneumonia. Even as he was being carried on board the *Old Colony* his body temperature was beginning to rise toward fever. Even the best attention by top medical people and the kindness and generosity of his hosts could not reverse the damage. In less than five days he would join the ranks of the dead.

Even the weather was conspiring to bring the city to its knees. It began with the storm on Friday, the day after the explosion, with more snow on Saturday and a fierce gale the following day that added an inch of rain to streets already slick with ice. On Monday morning a blizzard started, which would go on record as one of the worst storms in memory, depositing another six inches of snow on top of what was already there; in places the drifts were five feet high. The North End fires, still burning, had contributed a layer of soot that blackened the snow, desecrating even the cold, white blanket that lay over the ruins.

EVERYTHING WAS GONE. Everything she had known from childhood was completely shattered. From the corner of Duffus and Gottingen Streets she had a clear view to the Narrows. Every home, factory and warehouse was devastated. The ankle-deep snow was black from the soot of the fires still burning throughout Richmond and the North End. Sophye shivered from the cold and the biting wind, but more from a sense of impotence in the face of this overwhelming calamity. She stamped her feet to knock the snow off her overshoes, a hopeless gesture at best, as one step and she was again floundering in a drift almost to her knees. She had promised her father to look around the wreckage of their home and to ask people about her mother and the rest of the family. There was nothing to see and no one to ask. The only person in sight was a soldier on guard near the bottom of the hill. She spoke aloud. "This is a wild-goose chase, but I'll have to go through the motions. Daddy was badly hurt; he wouldn't have been lying here very long and he was probably unconscious. I don't think he has any idea just how bad it is."

She trudged downhill through the snow toward the lower end of Duffus Street and stopped where her home had stood. There was little to see other than blackened beams and bits of sidewall. It was late in the evening, the moon was obscured by cloud and there were no street lights. It was like looking into a bottomless pit. Never had Richmond been so dark. The sudden realization that little Clifford would almost certainly have been in the house, and quite likely her mother too, struck her like a physical blow. For the past few days she had held firmly to the hope that they had been injured and were lying in one of the many treatment centres. The physical evidence burst that bubble of optimism. Again she spoke to break the silence in this sea of death, "Oh! that poor baby! Poor, poor little Clifford!" She sobbed in anguish, imagining the horror of his death.

Sophye stood for several long minutes before the wreckage she was sure was now a tomb. She remembered the days of laughter, growing up in a home that had an Irish sense of fun and occasionally she smiled a bittersweet smile at some particularly fond memory. It was only when she was in her late teens that she had found the environment of Halifax too confining and had left for greener pastures. But the memories she treasured were now forever locked in this pathetic ruin. She dried her eyes and continued down Duffus to Barrington. She was standing in the heart of "Jacksonville" in front of the side-by-side wreckage of her Aunt Ada's and Aunt Margaret's homes when the soldier she had noticed earlier came up behind her. His footsteps had been muffled by the snow and Sophye, already spooked by the eerie surroundings, jumped and gave a yelp. The soldier stepped back quickly, lost his footing on the ice beneath the snow and sat down abruptly. Sophye backed away from him. "You frightened me. What do you want?" Ever the nurse, she added, "Did you hurt yourself?" Looking somewhat sheepish, the soldier regained his feet and busied himself brushing the snow from his greatcoat. He picked up his rifle and shook the snow from it too. "Not to worry, Miss, all I hurt was my dignity." Sophye's face softened slightly, "That's a new name for it, I'm a nurse and I have heard that bit of the anatomy called many names but never 'my dignity.' Who on earth are you and why are you here?" The soldier gave Sophye an appraising look and liked what he saw. "By some strange coincidence, my dear, these are the very questions I'm supposed to ask you. But, if it will make you feel better I'll go first. My name's George and my buddies and I were supposed to be going overseas when this thing happened. Now they want us on guard in the area to stop looters. Perhaps some general figured we should practice shooting a few people before we get to the front."

164

Sophye snorted indignantly. "So, do I look like a looter?" George smiled and arched his eyebrow. "Ah, but there's the rub. Even looters don't look like looters these days. That's why only the clever fellas, like me, get put on this patrol. The less someone looks like a looter the more likely she is to be one. We've been warned to be especially careful of pretty girls who dress up like nurses; they're the most dangerous of all. Now before I shoot you, would you be so kind as to tell me your name and what you are doing here?"

Sophye was not in a jovial mood. "My name is Sophye Jackson. I'm here looking for my family, they all lived in this part of the city. Those two houses there belonged to two of my aunts." My mother and father and my brothers and sister lived further up Duffus, and just around the corner on Roome Street is where my grandmother and two of my uncles lived."

At that moment there was a sharp crack, and the leaning wreckage of a house on the other side of the street shifted and fell into the basement, creating a shower of sparks. Sophye gave a cry of fear, "Oh my God, what was that?" The soldier put his hand on her arm. "It's okay, the fire in the coal bin in the basement just burnt through some of the beams holding up the wreckage and the whole thing caved in. It's happening all the time, that's why they don't want anyone going through the ruins until all the fires are out. Anyone still alive was rescued long ago and taken to the hospital. The bodies on the streets were taken to the morgues. If there are any bodies still in the houses, they'll just have to wait until it's safe to dig for them. It doesn't make much sense to get yourself killed trying to rescue a corpse."

Sophye shuddered and moved away from George, so that his hand dropped from her arm. Her tears started once again and he said softly, "I'm so very sorry you are faced with such trouble. Please try to hang on to hope. Many were only injured and are safe and sound in a hospital. It may not be as bad as it looks." Sophye turned away, "Thank you for your concern. I can't help here. I'll go back to Camp Hill at least I can make things better for some."

George was reluctant to see her leave, "Don't try to go back up Duffus, it's a sheet of ice under that snow and you could break your ankle. Go down Barrington to North Street and then up North." He tried to get her to smile. "You know, I'm from Cape Breton and the only hills I ever saw this steep are in the Highlands. Cape Bretoners would be far too smart to put hills like this right in the middle of a city."

His effort was wasted. Sophye moved south on Barrington toward the shell of the North Street Station. When she reached the wreckage of Hillis Foundry she turned and saw George still watching her. She returned his wave and continued on her way. She would only visit Richmond one more time.

Dartmouth faced many of the same problems as Halifax but on a much smaller scale. Fifty of the citizens were dead and hundreds had been injured but the medical facilities had been quickly organized. There were also many homeless, but not on the scale that now plagued the other side of the harbour. Nevertheless, even the loss of one precious life is a shattering blow to those who mourn that loss. The one single factor that mitigated Dartmouth's death toll was distance from the epicentre. The downtown area, the most heavily populated section of the town, was approximately the same distance from the Mont Blanc *as the South End of Halifax. At this point the force had lost all but a small fraction of its death-dealing strength.*

CHAPTER
16

THEY MET AT the morgue. Ada was examining bodies that had been delivered earlier that day, still looking for family members; Hugh Mills was helping to carry bodies from a truck to the basement. When he saw Ada he walked over and touched her arm, "Mrs. Moore, I don't know whether you know it or not, but your sister, Mrs. Hinch, is alive." Ada gave a startled cry, "Where? Where is she? We thought she had to be dead—her house is all smashed and there is no sign of her husband or kids. Where did they take her?" Despite many interruptions, Hugh managed to tell Ada of the rescue and the part played by the American sailors. "…So they took her to the *Old Colony* hospital ship. Her hip was badly hurt and might be broken, and her face was hit too, but last I heard she was going to be just fine. But they say the ship is going to transfer all their patients to other hospitals sometime this week because they have to go back on duty. You might want to check it out soon or it might get hard to find her again."

"Bless you, Hugh, this is the best news I've had since I don't know when and I need all the good news I can get; looking at these bodies tears my heart out and I've cried myself dry. I don't think I have a single tear left in me. Bless you again. Finding one alive is the best thing in the world, bless you again." Ada turned away and walked over to the last few bodies she had yet to check—a few of them were friends but none were family.

JAMES JACKSON HAD awakened before dawn. He felt a bit feverish. His forehead, when he touched it with his good hand, was hot. The pain in his left eye had subsided to a dull ache and his left arm, as long as he let it lay still, was not causing the pain he had lived with for the last four days. It was still painful to try a deep breath so he breathed shallowly to accommodate his mending ribs. But his mind had lost none of its sharpness. Sophye would be coming in soon and he was sure she would have good news about Margaret and the others. He had hated to ask the girl to do the job he should be doing, but there was no other choice.

The thought of Sophye brought a smile. She was really a great girl, a daughter any man could be proud of. When she had first talked of going to Massachusetts to take her nurse's training, both he and Margaret had been opposed. After all, there were places here in Halifax that had excellent training facilities, but the girl was adamant and they had eventually caved in. He grinned wryly. Almost everyone caved in to Sophye, but she managed it so nicely you wound up thinking that whatever it was she wanted had been your idea in the first place. She'd inherited her determination and no-nonsense approach from her Aunt Ada, but where Ada's rough manner backed people into a corner and triggered resistance, Sophye's firm but gentle approach almost always elicited full cooperation. She'd learned early that you catch more flies with honey than with vinegar.

And the girl was clever as well as pretty. She had passed the nursing course with flying colours and, as far as they could tell, she was doing well at that hospital in New York. Nursing was the ideal vocation for Sophye. Even as a little girl she never went to pieces in an emergency; she was never squeamish about blood or injuries, even her own. The cuts and bruises that are the normal part of childhood rarely reduced her to tears.

James chuckled, as he remembered the way she stood up to adversity the time they had all been at the beach one summer long ago. There were huge breakers rolling in and streaming up on the warm sand. Sophye was only about four and she was busy using a little shovel to fill a pail with sand. The pail of damp sand was then being dumped to build a castle. Unnoticed by the little girl, the tide was coming in; each wave was reaching higher than the one before. Suddenly a rogue wave came charging up the beach and not only flattened the castle but rolled Sophye over and over and dumped her on the sand. She never made a sound. Other girls her age would have gone running to their parents for comfort—not Sophye. The only indication she was upset was the lower lip thrust out in a pout. Without a word, she turned and marched determinedly across the beach to a pile of stones, picked the largest one she could lift and went to the water's edge and waited. When the next wave crested she heaved the rock at the breaker with all her might. He knew then she would be a fighter.

She certainly did not get this from her mother. Margaret was the gentlest of ladies and she was almost obsessed with the need to never hurt anyone's feelings. He tried to remember how the blast had hit them. They had been standing side by side, both facing the burning ship. Margaret had just said something that expressed concern for the men on board the *Mont Blanc* and he had half turned to answer when Minnie had called from the upstairs window. After that it was foggy. He had been hit on the left side with the most horrible blow he had ever received; he now knew that if it had only been the smallest fraction harder or if he had been facing fully into the blast, he would not have lived. Margaret would have been hit full broadside. He dared not dwell on that thought.

The nurse had just come into the room and taken his temperature. She read the thermometer with a frown. "You're running a bit of a fever this morning. I don't like to give the doctors more than they're already doing, but I'll check it again in an hour. If it is still up they better have a look." James was more interested in looks than fever, Sophye would be here soon and he wanted to look his best. "Would it be possible for me to have a shave?" The nurse frowned, "Of course it would be possible, but we are not going to do it. All of us nurses have bets on. With one eye covered by a patch and now the beard, you're starting to look like a pirate. Some are betting you're going to be the spitting image of Long John Silver, but I have my money on Captain Kidd. If we shave you it's going to throw the bets off. How about I get you some breakfast instead?"

After she left, James returned to the task of trying to remember exactly what had happened. It was a more painful task than the physical hurts he had suffered. He had been lying on the street amidst a pile of wreckage. Some of the debris was from his own home, but no, that couldn't be, it should have been blown away from him—not toward him. That didn't make sense. And Minnie had been blown out of the upstairs window when she should have been blown deeper into the house. But he was certain that she'd been sitting on a pile of boards about twenty feet closer to the burning ship rather than away from it. It was as if the house had exploded from inside and that didn't make sense. Minnie's arm was at an impossible angle, a shaft of metal pipe was stuck in her leg and her nightdress had been ripped off. He remembered his friend, Jim Ryan, putting a coat over Minnie and then coming over to him. But after that it was all a blank until he woke up in the hospital.

The nurse returned with his breakfast and placed it on the beside table. He did not feel like eating. He returned to his task. It would be impossible for a man to have two daughters more different than Sophye and Minnie. Sophye, even when she was young, always seemed to have a goal and moved relentlessly toward it; Minnie seemed to be always drifting as if observing life was enough for her, she asked little and seemed content with the simple forms of beauty. She loved music. She would spend hours playing the piano in the living room and she played it very well. Additional hours were spent playing her favourite records on the victrola.

James was beginning to tire. He ate a few spoonfuls of the breakfast and lay back on the bed, it just hurt too much to move around. He was finding it difficult to breathe, even shallow breaths hurt his chest and he was wheezing painfully. It was awfully warm in the room; sweat was running down his face and he wiped it away with his good hand. He was about to call for the nurse when she walked into the room. Again his temperature was taken and this time she did not hesitate but left to find the doctor. Her patient, James Jackson, was in the beginning phase of septic pneumonia. Some, who had survived the explosion, would die from the dread disease, James would not—a cruel and ironic fate had other plans for him.

It was not yet officially winter, that would not be until three days before Christmas, but reconstruction plans were already underway. While city officials were still concerned with the welfare of the victims, and the Americans were still deciding the type and volume of relief supplies needed, each group had the immediate urgencies sufficiently under control to allot some time to planning. The entire Richmond area and much of the North End would have to be rebuilt. It would have to be accomplished in two stages. First, of the greatest urgency, was temporary housing for the homeless; this need was only slightly cut back by the hundreds who emigrated from the city to live with relatives or friends outside the stricken city. Secondly, there was the necessity of planning proper, permanent housing for the future. Led by the Americans these plans were underway. The actual construction would have to wait for the expiration of a long, bitter winter, but when spring came the plans would be in place.

HARRIET BUNGAY SQUIRMED restlessly in her hospital bed. She simply refused to believe what her son was saying. She interrupted Charles before he could finish his sentence, "Gladys can't be dead, she wasn't more than fifty feet away from me, and I survived. No, someone found her after I was carried away and now they are looking after her. Didn't anyone answer the ad you put in the paper?" Charles sighed; if someone had answered the ad it would have been the first thing he told her. "No, Mum there was no reply." There was a long silence as Harriet digested the implications of his answer. "Well we'll just have to put the ad in the paper every day until we find her. Whoever has her must have missed it, it was only in one time. There's some money in my purse to pay for the ads. It was on the hall table, did you find it?" Charles sighed again. "Mum, there isn't any purse, there isn't any hall table, there isn't even any hall. The house was flattened and burned, there isn't anything." Harriet took a drink of water from the glass by her bed then held the glass against her brow. "Do you have any money to pay for the ad then?" The young man was becoming frustrated at the foiled attempts to get through her unshakable belief that Gladys was still alive. "The paper isn't charging for that kind of ad, they're free, it's a courtesy thing. I'll go down and see them again and ask them to put it in the paper a few more times, but don't get your hopes up. I'm still trying to find the others and I'm not having any luck there either."

Unknown to either of them at that moment, the bodies of Harriet's husband, Edward, and her son, Howard, had been found and were now resting in the Chebucto Road Morgue. Her other son, Edward Jr., was on board the *Old Colony* hospital ship, dying from pneumonia. Gladys was missing. Charles and his mother had yet to know the full extent of the tragedy.

The body of Gladys Bungay would never be found. If it had been in the Richmond area it almost certainly would have been during the clearing away of debris and the subsequent rebuilding in the following spring. Thousands of people had combed through the shattered homes and hardly an inch had not been searched. The only logical assumption is that her body was carried down to the Narrows in the wall of water that had flooded through North Albert Street. Many of the bodies, committed to a watery grave, never were recovered. And, herein lies the problem. Without a corpse it is difficult to accept the finality of death. There is room for hope, regardless of how unreasonable the hope may be. The process of healing is delayed, acceptance cannot be reached, uncertainty stands in the way of the normal process of grief followed by recovery.

Harriet Bungay was only one of many that used the process of denial to avoid thinking the unthinkable—to postpone the final acceptance of fact. In her particular case the denial was augmented by a modicum of guilt. She was the one who sent the little girl to the store and her death. The logic that no matter where Gladys had been in Richmond would have had the same result she did not see as a mitigating factor. Minnie McGrath also harboured denial that Clifford was dead. Only with the discovery of the child's body could she surrender herself to grief and begin the process of healing. Many people used the crutch of denial. Until her death, many years later, Harriet Bungay would sometimes sit quietly and question the world at large, "I wonder where my baby girl is tonight." To Harriet, Gladys would be forever young.

ADA WAS WRONG; she had plenty of tears left and she shed many of them in the first few minutes after she was reunited with her sister. But now they were tears of joy. Ada had spoken to the navy doctor before being shown to the room and had listened carefully to the description of her sister's injuries. "She received the blow on her right side—the side facing the exploding ship—and she has a severe haematoma on her right buttock and hip. It is one of the worst and largest I've ever seen. The blow must have been like getting hit with a sledgehammer. I think if it had been even a little bit harder, it might have shattered the bones. She's recovering nicely and we're pleased with the progress, but these things take about three or four weeks to clear and she must be kept very quiet. Please don't tell her anything that might cause her stress."

Now the two sisters were side by side quietly holding hands; the physical contact assured each the other was indeed alive. Ada had carefully evaded answering Mary Jean's direct questions about relatives and friends. However, her sister was extremely calm, making polite inquiries as if she was only an interested bystander. She became somewhat agitated only when Ada suggested that Joe and the children might possibly have survived. "Ada, Joe and the children are dead; all of them are dead. We must all accept that and be thankful that they are together again with the Lord." She said it with an air of calm finality. Ada was forever at a loss when confronted with unquestioning faith and wisely decided to change the subject.

"Dude, I arranged an ambulance for you. This ship has to go back to sea and all the patients still here are being transferred to other hos-pitals. I'm taking you to a hospital they set up in St. Mary's College. They call it the Massachusetts Relief Hospital. Seems all the names in the city are being changed to honour the Americans. To tell you the truth, I don't know where we'd be without them. They're everywhere, doing everything. I think from now on we should take the fourth of July as a national holiday."

Mary Jean was getting tired. She closed her eyes for a minute, "I won't argue with that, I've been treated wonderfully well since Hughie found me and the two American sailors brought me here. They both come to see me at least a couple of times a day and bring me little treats. They truly are fine young men. Everyone has been so good to me— why, even Father Gray came yesterday to hear my confession and give me communion."

Ada's first reaction was one of frustration. Confession? How in hell could Dude commit any sins lying in bed unable to even stand up? But she didn't voice the thought, saying instead, "I'm in a hassle with the Relief people. I want a house big enough for all of us and it's like hitting your head on a bloody brick wall, those people are so pig-headed. But I'm going to keep at it. Dorothy's alive. I haven't found her yet, but she was in school and some kids told me she made it. I found some of mine as well, and according to one of the Duggans, Hilda and two of the other Baker kids are in the hospital; Stanley at the Victoria General and Willie at the one in Truro. They haven't found little Leverette yet. As soon as I get a house I'm going to get us all together again, I promise." Her words fell on deaf ears; Mary Jean had fallen asleep. Ada continued to hold her hand, her mind racing as always. At least there was James and Dude and herself; they could come back from this, it was only a matter of time. But she would miss Emma; she would miss Margaret; she would miss her four brothers, the tears started again. This time they were not tears of joy.

On December 15th Edward Bungay Jr. died on board the Old Colony, *even as Mary Jean and Ada were in the midst of their tearful reunion. His injuries were not serious enough to cause his death; he died from pneumonia. Arrangements were made for the body to be transferred to the Chebucto Road Morgue. There, the body was reunited with those of his father and his older brother, Howard. All three awaited funeral arrangements.*

"FOR HEAVEN'S SAKE, woman, stop fussin' around. You're like a mother hen with a new chick." Sophye continued to tuck the blankets around her father and snapped back at him. "For a very sick man, still in the grips of pneumonia and hovering near death, you do hand out a lot of guff. Just remember, I'm your only nurse now, and I certainly don't intend to put up with the kind of sauce you were handing out to those other poor souls who were trying to take care of you at the hospital." With false gruffness James muttered, "With the likes of you looking after me I would probably be better off joining the army and recuperating in safety in the front lines." The taxi driver's eyes flickered uneasily between the injured man and the nurse, before deciding the young woman was in charge. "Where do you want to go ma'am?" Sophye finished tucking her father in and jumped into the front seat. "We are going to a house on Morris street. I don't know the number but I'll tell you when we are there." James caught the driver's eye, "But first, my son, I want you to drive up to Richmond so we can have a little look-see around." Sophye cut in firmly. "Driver, just go straight to Morris Street, please. Don't pay any attention to the rantings of this poor old soul. He's just been released from hospital and is under my loving care. He has a tendency to hallucinate—and I might also point out that I am the one with the money. This cab is going to Morris Street and nowhere else." The driver pulled sharply away from the hospital and wheeled south on Robie Street. The driver appeared eager to complete the trip.

EARLIER THAT MORNING Sophye had asked for and received her release from the Red Cross. She signed her father out of the hospital, to recuperate in the home of a family friend. As they drove along Robie Street she turned to look at her father and shook her head sternly, "You're not out of the woods yet, you know. There's still congestion in your left lung and we can't take any chances. Mrs. McKenna has a nice, bright, sunny room facing south ..." James interrupted, "How did she do that? It's overcast and looks like it is going to snow or rain or something." Sophye sighed, "You know full well what I mean, stop being silly. I saw the room the other night and it is beautiful. You'll be very comfortable there. Jim's going to drop in a couple of times a day to help me, and one of the hospital nurses promised to relieve me now and then so I can get some rest. "Oh, the saints preserve me, I'm going to have three angels of mercy pounding away at my frail old body." Sophye could keep a straight face no longer, with a large grin that gave lie to the words, she said, "If you don't stop acting up, this angel of mercy is going to dump your frail old body out on to the street, now behave yourself man." In mock submission James replied, "Yes, nursie, whatever you say, nursie."

Even with the help of the taxi driver it was difficult getting her father upstairs to his new room. Her brother arrived just as Sophye had put James to bed. His mood had swung from jocular to gloomy and for a few minutes he lay back against the pillows and looked at his son and daughter. "I think we need to talk." Sophye tried to divert him, "Dad, above all, you need to just rest. The doctor said you were as near to death as you could be. Now that you're recovering, the last thing we need is a setback, so you simply cannot exert yourself." Her father snorted with derision. "They always look for the worst. If they were with me on top of a boxcar they wouldn't last two minutes. I'm just a little weak, that's all. I'm going to be fine in a few days, so stop worrying. But, now, I want to talk, there are things we have to figure out." Jim sat on the side of his father's bed, "You should listen to Sophye. Like it or not, she's the nurse. We don't have to talk right now, we can talk tomorrow after you've had a good night's sleep." Sophye popped a thermometer in her father's mouth, "There, that'll keep him quiet for a minute." She turned to her brother, "I don't know how we grew up to be such wonderful children having such a stubborn and cantankerous father." Her words were met with a scowl and an indecipherable mumble.

James's temperature was down from earlier in the day and after informing him of this, Sophye reluctantly said, "Okay, old and wise one, go ahead and speak your piece." James closed his eyes for few minutes. Images and impressions whirled in his brain and he struggled to set them in order. Sophye sat on the opposite side of the bed and took his hand in hers. Finally he opened his eyes.

"Up until this morning I was clinging to the hope that your mother was still alive. Maybe badly hurt, but still alive. I can't kid myself any longer, and I think all three of us have to face the facts. That explosion hit me ten times harder than I've ever been hit in my life. Margaret was right beside me and she must have been blown back into the wreckage." He paused for a long moment, "If it is any consolation to you, I think she probably died instantly—she wouldn't have felt any pain."

There was a long silence. Both of the children had earlier reached the same tragic conclusion. Their mother's body had not been found; no one they asked had seen her after the blast. The only place she could be was in the burning and as yet unsearched wreckage of their home. James coughed a few times, took a deep breath and continued. "If Margaret is gone, so is Clifford." Sophye gave a sharp gasp that ended in a sob. Minnie's boy had been very special to her from the day he was born. She was forever sending toys to him from New York and during her visits home it was hard to tear the two apart; she loved him as she would a son of her own. Her father patted her hand, "It is God's will, girl, there is nothing we can do but accept."

Jim, partly to change the subject from the contemplation of Clifford, said, "I left early that morning, Dad. Annie was still home, did she get out of the house?" James turned to his son, "I'm not sure, she was there when I got home, but I went outside to watch the ship; she may have left for work without me knowing." Jim spoke again, "Ada said no one saw her, and even if she had left she wouldn't have gone far in the few minutes; anywhere close by would be just as bad." The acceptance of the finality of death descended upon them and it was long minutes, each engulfed in their personal grief, before the talk continued.

James led the way. "We have suffered much, but so has everyone we know. In a way we're more fortunate, Minnie is still alive, she's young and will probably remarry. Lew may be okay too. We haven't heard anything to say he isn't. The three of us are alive. It was a horrible blow but we don't have any choice but to live with it." Turning to Jim, he said, "Your wife, Mona, wasn't injured; the two of you have a whole life before you. You'll have children of your own and you've got to keep going, for each other, and for their sake." He was tiring rapidly from the emotional strain but, as always, he tried to lighten the sombre mood. He gave Sophye's hand a playful shake. "And you, girl, will go on to a good life. You'll marry too and produce a whole passell of squalling brats who'll make life miserable for their poor old grandfather." Sophye was quick to contradict his words as well as his light tone. "I don't think so, Dad. I saw what happened to large families here. There is no way I could stand the loss of even one child. I don't have the strength these people have. I'm not going to marry. Even if I do, it'll be long after I can have kids. I knew what I wanted to do with the rest of my life within the first few days of getting here. I found so much satisfaction in helping people who really needed me. I could never be happy again in a regular hospital, draining boils and fixing tummy aches; I could never be happy here, either. I hate this place now. I'm going back to the States to work in military hospitals where the patients are young people who have been injured in that other calamity—war. I'm staying here until you are on your feet and feeling well, then I'm going." No one dared argue with that.

It was one of the longest speeches Sophye had ever made and it clarified the thoughts and feelings that had been in her heart during the past week. She turned to her father, tears still streaming down her face. "We'll cry for all of them many times over the rest of our lives." At that moment the sun broke through the clouds. The room suddenly lived up to her expectations—it was sunny, bright and cheerful.

She walked over to the window and squinted against the brightness of the sun reflecting off the snow, "Isn't it a pity that people can't go from tears to happiness as quickly as the sky can turn from gloomy to bright."

CHAPTER
17

By mid-December there was no longer a deficit of medical personnel.
The scene at the hospitals had changed from almost hopeless, frantic confusion
to the usual hushed, orderly environments. Operations that had been
postponed because of the physical exhaustion of the doctors, were now
performed with routine efficiency and skill. Post-operative care was well
under control. There were still shortages and the most severe of these was the
shortage of men of the cloth.

The leaders of the four Richmond churches had suffered personal losses
along with the thousand or more victims who made up their congregations.
And now they had to pick up the pieces that were left.

In normal times, a clergyman might attend one or two funerals a week;
from the middle of December to the end of January the Richmond clergy
were faced with the task of burying a thousand times that number. Even
with the help of colleagues from around the city, the task was far beyond
their collective capacity. Many victims were never afforded the dignity of a
religious burial. Of great urgency was the need to re-establish a spiritual
presence to comfort the survivors of the disaster. The majority of those who
had suffered the loss of loved ones asked the same questions, over and over
again, "Why?" "Why me?" "Why would God allow the slaughter of
hundreds of innocent children?" They turned to the clergy for answers to the
unanswerable questions.

St. Joseph's Roman Catholic Church had suffered the most severe loss of
life among its parishioners. More than four hundred people had been killed
and hundreds more were injured. Only twenty families in the parish
survived the explosion unscathed. To re-establish a spiritual presence and
maintain a centre for celebrating the Sacraments until new facilities could be
constructed, a private home on Maynard Street (now Fuller Terrace) near
the foot of Ontario Street was pressed into service. The home was owned by
Mr. E. Delaney, who resided there with his daughter, Mrs. Mary (Mame)
Bouchard, and her family. The living and dining rooms were used as the

church and a remarkably beautiful sideboard was used as the altar. Fathers McManus, Buchanan and Gray held Mass and Communion there within days of the blast and continued to do so for many months until larger facilities were found. Months after the explosion, this sideboard, now truly blessed, found permanent residence at Admiralty House Navy Museum, only a few hundred feet from where it had served the parishioners of St. Joseph's Church in their time of great need.

Within a few days of the destruction of the Kaye Street Methodist Church and the Grove Presbyterian Church, the ministers, the Rev. Crowdis and the Rev. Swetnam, decided to co-operate in erecting a temporary church building. The Kaye Street Church had lost at least 107 parishioners and the Grove Church had lost 170, and it was felt that by combining the two congregations, each would be served better. Leading members of the Halifax and Dartmouth Methodist and Presbyterian congregations gave generous financial aid toward the construction of a temporary building. This building, nicknamed the Tar Paper Church because of its covering, was located on the south west corner of Young and Gottingen Streets. It was finished enough to hold services by mid-March of 1918, three and a half months after the explosion. Construction also started on the permanent church erected on the site of former Kaye Street Church. During the period immediately following the explosion, it would be known as the Kaye-Grove Church but the warmth of spirit that developed between both congregations led to it being eventually called the United Memorial Church.

Seven out of every eight members of the congregation of St. Mark's Anglican Church were either killed or injured. At least two hundred died. The church and all its contents were totally destroyed.

None of the four parishes had the time or the inclination to mourn their material losses; there was simply too much need for their spiritual guidance and practical service in the lives of their parishioners.

THE FARMS THEY passed, just before they reached Enfield, had the barren look of winter. It was a gloomy, grey day just nine days before Christmas. Even the beauty of fresh, clean snow forming undulating waves of white across the fields, failed to lighten the mood. The only sound was the rhythmic clickety-clack of the wheels, punctuated by an occasional mournful wail of the train's warning whistle for the level crossings. A black pall of engine smoke streamed past the window, momentarily obscuring her view.

Then it passed and Minnie suddenly noticed the beauty of the tranquil farmlands they were passing through. It seemed incongruous next to the terrible things Aunt Ada had been saying.

Ada had arrived in Truro on the early train, quickly found her and told her to get her things together for the trip back to Halifax. What things? Minnie had arrived at the hospital in Truro without a stitch of clothes other than the overcoat given to her by her neighbour. When she left the hospital she had been given some underwear, stockings, a black dress and a pair of shoes by the Red Cross people. She was wearing almost every material possession she had. A spare set of underwear and an extra pair of stockings were in the paper bag on her lap; Jim Ryan's overcoat was folded on the seat beside Ada. The bearer bonds were now in Ada's purse, to be returned to Jim Ryan, less the sixty dollars they had spent.

Minnie had listened to Ada for almost an hour, ever since the train had left Truro, but she only believed a bit of what she heard. She accepted that Aunt Mary Jean was alive and was now in the St. Mary's College Hospital and Uncle John's daughter, Dorothy, had been found injured but alive at St. Joseph's School. She believed Ada when other members of the family and friends she knew were named as being safe. Her father was hurt but would be okay and that her brother, Jim, was also safe and helping Sophye, who had somehow managed to reach Halifax on the Red Cross train from New York. But when Ada tried to tell her that her son, mother, sister and dozens of other family members had been killed, she was met with her niece's angry denial. Minnie was particularly vehement in her disbelief that anything could have happened to her son. "That's a terrible thing to say, Aunt Ada, and it's just an outright lie. You don't know that for sure, you're just guessing. Clifford will be alright, you'll see. Maybe he's hurt a little, but he'll be okay. Somebody must have found him after I left for Truro and taken him home with them. They'll be treating him real good. He can't tell them who he is because he's too young. All he can say is 'Tippy Daw' and that won't tell them much. But I'll find him. I'll go everywhere and ask everybody; somebody is looking after him and I'll find him, and I'll find him before Christmas, just you wait and see."

Ada fell silent with frustration in the face of such blind faith and ignorant hope. She had spent countless hours viewing the dead at the Chebucto Road Morgue and the city's funeral homes. She had been to every hospital, dressing station and orphanage a dozen times; she had asked hundreds of people the same questions again and again. Worst of all, she had stood before the burning homes of her family and friends, many times those first few days, listening to the finality of the crackling flames, smelling the sickening odour of burning flesh. She had little reason for optimism that any of the people in Richmond, who had not been found by now, were still alive. They remained silent until they reached Rockingham.

Ada reached over and took a bag of clothing she had prepared for Minnie and placed it beside her. "Here is an extra dress and some stockings, you take them." Minnie was still glowering. "We will be going to the South End Station, North Street Station was smashed. Your father is on Morris Street at the McKenna's house, Sophye is looking after him and we will walk there from the station. You may be staying there tonight, if they have room. If not you can come with me. I have a room at the Acadian Hotel while they get a rooming house on Barrington Street fixed up for me to run. The people there now will move out the end of the month and then it will take a couple of weeks to finish the repairs before I can have it. After it's ready you'll all be moving in with me for awhile. Now listen up, Minnie, and listen real good. Your father wasn't only hurt real bad, but he also caught pneumonia. I don't want you getting him excited. Don't tell him anything that I have told you about the rest of the family. If he asks you any questions tell him you just got back from the hospital in Truro and you don't know anything yet, okay?"

Minnie did not speak, but nodded her head impatiently. Ada didn't have to worry about it; there was no way she was going to tell her father a pack of lies like that. Both were silent as the train slowly moved through the railway cuts toward the South End Station. Minnie was lost in a fantasy where Clifford rushed to her arms and squealed with delight when she picked him up and hugged him close. And for a few minutes, Ada let go of the burden of trying to care for the rest of the family and descended into the morass of her own personal grief.

The home at sixty-six Veith Street had been within eight hundred feet of the Mont Blanc when the ship exploded. Partial shielding by the Hillis Iron Foundry on the other side of the street did little to prevent total destruction; in fact, the massive cement blocks from the factory were blown on top of the wreckage making rescue efforts both hazardous and difficult. The fires that started in the homes in the Richmond area were fuelled by the combustible wooden construction of the buildings and added to by the winter supply of firewood, coal and coke stored in every cellar. For those who had survived the blast but were trapped in the wreckage, fire became the agent of death; the wreckage of the homes, the crematorium.

The funeral pyre burned for more than a week. Another week would pass before the wreckage was cool enough, and there would be manpower enough to search. The majority of the men available had concentrated on searching any wreckage that might still entrap live survivors; the hunt for the dead was relegated to a lower priority.

FOURTEEN DAYS AFTER the explosion, a work crew assembled at the wreckage of sixty-six Veith Street early in the morning. The street itself was now clear of debris; their present task today was to remove the charred rubble and recover any bodies remaining inside. This same crew had already cleared the houses next door: the Frizzel family at number sixty-four and the Arnolds at number fifty-six. Six charred bodies had been found—three for each family—and sent to the morgue.

Both sixty-four and sixty-six Veith Street presented a particular dilemma to the crew. In both cases the wreckage of the houses themselves was pinned by massive pieces of the Hillis Iron Foundry. The crew was once again equipped with block and tackle, which had worked well on the wreckage at number sixty-four, and a team of horses was available should they need it. For the moment they simply stared at the problem and planned their attack.

There were eight of them, led by a man they called Charlie. They were not an exceptional lot, none were well educated, there were no college degrees among them. Four, including Charlie, worked on the waterfront, two were employed as freight-handlers with the railway and the other two were store clerks. They had all volunteered for this job from a sense of duty and responsibility. They worked hard and conscientiously, without bitterness at a job that can only be described as horrendous. All were family men whose own had been spared. By now, their fifth day at the job, they had acquired a certain immunity to shock; they had witnessed some terrible sights.

Charlie flipped his cigarette butt away and turned to his men. "This is going to be tougher than the one next door. That big block will have to be lifted on this end or it'll jam on the foundation. If we can pry it up about two feet we can get a sling around it. Eddie, see if you can find a couple of timbers that aren't burnt all to hell that we can use for a lever." Eddie wandered away toward some wreckage that had missed the flames. With some stout boards and using the edge of the foundation as a fulcrum, they levered the block high enough to pass a rope under it. "For gawdsake keep your hands out from under that thing," yelled Charlie. "We don't want to give the sawbones more work than they've already got."

Shortly before noon the large blocks had been removed and the larger debris had been tossed aside. It was extremely dirty work; most of what was left of the home had been reduced to charcoal and the men were coated with soot. There was little of the furniture that was identifiable. Only the piano keyboard and a few piano strings remained of the instrument that had provided so many hours of joy for a music-loving family. The burnt shell of a sideboard with shattered dishes and the cracked mirror of the hall stand where Mary Jean had primped, were barely recognizable. In the charred remains, forever lost, were the photo albums, books, records, personal papers and mementoes that had recorded the Hinch family's life. Nothing would ever be recovered. There was no sign of the matching teddy bears, intended for two five-year-old twin girls.

The first two bodies they found were above the basement, pinned in the wreckage. These had to be Clara and Lena Hinch, the two eldest girls who had been sick in bed when the blast occurred. By early afternoon the skulls and bones of eleven people had been recovered. The men, inured as they were to horror, still reeled at the enormity of this one family's loss. With great compassion they marked the skeletal remains and delivered them to the Chebucto Road Morgue. The remains were identified by Joseph's brother, David Hinch, and also by his sister-in-law, Ada Moore. Although the bodies were burned beyond recognition and definite individual identification could not be established, the proof of who they had to be was supplied by their wife and mother, Mary Jean Hinch; she had left one husband and ten children only a minute before the explosion. Eleven skulls were recovered. There was no one else they could be.

At the morgue, the largest remains, those of Joseph Hinch, were placed in one casket. The remains of all ten children were placed in another. On the following afternoon, under an overcast sky, the two caskets were taken to Mount Olivet Cemetery. After a brief and simple ceremony, they were slowly lowered into two adjacent graves in section two, plot P. The date was December 21, 1917. The following day would have marked Joseph Hinch's fifty-first birthday.

Not far from the grave of Joseph Hinch and his ten children another burial took place at Mount Olivet Cemetery on the very same day. Lewis Patrick Jackson, nineteen, was laid to rest in section two, plot S.

THREE DAYS BEFORE Christmas, Jim had come to the Morris Street home to see his father and sister. The atmosphere was more strained than usual and Sophye knew Jim had some bad news. On the pretence of helping her fetch some tea, he followed her from the room and whispered, "Sis, I have some really terrible news and I don't know whether or not to tell Dad. I'll tell you and you can decide; you know better than me how he'll take it." Sophye braced herself. With great reluctance Jim softly said, "On Thursday morning they started to dig through the ruins on Veith Street, they found all that was left of Mary Jean's family. There were eleven bodies but all that was left from the fire were skulls and a few bones. According to Aunt Ada, they put Joe in one casket and what was left of the ten kids in another. They were buried yesterday at Mount Olivet." Sophye gasped and clutched helplessly at the air. Jim put his arms around her tightly and awkwardly patted her back as he had done when she was small.

Still holding her, he said, "There is no way out of this, you have to hear the rest. They also found Aunt Margaret and her kids; except for Gordon they're all gone, Sis, God help us, they're all gone." For a long moment they stayed locked in each other's arms, their tears running together. Sophye moved back a step. "Was there any sign of Mum or Clifford?" Jim reached out and placed his hand on her arm. "No, not yet, they're still digging further down Duffus and won't reach our place for a few days probably. But I think you better prepare yourself for the worst. If they were alive someone would have seen them or found them by now."

Sophye wiped fiercely at her eyes, "This is so terrible. I just can't believe it. My God, we have to compose ourselves. We can't let Dad know the truth now. He is recovering okay physically, his eye is healing, he'll never have sight in it again, but he could take the eye patch off anytime now. He'll probably never have full use of his hand and arm again either. His ribs are mending, but catching pneumonia hasn't helped. He is recovering but much slower than I would like to see. It's his mental condition I'm worried about. He's given up hope. Younger people seem to snap out of it much better than people his age. For now there's no way we can let him know. I'm going to wash my face and then we go back in and talk to him. He should be going to sleep soon any-how—he sleeps a lot now." Jim wiped his own face with his handker-chief. "Okay Sis, you go wash, I'll wait here till you come back. I can't go in there alone right now. You know, after this is all over I'm running as far away from Halifax as I can get, maybe California. Go on now, wash your face."

Sophye splashed cold water on her face then held a damp flannel to her eyes. She could not let her father see that she had been crying. Jim was right, it would be best to leave and start somewhere fresh, some-where away from the memories of this place. Before coming back she had toyed with the idea of coming home and working in the Victoria General; she missed her family a lot. But she would never entertain that thought again. There was very little family left. She'd have to stay until her father was fully recovered and had regained some of his spirit, however long it might take. Surely he'd be able to go back to work when he got his strength back. He'd worked for the railroad for over twenty-five years, there must be something he could do for them other than as a brakeman. She would have to get Jim on her side and convince their father that life was not over yet.

Her professional side was intrigued by the ways in which people reacted to trauma. The greatest surprise was the people in the hospital; they were often cheerful, even jocular about their injuries. It never ceased to amaze her how each handled their problems in their own way. Some who never had been very religious suddenly embraced the comfort of the church; others who had been devout turned their back on God. There didn't seem to be any hard and fast rules. According to Vince McDonald, Minnie spoke of her mother and Clifford as if they would walk into the room at any minute; for her the explosion had never happened. Ada was barging around trying to bring everything back together as it had been before the blast. She took her wrath out on the, as yet unknown, "stupid bloody idiot that caused this." Whoever it was, hanging was too good, shooting was too good and she devised more painful methods of retaliation. Aunt Mary Jean had cried inconsolably for three days; she had known the fate of Joe and the kids long before it was confirmed. On the fourth day a calmness had descended over her spirit that was almost spooky. She had accepted the will of God. Vince was still ranting against what had happened to his world; she sensed it would be a long time before he recovered from his anger.

Sophye's reverie was interrupted by a timid tap on the bathroom door, "Sis, it's me, are you okay?" She took a deep breath and opened the door, "I guess I'm about as okay as I'm going to be. Let's go back in and try to cheer Dad up a little, if he asks about anyone just tell him they may be in a hospital out of town, maybe Truro or New Glasgow or Cape Breton—and then get him off the subject." The brother and sister walked back into their father's room, with strained smiles, trying to display a confidence neither of them felt.

The ruins of Richmond had cooled and enough manpower was now available to search for bodies. They were found in great abundance. The city's normal facilities for the preparation of the bodies had been swamped by the monstrous magnitude of the disaster. At the same time burials were taking place in private cemetery lots by relatives of those killed, about two hundred bodies of unidentified dead were being buried in a common grave in an area of Bayers

Road known as Potter's Field. Many of them had been very close to the epicentre and were obliterated beyond the possibility of identification. Faces had been destroyed. Clothing had been stripped from the bodies, leaving no papers or personal items to assist identification. In total over three hundred victims of the explosion were buried without positive verification. They will be forever nameless.

WITH HER FREE hand Sophye turned the collar of her coat up higher around her neck against the biting wind; under the other arm she carried a gaily wrapped package. Still dressed in a nurse's uniform, she thought longingly of the warm clothing she had left behind in New York. If she hadn't packed so many Christmas presents, most of which were now not needed, maybe she would have brought clothing more suitable to the weather. She glanced at the houses on Morris Street as she passed; they were a far cry from the day she had arrived. Most had new glass in the windows, broken boards and trim was replaced but not painted, smoke curled from the chimneys and there was a warm, snug look that indicated life in this area was beginning to approach normal once again. It would be a long time before Richmond reached this stage of recovery.

She had some relief from the wind when she turned the corner to Robie Street, it was only a few blocks to Camp Hill Hospital and the wind was now at her back. This mission she was on this morning should have been pleasant; she was taking the toy train, bought for Clifford, to a young boy she had tended in the first days at the hospital. He was about three, a year older than her nephew, and a very bright little fellow. His parents had been killed in their Richmond home and the boy had his left arm and left leg crushed by falling beams. His left leg had been amputated below the knee and it was still nip and tuck whether his arm would also be removed. The poor little guy deserved something nice, even if it was only a toy for Christmas. For a little while it might help.

With a heavy heart she counted the days since she had arrived in Halifax and found it hard to believe it was barely three weeks. It had been one horrible thing after another, and she doubted she could hear any more without losing her sanity. She had arrived on the eighth and today was two days before Christmas Eve. Some Christmas this would be. She remembered the horror of the first night at Richmond and the shock of seeing so many people she knew in Camp Hill Hospital. But the true devastation of the disaster's effect on her own family was only now sinking in.

Sophye turned into the entrance of the hospital. She walked over to the main desk and left the Christmas present with one of the nurses. She wanted to visit some of the Richmond people she knew and she didn't want to disappoint them by carrying a present that was not for them. She went first to see William Edmonds and found him sleeping soundly. For a few minutes she sat by the side of his bed. The bricks that had been packed around him were gone now and he certainly looked far better than he had when she was tending him. She looked out the window for a moment or two and then decided to leave without awakening him. As she turned to go, a nurse she didn't know came in. "Hi, you a relative?" Sophye replied, "No, just a friend. We live on the same street, or at least we used to. I also looked after him when I first arrived here." The nurse said, "He was thought to be dead, I heard. They brought him here straight from the morgue. He'll have some story to tell his children." Sophye smiled. "He was in real bad shape. He lost an awful lot of blood and for days we had to keep him packed in warm bricks to keep his body heat up. Believe me, it was nip and tuck to keep him alive." The nurse looked down on William for a moment, "They operated on that leg two days ago and trimmed the bone so he will be able to wear an artificial leg. He's coming along just fine, no infection or anything; he should live to tell the story to his grand-children even." Sophye chatted with the girl for a few more minutes and then left the room.

The hospital was different somehow. Then it dawned on her, the overwhelming sense of hopelessness was gone. There was still a feeling of urgency but it was controlled. The frantic, incoherent helplessness had been replaced by competence. There were far more doctors than there had been in those first few days and they walked with confidence in their ability to handle any medical need. When they talked with each other she recognized many had an American accent; many of these dedicated men were from the United States and Sophye felt a thrill of pride for her adopted country. The trainloads of medical equipment and personnel had made the difference. Why, just the other day, some-one had told her that one of the first trains from New York had enough medical supplies to fully equip a five hundred bed hospital! Imagine that! These doctors and nurses would be forever enshrined as saints to the people of Halifax. With a feeling of pride Sophye straightened up and stood a little taller, after all—she was one of them.

She glanced at her watch and realized she was running out of time. She couldn't leave her father for too much longer. Mrs. McKenna was looking in on him from time to time, but she wasn't a nurse. Sophye hurried back to the main desk, retrieved her parcel and made her way to the next floor.

The boy was awake. For a moment, when Sophye entered the room, a glimpse of recognition replaced the haunted look in his eyes. This look, as of a wounded animal, was common among the young children; they felt they were being punished and could not think of what horrible thing they had done to deserve this. Sophye leaned over the bed and lightly touched the side of his face, "Well, hello there. Are you my Johnny?" He nodded his head almost imperceptibly and for a brief instant he seemed about to smile.

The boy had been brought in the morning of the explosion, a few days before Sophye had arrived from New York. He had been heard crying in the wreckage of a house. When his rescuers released him from the debris he was brought straight to the hospital and his left leg was amputated just below the knee. When Sophye first saw him he was recovering after the surgery. His left arm was also swathed in bandages and his doctor told her it was highly likely it too would have to be amputated. Sophye had attended to him during the following week and the two had formed a rapport. Late at night, when the pain kept him awake, she would sit at his side for as long as she could, bathing his forehead and singing very softly:

"When Johnny comes marching home again,
Hurray, hurrah,
When Johnny comes marching home again,
Hurrah, hurrah,
We'll all be glad when
Johnny comes marching home."

He was still unidentified; either he didn't remember his own name or he was too traumatized to tell it to anyone. So for the time being he was Sophye's "Johnny." His already wide eyes grew huge as she placed the brightly coloured package on his bed. "This is a special Christmas present to you from a little boy named Clifford. The reason they call it special is because you can open it right now, you don't have to wait for Christmas morning." She smiled at him. "Go ahead, sweetheart, open it."

Slowly he tore the paper from the package and opened the box. The little engine had two freight cars and came with a set of tracks. He gazed at it in wonderment and for the first time in many weeks, he smiled. Sophye moved a small table over by the side of the bed and used enough of the tracks to form a small circle that just fitted the table; then she showed him how to wind the key and placed the engine and cars on the track. The engine ran round and round, sparks flying out of the smoke stack. The little boy gave it his undivided attention. When it needed winding, he held it down with the elbow of his injured arm and turned the key with his right hand. Away it went again and the little fellow hardly noticed when Sophye slipped softly from the room.

She walked along the hallway toward the stairs, but had to stop; her tears were blinding her. "Damn. Why must I always be crying? That poor little guy. I wish I could wave a magic wand and give him back his leg. Why do terrible things like this have to happen? Why is it always the nice ones who get hurt?" She wiped at her eyes with her handkerchief, but the people passing by paid no attention; they had seen many tears in the last few weeks.

By the time she was walking south on Robie street she had composed herself. "Everyone seems to have their own way of dealing with the grief, my way seems to become a bloody crybaby. I'm going to have to stop shedding tears; I have to be strong for Dad's sake. I think he'll have to lean on me for sometime yet."

ELLEN JACKSON HAD been seriously injured when her home collapsed on top of her. She had been placed on the first train to Truro on the afternoon of the explosion. In addition to her injuries, she suffered the trauma of not knowing where her husband and children were. Muriel and Florence had left the house to deliver Edward's lunch pail before going to St. Joseph's. She remembered having Gerald in her arms but he wasn't there when they found her. Charles and the baby had been in the house and were also missing.

On Christmas Eve, she was reunited with Muriel and Gerald. Both had suffered injuries but had been brought to Truro to be with their mother. Despite the horror stories of death and destruction she had heard from people visiting from Halifax, Ellen held firmly to the hope the others would also be found. Several more weeks would pass before her hopes were shattered. Her husband and the other four children were dead.

Muriel had been taken from St. Joseph's School to the Bellevue Military hospital on the morning of the explosion. There she was treated for wounds to her head, arm and leg. By the middle of the month it was assumed she was orphaned and she was moved to the Sacred Heart Convent. She remained there until December 20th, still being treated on an out-patient basis each day at Bellevue.

A picture of her and the story of the school was reprinted in several

American papers, which prompted a flood of letters from people in the United States, wanting to know how she was and if any of her family had survived. Some offered to adopt her.

Her younger brother, three-year-old Gerald, had suffered severe trauma. After the soldier had carried him to Gottingen Street and turned him over to the officer in charge, he was treated for some small cuts and sent to the home of Mrs. Curry on Jacob Street. He and his Prince were lovingly cared for until they located his mother. Gerald was far too young to understand what had happened and the events had left him extremely nervous and easily frightened. He grew more and more delicate, his pupils were dilated, which made him look even more terrified, and he had great difficulty sleeping. Once he was reunited with his mother he never wanted to be out of her sight.

When the authorities received the information that Ellen was alive and recovering from her injuries in the Truro hospital, the two children were sent to be with their mother. All three were taken care of by Professor and Mrs. Lorne DeWolfe at their home on Bible Hill, just outside of Truro. And now they were together again. Shielded from grief by the yet unknown reality that five of their family members were dead, the three survivors rejoiced in their reunion. They were among the very few that year who would find any happiness in the joyous season of Christmas.

LETITIA EDMONDS ALSO experienced at least one glimmer of brightness that same Christmas Eve. Arthur brought her the joyful news that William was alive. At least one of her sons had foiled the monstrous misfortune. The shock of Henry and Arthur Jr. being dead was at least slightly lessened. For a moment they could bask in the glory of victory rather than sink into the despair of defeat.

Throughout the city a few other families would find a modicum of comfort during this season normally associated with happiness. Children who feared they were orphans would find one or both parents. Mothers and fathers would be reunited with children they thought dead. Even in the midst of the most terrible tragedies there are glimpses of gladness.

Christmas day dawned cloudy and bleak, respecting the prevailing mood of the people. The spirit of Christmas was barely alive and it was extremely unwell. Some of the stores, their windows still battened by boards, had strung a few garlands of tinsel and hung a few ornaments in an effort to endorse the season. But the attempt fell far short of success. Most did not even pretend to celebrate. A day associated with the gathering of family and friends and the recollection of past Christmases was impossible to even contemplate. The neighbours next door would not be dropping by for eggnog. The aunts and uncles, the nephews, nieces and cousins would not be coming for dinner. Most would spend the day with sorrow as their only companion.

Richmond was silent now—still a sea of rubble. The fires were out, the burnt and broken bodies were still being extracted from the wreckage. It would be another month before the last were finally laid to rest. Richmond would take years to rebuild. Never again would the community achieve the closeness that was once its strength. The first days after the explosion may have been the most traumatic, but the days of Christmas week were the most sorrowful.

CHAPTER

18

By early January the majority of bodies still being recovered were from the burnt-out ruins of Richmond. The volume of funerals had finally dropped below the prohibitive numbers of the previous month but was still far beyond the norm for a city the size of Halifax. Grave-diggers and embalmers were at last able to keep abreast of the funerals and there was time now for the clergy to afford the explosion's victims the dignity of a proper burial.

NEAR THE END of January four skeletal remains were found at number one Roome Street. They were delivered to the Chebucto Road Morgue in a box. Only one body could be identified. The skull of three-month-old James William Jackson was distinguishable from the others by size. Elizabeth (Halloran) Jackson, aged sixty-seven and the matriarch of the Jackson family, and her two daughters-in-law, Louisa and Evelyn, could not be distinguished one from the other. Ada Moore identified all four bodies by the address on the box.

The last Jacksons were recovered at the end of January. Margaret Jackson, wife of James, their daughter, Annie, aged twenty-two, and their two-year-old grandson, Clifford McGrath, were unearthed in the ruins of eighteen Duffus Street. Once again, all three bodies were burned beyond recognition and only the baby could be identified by its size. They were buried together in section two, plot S at Mount Olivet Cemetery alongside Lewis Jackson, who had been buried three days before Christmas.

From the day after the explosion to the end of January, Ada Moore had borne the torturous burden of identifying the bodies of her family. She was the only one fit to assume the responsibility. It was an overwhelming charge. In addition to five of her own children, she viewed the charred remains of her mother, Elizabeth; her niece, Annie Jackson; her great-nephew, Clifford McGrath; her brother-in-law, Joseph Hinch and the ten Hinch children; her sister, Margaret and her seven children, son-in-law and two grandchildren; her sister, Emma, and one of Emma's children; two of her brothers and their children. The bodies of Ada's two other brothers, Frederick and Edward, would never be recovered, nor would Edward's daughter Florence. The only body she was not called on to view was that of her own husband, Charles Moore, who was identified by their daughter, Mabel.

In the midst of the torment came occasionally a small sparkle of triumph, as when she discovered that five of her children had survived and her sister, Mary Jean, was alive and on board the *Old Colony* hospital ship. Ada also managed to find six-year-old Dorothy Jackson, now the orphaned daughter of John and Louisa Jackson. Dorothy had sustained head injuries that would affect her hearing for the rest of her life, but she had survived. Using her powers of persuasion and perseverance, Ada obtained a large house from the Halifax Relief Commission under whose roof she gathered the remaining members of the Jackson family. During the following months almost all of them would spend at least some time with Ada while they tried to rebuild their lives.

The crisis caused by the Halifax Explosion launched both the city and its citizens on the road to recovery. They did not travel together on the same track. Being inanimate, the city had a major head start. It did not need to mourn the dead, suffer the torment of lost family and friends or allow time to heal broken bodies. Its damage had been confined to smashed buildings, broken bricks and shattered glass; all could be repaired or replaced. For the city, the process of healing began almost instantly, starting with the transportation services and the waterfront.

The gods of war are immune to the suffering of mere mortals. They do not allow time for the grief of the victims. In Europe and other parts of the world, young men continued to die or be hideously maimed. Many of them were Canadians. The gluttonous appetite of death demanded many more of those who had paid the ultimate price in the pursuit of freedom and peace. Their replacements must be sent on troop ships, from the East Coast Canadian Port. The same ravenous hunger of destruction had consumed mountains of materials that must now be replenished. It was imperative, to satisfy the gods of war, that Halifax quickly regain its position as a major wartime port. And it did.

Within weeks the docks, sheds, rail lines and other facilities were repaired and functioning, at least at a satisfactory level, and plans were being drawn for new wharves, equipment and machinery, that would exceed in efficiency those that had been destroyed. The Halifax waterfront would rise again, better than before.

In the first few days of panic and confusion the urgency had been the treatment of the injured. After the cries for outside help had been heard and were answered, the obvious next priority was housing for the homeless. This fell into two categories: temporary and permanent. The first temporary shelters were those buildings still habitable and not needed as medical facilities. Schools, universities, churches, church halls, large buildings were immediately set up as housing. Everything the imagination could conceive as housing was utilized. Boxcars on sidings became home for one, two or even three families. The tent city set up on the Halifax Common had proven sadly inadequate after the toll of twelve dead from freezing during the first night. Even with the tents upgraded to withstand the weather, many were reluctant to occupy them. Even before the final bodies were buried, plans already formulated for emergency housing on the Exhibition Grounds were in motion. This would be hindered by the worst weather in years, but by early spring, temporary housing had been built for over one thousand people, five thousand remained in emergency shelters and the remainder had found accommodation with friends and relatives in the city or elsewhere. And before this temporary construction had even begun, the Americans, who had descended on the ravaged city with such massive aid, had already drawn the plans for permanent housing that would be constructed in the devastated area, to be known as the Hydrostone District.

For the city planners, engineers and architects, it was the ideal redesign project—there was little left of Richmond and the North End to obstruct their vision. The impossibly steep hills of Richmond were remedied by a boulevard, Devonshire Avenue, which dissected the area from Barrington to Gottingen with a subtler gradient, making access over the hill much easier, particularly in the icy winter conditions. Free from the encumbrance of having to plan around existing houses or to expropriate properties, roads were widened to allow for the ever increasing flow of traffic. Areas were set aside as green belts and the entire north end of the city started on a course of improvement that would not have been possible under normal conditions.

Property owners built their new houses according to higher construction standards set by the city; building materials and fixtures had come a long way since the construction of many of the previous homes. The residential areas were not reconstructed as quickly as the commercial and industrial zones. But what was truly amazing was that despite the devastation of their homes and families there, the majority of the residents in the Richmond area showed little interest in building or buying anywhere else.

The immediate surge of reconstructing was largely triggered by the massive help rendered by the people of the United States, in particular the people of Massachusetts. Without their largesse it certainly would have taken much longer to rebuild the shattered parts of the city; there probably would have been little enthusiasm for the enormous task without them leading the way. Their example spurred the people of Halifax and Dartmouth to join in the task of rebuilding.

As soon as two days after the explosion, a pair of ships loaded with relief supplies set sail from Boston for Halifax. On board were ten trucks, an outright gift to the city from the State of Massachusetts, complete with drivers and drums of gasoline. In addition to the trucks there was food, 510 cases of second-hand clothing, 1,045 cases of boots and shoes and additional medicines and medical supplies. Something else had been added. There were 837 cases of glass, putty and glazier tools, drums of cement, 2,083 packages of beaver board and 51 kegs of nails. Without being asked, the Americans had foreseen the urgent need for reconstruction.

Skilled salvagers arrived to help clear the wreckage and recover the remains of the victims. Twenty-five glaziers arrived from Boston to begin replacing the city's windows, almost every one of which had been smashed.

Each year in Nova Scotia, a committee searches the province for a very special Christmas tree. Generally it is about fifty feet tall and perfectly proportioned; it must be the best tree in the province. In late November the tree is cut, wrapped and shipped to Boston, where it is decorated with thousands of lights and erected as a reminder of Nova Scotians' gratitude for the unstinting aid showered upon them by their generous neighbours to the South.

AS JAMES JACKSON gradually recovered, Sophye began thinking of returning to New York and the life she had put on hold. But before she left she knew she must visit Richmond one last time and lay her ghosts to rest. It was a fine, bright afternoon in mid-March, more than three months after the explosion. Sophye stood on Duffus Street near where her family home had been. There was hardly a ripple on the waters of the Narrows and the surface of Bedford Basin was only disturbed by the wake of a small motor launch. A light, gentle breeze from the South ruffled her hair and the warmth of the sun bespoke the promise of an early spring. The silence was broken occasionally by the pounding of nails or the rasping of a saw on wood; reconstruction had already begun on some of the foundations. The charred wreckage had largely been carted away and while a ghoulish atmosphere no longer pervaded the neighbourhood, its barrenness struck Sophye with a chill.

In early February, soon after the bodies of her mother, her sister Annie and little Clifford had been recovered and buried, there had been an impromptu gathering at Ada's home on Barrington Street. The mood was sombre and the void caused by absent spouses, children and siblings was painfully evident. For much of the evening, Ada tried to convince Sophye that she had a responsibility to stay in Halifax, to remain with what was left of the family. Sophye turned a deaf ear; her mind had already been set. Her experience at Camp Hill Hospital had transformed her feeling towards nursing. She'd found tremendous satisfaction in treating the victims of the catastrophe. To bring relief from suffering to the innocent victims had been the most rewarding experience of her life. It was far more intense than working in a regular hospital. Her plans were made, and they were inflexible.

Her resolve was strengthened by the few words she had with Mary Jean near the end of the evening, "Child, you must follow your own heart. You're so young and have so much still ahead of you. Anything you want can be yours if you only work for it. We will recover and find our own way here; you've no need to feel responsible for us. You're a good girl. No matter where you go or what you do, God will bless you and guide you. If you stay here you will probably marry and have children. That was all I ever wanted out of life, but I think you would be happier using your great blessings to help hundreds of people, much as you've been doing since you came back here. You are alive and free. Don't pay any attention to Ada or anyone else, but go where you must go, do what you must do and may God bless you."

Sophye turned up the collar of her coat but the chill persisted. She took a final look at Bedford Basin, the wake of the motor launch had subsided and now the surface of the water was like a mirror, reflecting the blue sky. Mary Jean's words came back to her as she took a final look at the bare foundation of her home, where her mother, Annie and Clifford had died. A few tears rolled down her cheeks, but she did not bother to brush them away, "These are the last tears I shall shed for Richmond. I will let them flow and then I will get on with my life." Slowly she turned and walked up the hill toward Gottingen Street, letting the gentle breeze dry her face. She would return to Halifax many times over the years to visit friends and relatives, but she never again returned to Richmond.

"Those who give of themselves
To help the unfortunate,
Receive far more than they give.
They gain enrichment of spirit,
And a sheer delight in living."

Once tasted, the nectar of service to humanity becomes the favourite
nourishment for the soul. All of those who helped the victims, undoubtedly
good people to start with, became better. They had made an investment of self
in those they had helped. This investment would pay handsome dividends for
the rest of their lives. They were imbued with an expanded feeling of
self-worth, and in their remaining years they would seek opportunities to
reinforce and augment this marvellous formula for living.

ALTHOUGH HE WAS not from Richmond, Hugh Mills knew and was
friends with many of the residents. When he was fifteen he came to
Halifax and found work the very same day at Moir's Candy Factory. By
age twenty-one Hugh Mills saw his name raised above the door of his
own shop on Spring Garden Road. Mills Brothers rapidly became one
of the most prestigious clothing stores in the country. It remains so
today, more than three-quarters of a century later. Hugh built his
dream wisely and well. But, three years before that opening day, the
Halifax Explosion occurred, an event that would shape the rest of his
life. Always in his mind was the spectre of the children he had seen that
terrible day. Never could he forget the horror of witnessing young
bodies cut down by explosion, fire and flood, dead before they had a
chance to live. He could not help them then; he could not help them
now. But there were many others he could help.

With his business on a firm footing and a loyal staff who were
capable of relieving him of many of

Photo courtesy of Jane (Mills) MacLellan and Heather MacLellan

Hugh O. Mills, left, and his brother
Willett J. Mills, right, in a photo taken
many years after the explosion. Hugh
Mills was instrumental in rescuing Mary
Jean Hinch from the wreckage after
which she was taken to the American
hospital ship, Old Colony.

the duties of management, Hugh Mills was at liberty to pursue his life-long dream. For the children, to give to them some of the pleasure that had been denied the others, he turned to his love of show business. In 1934 he started a radio show under the pseudonym "Uncle Mel." It aired as a top children's program for almost three decades, and provided countless joy for thousands of young people who were given the opportunity to sing, recite poetry, tell stories and develop the many talents with which they were blessed. Hugh Mills quickly became one of the best loved radio personalities of his time.

During World War Two, Hugh Mills raised money for the war effort through the "Uncle Mel Safety Club" and organized the Halifax Concert Parties Guild to provide entertainment for servicemen at home. Near the end of the war he travelled to Britain and Europe to entertain the Canadian troops himself. In 1946 he was awarded the MBE in recognition of his services.

The second outlet for his enduring compassion and altruism was prompted by his memories of the blood. He had been shocked by the number of people who bled to death. In some cases, the rescuers had managed to staunch the flow and save the victim from death, but with neither blood supplies nor facilities for transfusions, for many there had simply been no hope. At the time there was little he could do for them. But after the explosion, people would continue to suffer blood loss, during surgery and through accidents. There would always be a need for blood. In 1985 Hugh Mills was awarded a special certificate in honour of his four decades of volunteer work with the Red Cross. He served as president of the Halifax branch of the Red Cross for four years, was instrumental in building the city's Red Cross Lodge in 1948 and was its chairman for many years. He was also a driving force behind the establishment of Halifax's Sir Charles Tupper Medical Building in Halifax.

Hugh Mills died at the age of eighty-eight on February 16, 1987. Few have been blessed with a life as rich as his. Few have contributed as much to their friends, associates and community. He is still mourned and missed by those whose lives he touched.

SOPHYE JACKSON WAS profoundly affected by the Halifax Explosion. Returning to her hometown to help treat the victims of the blast, she was confronted with the devastation of her home and family. Though she resigned from her duties with the Red Cross in order to tend to the needs of her father, the weeks she spent in Camp Hill Hospital forever altered the direction of her professional vocation.

In April of 1918, she returned to New York just long enough to enlist in the American Public Health Services. After receiving a commission, she worked in United States Marine Hospitals throughout the country for the next thirty years, serving during two World Wars and becoming an American citizen in 1923. Sophye served with distinction as a Senior Assistant Nursing Officer until her retirement and honourable discharge in 1951. During those three decades she experienced the satisfaction of ministering to American Marines and victims of war, and with her skills and compassion had eased the suffering of thousands. In early November of 1943, at the age of forty-eight, Sophye married Herbert Thompson. They had met many years before in a Marine Hospital, she as a nurse and he as a patient. Their marriage lasted for thirty-two years until her death on August 10, 1975. Her husband died six years later on December 11, 1981. They are buried together in Floral Hills Cemetery, near Seattle, Washington, a very long distance from Richmond.

Epilogue

In January the sporadic aid being administered by the civic authorities was organized under a single bureau, the Halifax Relief Commission. This agency took over the function of twelve separate committees and would eventually receive international recognition as a model for similar relief organizations. However, in the beginning it was on shaky ground. Although massive amounts of money had been pledged—from the carefully hoarded pennies of children to hundreds of thousands of dollars sent by corporations and millions committed by foreign governments—caution was the order of the day. The money would have to last a long time. There were hundreds of widows, most with children, who would receive pensions until they either died or remarried. Hundreds of blind and critically injured victims would require institutional care for the rest of their lives. Thousands had to be compensated for property destroyed or the expense of repairs to their home. But until the financial picture was solidified, available resources were distributed sparingly, primarily where they were most needed—food, clothing and temporary shelter for the homeless. Compensation for losses of real property would have to wait. This did not sit well with many of the survivors.

The majority of the dead had been found and buried by the end of January. Physical injuries had healed or were healing, the trauma had subsided slightly and most of the people, though still in a state of shock, started to feel a stirring of interest in their future. They were starting to emerge emotionally from personal crisis. Along with the emergence of the city from the ashes of destruction, the people would also arise from the catastrophe. Just as the civic leaders and the American benefactors provided the impetus for the city, the Halifax Relief Commission became the catalyst for the victims to begin their lives anew.

One of the Commission's most successful strategies was to assign case workers to individuals. Except for a few instances, where there was a clash of personalities, this system was ideal. The case worker came to know the individual people they served. They knew who was most in need, who was trying to put something over on them, who needed help but was too proud to ask. Aid was rendered on a person-to-person basis; no one ever became just a number lost in a complex system. This commission existed until recent times, still disbursing funds to the long-term victims who had been blinded or otherwise rendered incapable of earning a living. It received full marks for *fulfilling its mandate to the people of Halifax and Dartmouth. But it could only serve the more practical necessities of recovery. Deliverance from emotional trauma depended upon the will and spiritual resources of the victims themselves.*

The survivors were as veterans of a war. There developed among them a strong sense of comradeship; from the greatest to the least they had suffered together and established a closeness that will never be known by most people. In Richmond the spirit of togetherness still existed, and for that generation it became even stronger. Many would become better people than they had been; they developed a greater empathy for the troubles of others and acquired a remarkable gentleness of spirit.

And now began the process of rebuilding shattered lives. For some the process would be painfully slow; they would resist the changes that were necessary. Others, after a normal period of mourning, found the courage to accept the unacceptable and start anew. Each handled the task of rebuilding their lives in their own way. There were almost as many means as there were survivors, but some methods found acceptance for many.

One method of combating the loss was for the widow of one family to marry a widower from another.

VINCENT MCDONALD, SLOW to recover from his great loss, married Ellen Jackson, Edward's widow. This provided a step-mother for the only surviving child from his first marriage, nine-year-old Gordon. In return the two surviving children of Ellen Jackson, Gerald and Muriel, acquired a step-father. This marriage produced three children. Vincent McDonald died March 14, 1962 at age eighty-nine. He was pre-deceased by his wife, Ellen, who died at age seventy-one, on July 4, 1953.

ADA MOORE MARRIED Howard Sperry and, for awhile, moved away from the city. Mary Jean Hinch married James William Mahar. Vincent Coleman's widow, Frances, married James Jackson. All the families had been friends long before the explosion and the surviving members of each now became as one.

Widows and widowers of many other families in the Richmond area also married each other; there was a strong reason this was so. By joining together they minimized the trauma of loss. By being together each could comfort the other; they shared the other's burden of grief. Some simply left the area. They believed healing was faster if you were removed from an environment that

*stimulated the process of memory. But the scars were within themselves and
could not be diminished by distance.*

JAMES JACKSON JR. and his wife Mona, moved to California. He
applied for and received a job with the railroad in that state. When his
position was firm, and he was financially stable, he sent for Dorothy
Jackson, the orphaned daughter of his Uncle John and Aunt Louisa. He
cared for the girl until she was a young adult.

*The vast majority had been through the most troublesome times they would
ever face. Nothing that occurred in the rest of their lives would inflict as
much pain as they had already faced and conquered. But, for a few, fate was
not finished. Destiny sometimes seems to have a propensity for irony. Just as
some of the survivors of that terrible day emerged from the depths of despair
and had reached a state of happiness, diabolic misfortune struck again. James
E. Jackson and Minnie McGrath were unfortunately in this category.*

FOUR MONTHS AFTER the explosion, James Jackson made the first
moves toward beginning a new life. He went back to work for the railroad. Almost seventy workers in the Richmond Railyard had been
killed; there was a severe shortage of qualified men and the company
was only too happy to have him back. In 1919 he was promoted to Yard
Master and Foreman of all brakemen. He earned the respect and good-
will of everyone who worked with him.

After spending a month with Ada, James used the compensation
from two of his four properties and bought a duplex on Oxford Street,
retaining one of the Richmond properties with the intention of eventually rebuilding. His son, Jim, and his daughters, Sophye and Minnie,
moved in with him. He also took in his niece, Dorothy, the orphaned
daughter of John and Louisa Jackson.

Nine months later, James then took a second step toward recovery.
The Jacksons and the Colemans had long been family friends. Both
belonged to Saint Joseph's Church and both had strong ties to the railroad. Vincent Coleman as a telegrapher, while James and others of the
Jackson family worked as brakesmen and yard workers. On January 25,
1922, James Jackson married Vincent's widow, Frances O'Toole
Coleman. Both widowed by the explosion, James and Frances shared a
common suffering. Frances, too, had been seriously injured. She had
sustained internal injuries, a displaced collarbone, and problems with
her back, shoulder and arm. She had to wear a rigid back brace; and,
even as late as the summer of 1918, she was unable to do her own

housework. She had also lost her property. The Coleman's home on Russell Street, nine rooms and a pantry, had been demolished and burned along with all their clothing and furniture.

Frances could never be happy in Richmond again, there were too many memories. To begin their new life together they moved across town to Jennings Street, in the south-west end of the city. From there they could not see the Narrows, the Basin or the harbour. James settled down to devote himself to Frances and his four new stepchildren. But two weeks after their first anniversary Frances (Coleman) Jackson was once more a widow.

On the morning of February 8th, 1923, James Jackson was riding the boxcars, swaying gently to their rhythm as he joked with one of his men. He seldom missed a chance to feel the

Vincent Coleman gave his life to save the lives of hundreds. Several years after the explosion his widow, Frances Coleman, married James Jackson.

Photo courtesy P.A.N.S. (N-6198)

movement of the train beneath his feet. Despite his comeback, James was not the man he'd been six years before. He had sight in only one eye, his hands had lost their strength and his reflexes were slowed. His uncle and best friend, George Jackson, was standing a few hundred feet away, ready to wave if James had looked his way. The car lurched as it struck a switch and George saw his nephew lose his balance. As he fell he appeared to grab the top of the ladder but either he missed or his weakened hands could not hold his grip. James Jackson fell under the freight train and was killed.

Frances O'Toole (Coleman) Jackson never married again. She devoted the remainder of her life to caring for her children and her garden. She was actively involved in various charities as well as her church. Frances donated Vincent Coleman's pen, watch, and the telegraph key he'd used to warn the trains and save about 350 lives at the cost of his own, to the Provincial Archives of Nova Scotia. They remain there as a reminder of his great courage.

Frances died at the age of ninety-two. On June 15th, 1970, she was buried beside her first husband, Vincent Coleman, and their eight-year-old son, Cyril, who died one year before the Halifax Explosion. A tall headstone marks their place in section two—plot V at Mount Olivet Cemetery. The base of the headstone is marked with the names of Vincent and Frances on one face, their son, Cyril, on another, and James E. Jackson on the third. There is some doubt that James is actually buried in this grave. But if not, he is close by. Only a few feet away is an unmarked grave containing the bodies of his first wife, Margaret (Topping) Jackson, their son, Lewis, and their daughter, Annie. In this same plot, also unmarked, are the graves of their son-in-law, James Clifford McGrath and their grandson, Clifford. It is more probable that James E. Jackson is buried in this plot.

THE LOSS OF her two-year-old son shattered Minnie's universe. Still mourning the loss of her husband in the previous year, she remained in denial of Clifford's death until finally confronted with his skeletal remains.

After several years of mourning, Minnie married her second husband, Frederick C. Walker. Following the example of her brother, Jim, and his wife, Mona, they moved to California, away from the scene of Minnie's nightmares. Like his brother-in-law, Fred Walker found employment as a brakesman with the state railroad and for some years they lived in happiness in the Golden State with their five children. But the call of home brought them back to Halifax in the winter of 1931.

They stayed with Fred's mother at sixteen South Street, for several months, while he studied and wrote the qualifying exams to work on the trains. He passed and began work in Halifax. At age thirty-five Frederick Walker

Minnie (Jackson) (McGrath) Walker and the children from her marriage to Fred Walker.

Photo courtesy of Diane Walker.

was killed in an accident within an hour and a half of starting work his first day on the job.

For the third time in her young life, Minnie found happiness torn from her grasp. She never remarried. For the rest of her life she devoted herself to her children and the simple pleasures that gave her life meaning. She died August 9, 1973, at age eighty-three and was buried in Mount Olivet Cemetery.

Many survivors who escaped death had to contend with long periods of recuperation from physical injuries. Some would never fully recover. In many cases the children suffered a particularly intense trauma. Torn from the arms of their parents their sense of security was shattered. They were deprived instantly of the comfort of parents and family and thrust into a world of pain and uncertainty. The syndrome, now known as "security anxiety," would prevent them from regaining faith, trust, and the feeling of security for many years.

GORDON MCDONALD'S FACE had been hideously scarred. Despite many operations it would remain so for the rest of his life. The boy continued his schooling, but the taunts of thoughtless children caused deep emotional scars. From the time of the explosion he could not bear to be separated from his father. At age fifty he married his second wife, Dorothy Thompson, a kindly, understanding woman who led him away from his lifestyle of semi-recluse. It was only during those years that Gordon finally began to enjoy the normal pleasures of life. Gordon worked at the Halifax Dockyard for forty-three years. He died August 23, 1990, at age eighty.

WITH THE DEATH of her mother, Mildred Hale was one of the many orphans created by the blast. Shortly after the explosion her grandfather, Hugh Hale Sr., arrived from Amherst and took her under his control. He was a very old man and unable to properly care for her, her brother Ralph and her sister Thelma. Mildred's aunt, Mrs. Stanton Wheeler, arrived from Oxford, Massachusetts, and with Mr. Hale's permission took the children back to the States. Mildred was in hospital for the better part of a year from explosion-related injuries. She married Joseph Hadley, and lived her life in Massachusetts. They raised three children. Mildred Hale died in 1986 at age eighty.

DOROTHY JACKSON LED a very unsettled life. Orphaned by the explosion she lived for a short time with her Aunt Ada and for another short time with her Uncle James Jackson. She was sent for by James Jr. and his wife Mona, and lived with them in California. Her life was plagued by the hearing problems created by the explosion, her schooling suffered and she never felt fully accepted into the family life of Jim and Mona. By young adulthood she left the family and the best research efforts have been unable to trace her whereabouts.

IN THE CONFUSION following the explosion, Letitia Edmonds and her son, William, were officially listed as dead. She was severely burned on her neck and arms and William sustained lacerations as well as the loss of his left leg. However, they were both very much alive. This family was unique, it cheated the grim reaper, not once but twice.

On the night when William "came back from the dead" he was taken from the Chebucto Road Morgue to Camp Hill Hospital. Initially he was listed simply as an "unknown child." About a week later, when he was lucid, William looked up to see his Aunt Emily pass by his room. Soon after, Arthur was reunited with his son.

The Edmonds had lost two sons to the explosion, but their daughters had both survived and William, at least, had been returned to them. Letitia's wounds would heal and Arthur was still capable of earning a living to support his family. However, his means of livelihood, his horses, wagons, sleds and all the harnesses had been destroyed by fire. And Arthur was middle aged; as with many men his age, the loss of the material possessions accumulated over years of sweat and labour came as a deep blow. As he mourned the death of his sons, he would also mourn his home and business.

Arthur entered into a prolonged battle with the Halifax Relief Commission for compensation to recover his means of employment. Eventually he was reimbursed for his losses and once again was able to provide for his family.

Temporarily housed in the Exhibition Grounds, once the new Hydrostone homes were completed, Arthur and his family moved into twenty-five Stanley Place. By then he had acquired four horses and was hauling stone for the reconstruction of St. Joseph's Church, school and convent.

WILLIAM SUFFERED through a great deal after the amputation of his leg. He was hospitalized for nearly a year and subjected to at least a half-dozen operations in an attempt to prepare the stump for an artificial leg. On several occasions he faced the threat of gangrene and it was only after a specialist from England performed one more operation that the

Photo courtesy of his son, James R. Edmonds.

William Edmonds and his wife Marjorie (Wilson) Edmonds taken in the summer of 1930. He led a full and active life after the pain and trauma he experienced in the Halifax Explosion.

boy was out of danger. But, it would be many years before he could be fitted with a prosthesis. He attended Bloomfield School to grade nine and then passed a course in wireless telegraphy. Unable to find work in this field, he and his father joined forces in 1927 to run a grocery store. In 1929, William married Marjorie Alice Wilson with whom he had eight children. He left the store to work as elevator operator in the Provincial Building and from there he followed in his father's footsteps and set up a fruit and vegetable wagon. In 1947 he returned to the Provincial Building as foreman of the cleaning staff. He died March 28, 1960, and is buried in Fairview Cemetery along with his parents.

ADA (JACKSON) MOORE may well have been born a hundred years too soon. Her lack of real power, including her inability to vote, was a constant source of frustration. Quick and clever, she also had a passion for organization and most of the Jacksons were content to sit back and let Ada take charge of the constant stream of family weddings, births, birthdays and anniversaries. She possessed a remarkable memory for dates and kept a mental dossier on every relative—adult or child—and so could organize a gathering in moments.

Possessed of a fierce family loyalty, it was she who labelled the lower reaches of Richmond "Jacksonville" partly in jest, but with a grain of truth—over seventy Jacksons and descendants of Jacksons lived in the area from Veith to Duffus Streets. Three weeks before the explosion, at a family gathering to celebrate Emma's marriage to Lawrence Boutilier, Ada's youngest brother, William, had amused the gathering by saying, "Did you know that Ada's designing a Jackson flag? When she gets it sewn together we'll all march in uniform to City Hall and the General herself will demand the surrender of the city and appoint herself Mayor. Won't that be fun?" While this was highly amusing to the guests, it was very unfair to Ada. Her concern for the welfare of her family was not self-serving but based on a deep love and allegiance to them all.

As it had been for so many others, the violent explosion of the *Mont Blanc* changed her life forever. Of her eight siblings, four of her brothers and two of her sisters had been killed outright. James and Mary Jean had sustained severe injuries; only Ada had escaped with a few minor cuts and bruises. Her husband was dead. There would be much for her to do.

The burden of identifying the dead and locating and gathering the survivors fell on her shoulders. She bore it with characteristic courage and determination. There was one bright spot during those days of despair and sorrow. Four of her children, who had been on their way to school, were found injured but alive; part of her life was restored to her.

As might be expected, Ada clashed with the authorities almost immediately. Realizing that her primary need was a place in which to unite her shattered family, she began to haunt those in charge of providing accommodation. By the time she was dealing with the Halifax Relief Commission she was beginning to provoke some animosity. One of the case workers, who had described Mary Jean as "a wonderful person," labelled her sister as "somewhat pushy." Ada was unconcerned; the Jacksons needed a house and if it took "pushy" to get it, then "pushy" she would be.

In January, Ada won the battle. She was allowed to rent a large house at 982 Barrington Street, south of North Street. To generate some income, she turned it into a boarding house as well as a gathering point for the surviving family. All of them stayed with Ada at some point during their recovery. But each had plans of their own and, despite her most persuasive arguments, she could not generate any enthusiasm for a return of the family to Richmond. The spirit of "Jacksonville" had disappeared, along with the *Mont Blanc*, in one millisecond on December 6th, 1917.

AFTER THE OTHER Jacksons moved on, Ada left Barrington Street to live in the temporary housing on the Exhibition Grounds. Two and a half years after the explosion, she followed the example of many other widowed survivors and took the first step toward a new life. On April 1st, 1920, Ada married Howard Frederick Sperry. Howard had boarded at number one Roome Street, but had been out of town on the day of the

Photo from the author's private collection.

catastrophe. With her four youngest surviving children, Ada was once again surrounded by the comfort of a large family. Mabel and her husband, Francis Shanks, had a place of their own after the war and they had six more children. Her husband served in both world wars and their son, Harold, who survived the explosion, was killed in Word War Two at the age of thirty. Mabel, now a Silver Cross Mother, died in 1989 at the age of ninety-two.

After the death of her brother James in 1923, Ada finally put to rest forever her fantasy of rebuilding the Jackson family. There were now only two of the original nine, Ada and Mary Jean, and the two sisters had lost the intimacy that marked their relationship before the explosion. Over the following years they remained friends, but their relationship was irretrievably diminished. The explosion had shattered more than houses. On April 8th, 1954, fifteen days before her seventy-sixth birthday, Ada Agnes (Jackson) (Moore) Sperry died. She was buried in Mount Olivet Cemetery. And now there was only Mary Jean.

DURING THE MONTHS following the explosion, Mary Jean's rosary was her constant companion and her sole comfort. Her faith, always firm, became even stronger. Her trust in God would be a source of constant exasperation to her sister Ada but Mary Jean's faith was unshakable. She now had only one goal and it precluded any distractions or doubts. The baby would be born in April and she would need to be fit and strong for that event. Turning her back on what had been, she faced an uncertain future with the certainty of her faith.

By mid-December, when she was transferred from the American

Mary Jean (Jackson) (Hinch) Mahar. This is one of the very few available pictures of her and was taken by the author about 1935.

Photo from the author's private collection.

hospital ship, her hip had healed to the point where she could walk a little, albeit painfully. Her teeth were still loose and an infection had set into her gums. Ada had arranged her transfer to the St. Mary's College Hospital and was in the midst of organizing a home for the few surviving family members. Mary Jean moved into her sister's boarding house on Barrington Street and stayed there several months.

In the meantime, the infection in her gums had escalated. In March, Mary Jean faced the extraction of all of her teeth, the only guaranteed method for suspending gum infection at that time. At eight months pregnant there was the possibility of harming the baby if she underwent anaesthesia. One day in the middle of March, she sat in the dentist's chair and had sixteen teeth extracted without the relief even of painkillers. A few days later she returned and had an additional fourteen teeth removed. She may have been a very gentle lady but she had a core of steel.

On April 20th, 1918, she gave birth to her fifteenth child, Hubert Benedict Hinch, a fine, healthy baby boy who became her only physical link with the past. The birth of her son provided the impetus to reach forward to a new life.

Mary Eugenia Jackson Hinch married James William Mahar on September 29th, 1919, at the partially reconstructed St. Joseph's Church in Richmond. Shortly afterwards, they moved to a new home at 148 Chebucto Road, between Oxford and Kline Streets. There, on September 19th, 1923, at the age of forty-six, she gave birth to her sixteenth child, James G. Mahar.

Mary Jean survived her second husband, who died in 1944. She lived alternately with her two sons, serenely tending to her garden, grandsons

Photo from the author's private collection.

James William Mahar and his wife, Mary Jean, taken approximately 1938.

and church until August 8th, 1958, when she died of cancer at the age of eighty-one. Her funeral mass was said at St. Theresa's Church and she was buried in Mount Olivet Cemetery beside her second husband. She is not far from the unmarked grave containing the bodies of Joseph Hinch and her ten children; within thirty feet lies her brother James E. Jackson. She is in good company.

Before the casket was closed, the rosary that was blessed by the Pope and given to a very young bride over sixty-five years earlier, was draped around her fingers and buried with her.

AUTHOR'S NOTE

As her youngest child I was privileged to know Mary Jean for thirty-four years. In addition to the trauma of the Halifax Explosion, she would face many other periods of adversity: the tragic death of the last of her five brothers, James Jackson, in 1923; the Great Depression of the early thirties; World War Two and the anxiety of having her two remaining children serving overseas during that war; and being widowed for a second time with the death of my father in 1944. Throughout a life fraught with tragedy she remained a calm and gentle person.

Her serenity was maintained by an unshakable faith in God and a deep-seated quiet courage. I never once heard her complain or grieve aloud over her losses; in fact, I was not even made aware of her tragedy until the age of twelve, when I heard parts of the story from other people. Occasionally, when I was that age I would come home from school and know she had been crying. At that time I did not know why. When I grew older and knew the details, it was apparent she had been visiting a place in her heart that was closed to all others. But she did not dwell there, when the solitary visit ended, she always returned to us, with renewed peace and composure.

I grew up in a happy home. My father had six surviving children from his first marriage but all were many years older than I. Most were married and away from home, and in my early years we were a family of five. My mother and father, my half-brother, Hubert Hinch, my half-brother, Arthur Mahar, and myself. Since Hubert was her son, Arthur was his son and I was their son, we were referred to as "hers," "his" and "ours." There was never any but a jocular treatment of the division and the three of us grew up as brothers.

My father was boss of the stevedores at Furness Withy and was a firm but fair man who earned the respect of all who knew him. He also had a delightful sense of Irish fun and there was much laughter in our home.

During the years of the Depression there was great hardship in the land. Men who were travelling the country looking for work would come to our door begging for food. My mother, then in her mid-fifties, never turned anyone away. She would make them sandwiches and tea and I would sit on our back porch with them while they ate. I often wondered why they didn't go to the other houses in the neighbourhood, and it wasn't until years later that I learned our front steps had been marked with a symbol that said to all other vagrants: "This is a good place." It surely was.

With the advent of World War Two, Hubert joined the day after war was declared and went overseas with the Royal Canadian Engineers at the end of January 1940, the first contingent to arrive in England. I had to wait until I was eighteen to join the Canadian Air Force and went overseas in January 1943. I was attached to and served with the Royal Air Force after arriving in England. In November 1943 I was posted to Africa. In April of 1944 I had a letter from home with the news of my father's death. My mother was once again a widow, with neither of her two sons there to comfort her in her loss.

After the war the family house was sold and for the rest of her days she lived for a few months with one son and then a few months with the other. Her main interests in life were the church, flowers, bingo and her grandsons. Even in her late seventies she was still a remarkably pretty woman and still dressed to merit the nickname "Dude" that Ada had bestowed upon her so many years ago.

The Halifax Explosion was only mentioned in our home on one day of the year—All Souls Day. From the time I was old enough to write and until the year she died, my mother named the names of the dead who were to be prayed for at that special mass. She named them softly, slowly and lovingly, without any emotion other than perhaps a slight tinge of sadness. It was as if she were far away, with them, in another place, at another time. As young as I was I sensed these were very special people and this was a very solemn occasion. There were far too many names to fit the form supplied by the church; they were listed on two sheets of writing paper. In my best penmanship I carefully copied each name—the grandmother, uncles and aunts, half-brothers and sisters and all the cousins I never knew. They were always in the same order; she never forgot even one.

There were fifty-four names.

Sources

Anglican Diocesan Centre—Rev. William Bishop and Staff
Archdiocese of Halifax, Catholic Pastoral Centre—
    Rev. Martin Currie, Vicar General and Chancellor;
    Karen White, Archivist
Calvary Cemetery, Los Angeles, California, U. S. A.—Staff
Catholic Cemeteries Commission, Halifax—Staff
Church of Saint Peter and Saint Paul, Wilmington, California,
    U. S. A. —Father G. Peter Irving, Pastor; Helen Workman Mora,
    Archivist
Dalhousie University Archives, Dr. Charles Armour, Archivist:
    Explosion material—scrapbook; Archibald MacMechan material;
    J. MacAloney notes; Dr. Howard L. Bronson material;
    Creighton family letters on microfilm
Fairview Cemetery, Halifax—Staff
Floral Hills Cemetery, Alderwood, Washington, U. S. A.— Staff
Halifax Regional Fire Department—Capt. Donald R. Snider
Halifax Regional School Board—Dr. Donald Trider, Superintendent
Halifax Regional Municipality Library System (Halifax & Dartmouth
    Branches)—microfilm; city directories; computers
IMPACT Videographic Services Limited—Versteege
Los Angeles Times, Dave Laventhol, Publisher; Jonathan Miller, Ad Sales
Maritime Museum of the Atlantic—Graham McBride and Staff
Mount Saint Vincent Motherhouse Archives, Sisters of Charity,
    Sister Mary Martin, Archivist
New York Times, NYT Pictures, Photo Syndicate, New York, N.Y.,
        U. S. A.—Staff
North End News, Volume 9, Number 13, March 14, 1997
(Personal collection) *The Halifax Herald* Limited—Computer disk on
    Halifax Explosion; Computer disk for obituaries; Herald Online
    Services—Genealogy
(Personal collection) Family information, papers, photographs
Public Archives of Nova Scotia, Halifax—Carman Carroll, Provincial
    Archivist, and Staff
Special mention: Lois Yorke, Archivist, Manuscript Division; Garry
    Shutlak, Archivist, Maps and Photographic Division—photographs
    from P.A.N.S. collection "A Vision of Regeneration," location
    number 44.6.7

P.A.N.S.—Halifax Relief Commission information including: MG20, MG27, MG36; files; microfilm, newspapers

P.A.N.S.—microfilm (newspapers available on the Halifax Explosion)

P.A.N.S.— numerous microfilms researched: church records; cemetery records; births; marriages; deaths; city directories; census; biographies; etc.

P.A.N.S.— The Lorne Club (L.A.A.C.); C.H.N.S. Radio collection

St. Agnes Roman Catholic Church, Halifax—Rev. Lloyd J. Robertson

St. John's Cemetery, Halifax—Staff

St. Joseph's Roman Catholic Church, Halifax—Father Gordon MacLean; Thelma LeBlanc, Secretary

St. Mark's Anglican Church, Halifax—Rev. J. Smith

St. Mary's University, Halifax—Professor Paul A. Erickson

St. Patrick's Roman Catholic Church, Halifax—Father John Hayes; Catherine Hutt, Secretary

St. Theresa's Roman Catholic Church, Halifax—Rev. Lloyd E. O'Neill

Songs:

"The Band Played On"—words by John F. Palmer; music by Charles B. Ward

"After the Ball"—by Charles K. Harris

"When Johnny Comes Marching Home"—Traditional

Hymn:

"Bringing in the Sheaves"—words by Knowles Shaw; music by George A. Minor